The Teachers' Notes to
Reading Greek

THE JOINT ASSOCIATION OF
CLASSICAL TEACHERS' GREEK COURSE

The Teachers' Notes to
Reading Greek

CAMBRIDGE
UNIVERSITY PRESS

PUBLISHED BY THE PRESS SYNDICATE OF THE UNIVERSITY OF CAMBRIDGE
The Pitt Building, Trumpington Street, Cambridge, United Kingdom

CAMBRIDGE UNIVERSITY PRESS
The Edinburgh Building, Cambridge CB2 2RU, UK   http://www.cup.cam.ac.uk
40 West 20th Street, New York, NY 10011–4211, USA   http://www.cup.org
10 Stamford Road, Oakleigh, Melbourne 3166, Australia
Ruiz de Alarcón 13, 28014 Madrid, Spain

First published 1986
Reprinted 1989, 1993, 1996, 2000

Printed in the United Kingdom at the University Press, Cambridge

British Library Cataloguing in Publication data
Joint Association of Classical Teachers.
The teachers' notes to *Reading Greek*. –
(The Joint Association of Classical Teachers' Greek Course)
1. Greek language
I. Title   II. Joint Association of Classical Teachers. *Reading Greek*
III. Series
488   PA258

Library of Congress Cataloguing in Publication data
Main entry under title:
The Teachers' notes to *Reading Greek*.
(The Joint Association of Classical Teachers' Greek Course)
Includes index.
1. Greek language – Study and teaching.   2. Greek language –
Grammar – 1950–.   3. Greek language – Readers.   4. *Reading Greek*.
1. *Reading Greek*   II. Series
PA231.T53   1985   488.2'421   85–15147

ISBN 0 521 31872 6 paperback

Cover illustration: detail from an Attic red-figure cup.,
Musée du Louvre G 448. Photo: Chuzeville

CONTENTS

PREFACE

The Publications of the Joint Association of Classical Teachers' (J.A.C.T.) Greek Course

The constitution, aims and working of the Project team which produced the J.A.C.T. Greek Course are set out in the *Text* of *Reading Greek*. Project publications to date are:

Reading Greek (*RG*) – an intensive introductory course in Ancient Greek for mature beginners, to be completed in about one year, which covers all the basics of classical Attic Greek, Herodotus and Homer. There are three units: *RG* (*Text*), *RG* (*Grammar, Vocabulary and Exercises – GVE*) and Morphology Charts (all C.U.P., 1978).

A World of Heroes (*WoH*) (C.U.P., 1979) and *The Intellectual Revolution* (*IR*) (C.U.P., 1980), which follow *RG* with selections from Homer, Herodotus and Sophocles (*WoH*), Thucydides, Euripides and Plato (*IR*). Both texts have vocabulary glossings on the facing page and are intended to help the intensive beginner to read widely in Ancient Greek.

Greek Vocabulary (*GV*) (C.U.P., 1981) – which contains the total learning vocabulary of *RG*, *WoH* and *IR*. This is a useful learning aid in its own right but also makes *WoH* and *IR* accessible to anyone *whatever introductory course he or she has completed*: any words not glossed on the facing pages of these texts will be found in *GV*.

Speaking Greek (C.U.P., 1982) is a pronunciation tape to accompany the course. It features readings from *RG* by David Raeburn and the cast of the Cambridge University Greek play of 1980, and further readings, a discussion and examples of pronunciation by Professor W. S. Allen, the author of *Vox Graeca* (2nd edn, C.U.P., 1974).

The World of Athens (*WA*) (C.U.P., 1984) is a cultural and historical introduction to fifth-century Athens for the mature beginner which serves as the background book to *RG*. It requires no knowledge of Ancient Greek, and it will also be found useful in its own right as a thorough, lively and up-to-date appraisal of the culture and achievements of fifth-century Athens. Reference is made to this volume throughout the *Teachers' Notes* and it is an *essential* tool in the teachers' hands. If each student cannot have a copy, several should be available for use in the library.

Teachers' Notes to *Reading Greek*

1. A general introduction to *RG* as a whole.

2. The *Teachers' Notes* to *RG*, with preface, written by James Neville, Head of Classics at Tonbridge Girls' School, Kent. James Neville has used *RG* from its earliest trial versions, in a wide variety of teaching conditions.

3. Notes on the illustrations in the Course, contributed by Dr Brian Sparkes, Professor of Classics at the University of Southampton, who was responsible for their selection, and notes on Attic vases and vase-painters in general, again by Professor Sparkes.

4. Sample examination papers for students who have been studying Greek (i) intensively for one year at university, using only *RG*, and (ii) intensively for two years at school (sixth-form, or 11–12th grade) with a view to taking an examination based on *WoH* and *IR*.

5. Two year-plans for *RG*, derived from British universities, and one school year-plan.

6. An Appendix of regular verbs, nouns and adjectives, by section, taken from the learning vocabularies of Sections 1–6, which can be used for constructing rehearsal or practice exercises where needed.

7. A comprehensive index to the *Grammar* of *Reading Greek*.

I should like to offer the Project's warmest thanks to James Neville for writing the bulk of these notes; to Brian Sparkes for the picture notes; to Professor Edward Phinney of the University of Massachusetts at Amherst for bringing the book into line with the needs of the American market; and to Mr John Muir (Faculty of Education, King's College, London) for reviewing the whole book in typescript, to its very considerable advantage. One final act of thanks must be made to Professor W. K. Lacey and his students at The University of Auckland, N.Z., for the index to the *Grammar* volume of *RG*. All responsibility for all errors of omission or commission rests entirely with the Project.

> Peter V. Jones
> (Director, J.A.C.T. Greek Project) Department of Classics,
> The University, Newcastle upon Tyne NE1 7RU
>
> October 1984

ABBREVIATIONS

GV = *Greek Vocabulary* (C.U.P., 1981)
GVE = *Grammar, Vocabulary and Exercises* to *Reading Greek*
IR = *The Intellectual Revolution* (C.U.P., 1980)
RG = *Reading Greek* (C.U.P., 1978)
Text = *Text* of *Reading Greek*
WA = *The World of Athens* (C.U.P., 1984)
WoH = *A World of Heroes* (C.U.P., 1979)

See pp. vii–viii for a description of these books.

BASIC METHODOLOGY AND
LESSON PLANNING

As *GVE* explains, the first grammar section covers the *Text* of Section 1A–G. Consequently, the first task is to read and translate the *Text* of 1A–G as quickly as possible, pausing only over passages which cause difficulties, or passages which exemplify new or reinforce old grammatical points.

Methodological guidelines

Two general guidelines are important: (1) Underline or colour with a highlighting felt-tip pen those sentences, clauses, phrases or words in the *Text* which illustrate the grammatical points to be stressed by you for the students. (2) Teach *only* the grammatical points recommended in each section or sub-section of *GVE*. For example, the Course introduces only the nominative and accusative of nouns to start with. Genitive plurals come in Section 2, genitive singulars in Section 7 and datives in Section 8. If you teach genitive and dative forms ahead of time, you may confuse the learning process unnecessarily. However, if you prefer, list for students ahead of time for example the forms of the genitive and dative (especially the definite article), without going into detail about their meaning or use. Throughout the book the running vocabularies give students all the help they need to understand unusual words or constructions: i.e. they *omit* everything students should have learnt, and *include* everything which is new.

Lesson plans

A procedure for starting the Course might be as follows: Lesson 1 could cover *Text* 1A in class; home preparation would be to learn the learning vocabulary of 1A and prepare ahead 1B–C; Lesson 2 could cover translation of 1B and C, and push on into D: home preparation would consist of learning the vocabulary of 1B–D and preparing 1E–F. And so on. During translation, the grammar of 1A–G should be pointed out and reinforced, and when the text has been translated in this way and the vocabulary learnt, turn to the grammar section for 1A–G and go through it in detail with the students, ensuring that it is understood by asking questions or drilling with simple practice exercises. The grammar must then be learnt by heart.

As for practice, the teacher should assign whichever exercises in *GVE* are judged to be necessary, supplementing these in class with brief, oral 'transformation', 'substitution' and 'expansion' exercises (see pp. 25–6). Finally, the teacher should set, or assign, the Test Exercise for translation at sight.

This is a useful general pattern for daily lesson plans and can be used with most sections. For year-plans, see pp. 204–6.

Basic format of instruction

The methodology and general lesson plan suggested should not, of course, be rigidly followed, but (1) rapid reading of the *Text*, (2) regular vocabulary drills or quizzes, and (3) appropriate exercises in the grammar are a good format for progressing through the Course.

Year-end goals

The readings in the *Text*, unlike those of many other textbooks, are numerous, culturally and grammatically full, and sometimes lengthy. Accordingly, limitations of instructional time may force the teacher to cut back the amount of *Text* which students are to cover. Because presentation of new grammar effectively ends with Section 16, this section may well end the first year. With slower groups, the teacher should aim to finish Section 13 (*Neaira*) – a sizeable (and attainable) target for those who have difficulty learning a second language. For year-plans, see pp. 204–6.

Mainly for university teachers

It may be useful to make some general remarks about the use of *RG* (which could, *mutatis mutandis*, be extended to any reading course). *RG* was written on the following principles:

1. Learning to read a language involves far more than merely memorizing grammatical rules and vocabulary words. Intuitive grasp of structure, 'feel' for the language, are as important as knowing formal grammar, and

both skills must be learnt if quick progress is to be made towards comprehending unadapted texts. Hence the long reading passages of *RG*, which not only illustrate the new grammar but also provide practice in reading continuous texts.

2. Students do not need to know every detail of Greek grammar before reading an original text.

3. Translating from Greek into English requires a different grasp of grammar from the reverse process. A grammar written for translating Greek into English can rationalize and simplify in a way which is impossible for a grammar written for translating English into Greek (consider what you need to know to teach the rules of πρίν and ἕως successfully in either case).

4. Learning a language should not be divorced from understanding the civilization which produced it. Therefore all reading is based on original Greek texts and requires constant reference to background material in *WA*.

To conclude from this, as some have done, that there is 'no grammar' in *RG* or (even more incredibly) that 'there is no need to teach grammar if you use *RG*' is to miss the whole point: namely, that 'grammar' is on the whole got by memorizing (though practice helps), and that 'feel for structure' is got by reading (though grammar helps), and that what *RG* attempts to do is to *combine both operations so that one supports and helps the other*. Thus, for example, it is extremely helpful for memorization if examples of the new forms or rules to be learnt have already been met many times in a carefully-controlled reading passage; it is extremely helpful for reading if common structures are frequently repeated using known words and constructions in a cultural context which gives them real meaning in Greek terms. To the contrary, to use *RG* to teach only grammatical structure and vocabulary is to throw away the third prop indispensable for comprehending a language – the culture of the people who used/use it. As every successful student of a modern second language knows, one can be as technically fluent as a native, but it is not until the culture is actually *experienced* in real life that one starts to speak the language idiomatically and authentically. We do no justice to the ancient Greeks or their language if we do not at least try to make the Greek experience of the ancient world our students' constant point of contact with the language. Otherwise, Ancient Greek becomes merely a dead language misused in a twentieth-century cultural context.

If teachers feel uneasy with this *entire* approach, then they should not use *RG*, because they will fight the Course rather than co-operate with it, students will become disoriented. (since teachers will say one thing, the book another), and the results will be unsatisfactory. In the case of partial disagreement, teachers may modify the Course in one way or another; e.g., they may emphasize grammar further by inventing more exercise work. But modifications should not substantially alter the basic methodology or plan of the Course, nor the pace at which it must be completed. It is all a matter of balance.

Another consideration in deciding whether, and how best, to use *RG* is the ability of your students. What is your honest assessment of them? What is their *aptitude* for learning a second language? What is their *need* to get to point X in the Course during one year (and thus their likelihood of reaching the target)? Given that it is *possible* to soft-pedal the grammar in *RG*, and to play up its high cultural content, *RG* is ideal for students whose linguistic aptitude is limited, but who are highly motivated to learn about the ancient world. Given that *RG* is wherever possible streamlined grammatically (by concentration on essentials and use of analogy), and that the *Text* encourages fast, accurate reading, it is ideal for the gifted linguist who wants to move rapidly and does not worry if some things remain unexplained to the *n*th power. On the other hand, *RG* is less likely to be successful with the perfectionist – the highly methodical learner who must know precisely where he or she is at every step.

The third crucial consideration is the time available. How many hours a week can be spent on Greek? Is it a major or minor subject? How much homework can reasonably be expected? Together with the previously-mentioned consideration, this third question will help you to arrive at a satisfactory answer to the question: How much Greek do you want students to learn in one year and what sort of grasp do you expect them to have of it? How much Greek do they actually *need*? How will *RG* help or hinder them to reach those goals? Should you think afresh about goals as a result of past experience with *RG* (or any other course)? These questions are extremely important, because in answering them you are helping to define your *goals* (in their most obvious form, an examination) and the better you can define them, the more chance you have of guiding your students towards reaching them. One approach is to consider your *ideal* end-of-year examination for a beginner in Greek, and then see which course guides you towards it best. If it contains no questions about the Greek world, puts strong emphasis on English-into-Greek and demands the ability to generate (rather than recognize) forms of, say, ἵστημι, perhaps you should not select *RG*. Such an examination, however, might cut down dramatically the number of people who could genuinely benefit from a year of Greek (and might be lured into doing it longer) – but that is another question, though in these days its importance grows every year. (For possible examinations, see p. 186.)

Whichever answer you give, a fourth and final consideration may also play a part in formulating it: What do the students *do* next? Is one year of Greek all they will study? Will they be expected to read prose authors next year? Or to read widely in, say, Homer? Will the second year's work be a frantic gallop through 6,000 lines of Greek, or a more leisurely stroll through 3,000, with more time to appreciate the poetry and study the cultural background? How far are the first and second years' work in Greek compatible? Does *RG* suit the tone and tempo of the second year's work or not? The problem becomes all the more acute when there is a mixed class consisting of those who study Greek for one year only (obvious advantages in the broad cultural and linguistic sweep of *RG* here) and those who need to be ready for intensive reading of Aristotle for a philosophy major next year.

(For an examination which attempts to cater for the less linguistically minded, see p. 187, with discussion.)

Mainly for teachers of sixth-formers (11–12th graders)

The considerations which face university and college teachers, sketched above, tend also to face school teachers, only usually more acutely. In the United Kingdom, this is especially the case if students begin Greek in the sixth-form and wish to take an 'O'- or 'A(lternative) O'-level examination in it, or even an 'A'-level, after one or two years in the sixth-form. Such students, with perhaps three other 'A'-levels to cope with, will probably be lucky to have two hours a week in their schedule for Greek. In the United States, this is especially the case if senior high-school students are studying Greek in addition to other languages and subjects in which they will take as many as four to six different College Board Achievement examinations. Because there is no College Board in Greek, students will be likely to fit Greek into the margin of their other studies (especially of Latin, in which there *is* a College Board); for this reason, Greek in American high schools is frequently taught during breakfast or lunch periods as an 'overload', and the only national examination in Greek available to American or Canadian high-school students is the short, norm-referenced National Greek examination, sponsored by the American Classical League. Under such conditions, secondary-level students and teachers in both the U.K. and the U.S.A. need all the help they can get.

James Neville's notes should be particularly useful in pointing out the short-cuts that students can (and sometimes *must*) take. In the U.K. probably the most useful tactic is for students taking intensive courses within a limited time to go to a summer-school or short course. A summer-school course *before* the start of the sixth-form course will bring the student to *RG* Section 9 or 10. The ground covered will need revision at the start of the first year in the sixth form, but even so, *RG* should easily be finished by the end of the first year, and in a second summer-school *WoH* and *IR* and easy texts of Homer, Plato and Greek tragedians should be assigned. This leaves the whole of the second year for the study of the books set for the 'O'-level examination. Even one summer-school can make all the difference. (For details of the special J.A.C.T. 'AO' examination in Greek, based on *WoH* and *IR*, see p. 000; for the syllabus, write to: The Secretary, Oxford and Cambridge Schools' Examination Board, Elsfield Way, Oxford OX2 8EP. For details of summer-schools and short courses for students and adults, and grants available – teachers are advised to use these courses to brush up their own Greek – write to: Dr P. V. Jones (see Preface for address).)

In the United States, at the time of writing, there are no summer-school programmes in Greek designed specifically for high-school students. Several programmes exist, however, for university and college undergraduates or for high-school teachers who have no previous knowledge of Greek or who wish to review their earlier study of it. The oldest and best known of these are the New England Classical Institute and the C.U.N.Y. Latin/Greek Institute. For further information about these institutes, write to: (N.E.C.I.), Department of Classics, Tufts University, Medford, MA 02155; (C.U.N.Y.-L/G.I.), Dept. T, City University Graduate Center, 33 West 42nd Street, New York, NY 10036. The National Greek examination, sponsored by the American Classical League, has been placed on the Advisory List of National Contests and Activities maintained by the National Association of Secondary School Principals, and this List is distributed to all secondary schools in the United States early in September. For further information, write to: Professor Edward Phinney, Department of Classics, University of Massachusetts, Amherst, MA 01003.

Another course in which *RG* can be used in the sixth-form or senior high school (given the staff and curricular space) is the General (Classical) Studies course for a term, semester or even a full year. The linguistic pace of the course can be slowed right down and heavy emphasis placed on culture, history and word-derivation (*WA* comes into its own here). With a modest linguistic goal in view (e.g. Sections 4 or 5), the teacher can work wonders. The same goes for Adult Education classes, which teachers should propose if they have not yet taught them. These classes are enormously stimulating and revivifying. Adults who feel they have missed something of great value in the past and now wish to acquire it are an object lesson in determination, application and inquisitiveness. τοιοῦτοι εἰ πάντες γένοιντο...

Practical guidelines for all

1. *Reading and writing Greek*

It is of the highest importance, especially for weaker students, that Greek is read *aloud* and *written* as much as possible during the first month of learning the language. This may seem to slow down progress, but the rewards are immense, in accurate recognition of words and forms, in speed of learning vocabulary and general confidence in handling the language. Here are some suggestions on how to encourage reading aloud and writing.

(*a*) Read out a sentence or clause, and ask the entire class to repeat it after you; then choose smaller groups to imitate you; then individuals. (On choosing between dynamic and melodic accents, see below, pp. 10–11.) Then ask them to read another sentence or clause alone, without your prompting, after they have first prepared it; finally, ask them to read aloud at sight. Always read aloud, or have read aloud (preferably by the student about to do the translating), the Greek that is to be translated. The *Speaking Greek* cassette is invaluable for practice at home in pronunciation and accentuation (particularly in the first month, when special attention should be paid to Professor Allen's talk, on Side 1 of the cassette, 'The sounds of Greek').

(*b*) In the first month and periodically thereafter, students should write out in Greek, with diacritical marks, the passages they are translating, and, perhaps without diacritical marks, the exercises and their answers. These papers should be checked by the teacher for accuracy. It is astonishing what kinds of problem are revealed, and how easily they are cleared up, by this simple, though time-consuming, device.

2. *Grammar*

Only teach the grammatical points which *GVE* specifies as requiring to be learnt for any section. Everything lying outside that listing is glossed in the running vocabulary and can be ignored until the time comes for it to be taught fully. Underline in your text all examples of the grammatical point(s) to be learnt for each section, so that you remember to emphasize it/them and treat it/them with special care during the reading.

Some teachers prefer to give students a fuller picture of the grammar than that specified by *GVE* at any one time (e.g. ask students to learn *all* the cases at once). The Reference Grammar at the back of *GVE* gives the *full* picture, and should be consulted if required.

3. *Definite article*

Insist that the definite article be mastered thoroughly, by heart, at the beginning. It is used generously in *RG* and gives immediately the key to case, gender and number of any noun (irrespective of type) to which it is attached. This gives much help to the student when learning noun-types.

4. *Morphology charts*

Insist on students using the morphology charts, either as they go along, meeting new forms and filling them in, or as revision, or review, sheets at the end of each section. These charts cover all morphology and contain also a principal-part sheet of the most important sixty verbs in Greek. The charts are arranged so as to encourage the students to see the connections between forms. They may prove to be a little cramped in one or two instances. Fill in just the endings if no more room is available.

James Neville recommends drawing on the blackboard or projecting from a pre-drawn overhead transparency an empty 'grid' of new forms to be met in a day's class. The grid is filled in as the forms are met in the readings and understood by the student. The forms in the grids can then be transferred to the morphology charts. (The advantage of grids on overhead transparencies is that the transparencies can be kept from day to day or even year to year and reused after being wiped off. Draw the grids with indelible inks, and fill in the forms with water-soluble ones.)

5. *WA*

Contains full cross-references to *RG* in an Appendix. Constant reference is made to *WA* throughout these *Notes*.

6. *Vocabularies*

Constantly check that students are learning at every point the vocabularies set in *GVE* to be learnt. The result will be a much greater confidence in translating and a considerable saving of time.

Peter V. Jones
Edward Phinney

THE *SPEAKING GREEK* CASSETTE AND THE
TWO ACCENTS OF ANCIENT GREEK

The cassette

Choosing between the accents

Before the teacher can read the Greek aloud, he or she must choose between the *melodic* accent, used before A.D. 300, and the *dynamic* accent, used later (and still in modern Greek). The differences between these two accents is explained by W. S. Allen in the last half of his talk, 'The sounds of Greek', on Side 1 of the *Speaking Greek* cassette which is sold with the RG Course. (See also the written explanation of the two accents in Chapter 6, 'Accent', of Allen's *Vox Graeca* (2nd edn, C.U.P., 1974).) Teacher and students alike may hear the difference between the two accents by listening, for prose, on Side 1 of the cassette, to W. S. Allen reading a selection from Section 6c (= *Text* p. 49.1–9) with a dynamic accent, and, on Side 2, to D. Raeburn reading the same selection with a melodic accent; for dactylic hexameter verse, on Side 1, to Allen reading a selection from Section 19E (= *Text* p. 176.8–20) with a dynamic accent, and, on Side 2 again, to Raeburn reading the same selection with a melodic accent.

By listening to these comparative readings, the listener will note that the melodic accent, though it contributes to vivid performance, is difficult for English speakers and demands considerable practice before perfected. However, if the class has time and determination to practice melodic accents, this will reinforce students' knowledge of written accent marks, since only the melodic accent differentiates between acute (Allen's 'rising tone'), circumflex (Allen's 'rising and falling tone') and grave (Allen's 'modified tone') sounds. The dynamic accent, when properly emphasized on the syllable marked by acute or circumflex, will reinforce students' memory of the syllable on which to position an accent mark, but not of *which* mark to use. Despite this mnemonic disadvantage, many students prefer to practise dynamic accents since they are also used in English and therefore come more easily.

Because practice of both accents is beneficial, the teacher may want to use both with students, but at different times. Pitching ('intoning') accents is recommended in the early months of the course when students are learning both accent position and accent mark of basic words, or in later months when texts are unadapted and particularly beautiful to hear (notably Section 14A–C (from Euripides' *Alcestis*), Section 17A–E (from Plato's *Protagoras*) and Section 19A–G (from Homer's *Odyssey*)). Stressing ('breath-emphasizing') accents is recommended when students are secure with accent marks and their position, and the text is adapted prose. Using both accents together is not recommended, since, as Allen states in his recorded talk, English-speaking readers tend to stress the syllable they intone. The position of stressed, as opposed to intoned, syllables in classical Greek prose is unknown; in verse, stressed syllables are marked by poetic beat, or ictus. Thus a reader, when reading verse aloud, who stresses beat *and* pitched tone can distort the rhythm; for verse has stress (= ictus) separate from intoned syllable (= marked with acute or circumflex). Too many stressed syllables in orally-read verse can change, say, the potential 'THUM pe ty THUMP thump' of the dactylic hexameter into an even thumpier 'THUM PE TY THUMP THUMP'.

Edward Phinney

TEACHERS' NOTES TO *READING GREEK*

Introduction

The notes in this book are designed to help teachers to use *RG* in such a way that their students may be able to read fluently and competently some of the finest works of one of the greatest ages the world has seen.

If the Course is used for 'reading purposes', i.e. to enable students to read and appreciate Greek literature, some of the detail which tends to fill traditional courses may be omitted. To some traditionalists this approach may seem carefree, even slapdash and slovenly. I admit that it is less explicit than the detailed way in which most of us teachers learnt Greek; I cannot, however, agree that an appreciation of Greek literature is seriously impaired by ignorance, say, of the duals of φημί (any more than I considered my response to the literature inadequate when I discovered my ignorance of the fact that a Greek verb can have a future perfect passive participle, which I had never learnt at school). It is a question of where you draw the line.

Throughout this Course the 'inductive approach' is used: this (a) fixes new points more firmly because the students can deduce the form or rule for themselves, and (b) makes them do the thinking all the time, with the teacher as guide or midwife.

Some preliminary recommendations: (1) Do not allow students to have *GVE* open during lessons; this book is to be used strictly for help with rereading, preparation ahead, exercise work or the understanding and formal acquisition of grammar. (2) Underline the first occurrences of examples illustrating new grammatical points in your own text. (3) In the early stages (a) stress that endings, not word order, determine sense; (b) watch for a tendency to look at the first few letters and guess the rest. (4) *Practise* reading aloud and writing, especially in the first month.

All these imperatives are a shorthand way of saying 'this is what I do or have done'. In a sense, these notes are counterproductive: the aim throughout is to allow the thoughts to arise from the text, not to stipulate what you should do. Many other and better thoughts may occur to you as you use the Course.

James Neville

Section One A

Background (all references to *WA*)

Survival of Greek literature   7.5
Greek alphabet   7.2–3
Ships and sailing   1.4, 15
Rhapsode and festivals   2.45–8
Grain trade   HI 23, 40; 1.20; political importance of   5.74–7
Trade   4.55–8; 5.69
Loans on ships and source of this story   4.59
Peiraieus   HI 15, 24; 1.20–4, 32
Parthenon   HI 27; 1.18; history of   1.25–7, 30–1, 34; art and   7.78; temples and sanctuaries   2.38–9

It is, of course, possible for the teacher to mediate the background material to the students. But it would be far preferable to get individual students to prepare this beforehand and be responsible for reporting to the class on cue from the teacher. Two or three copies of *WA* in the library are a minimum requirement for this.

Grammar Sections 1A–G

Present indicative active -ω, -άω, -έω
Present imperative active -ω, -άω, -έω
The definite article ὁ ἡ τό (nom., acc.)
καλ-ός, -ή, -όν (ἡμέτερος) (nom., acc.)
ἄνθρωπος, ἔργον (nom., acc.)
Some prepositions (εἰς, πρός, ἀπό, ἐκ, ἐν)
μέν...δέ
Adverbs in -ῶς, -έως

Discussion

Make sure that the Greek alphabet and pronunciation have been revised or reviewed with many simple Greek–English and English–Greek examples on the board. Tell a well-known Greek myth, e.g. the story of Odysseus, or an incident from Greek history, writing the names of the participants on the board in Greek, and demanding their recognition.

For suggestions on pronunciation and writing, see p. 7 of these *Notes*.

Preliminary material

Use the map and the pictures on p. 2 of the *Text* and *WA* (see references on p. 13) to supply some background material to the first episodes in the story. For example, the map is useful for talking about the grain trade: the poor quality of the soil in many parts of Greece and its unsuitability for cereal crops, the necessity for importing grain and the main grain-supply routes. The map can also be used to talk about ancient ships, sea-routes and the universal practice of sailors staying in sight of land as much as possible (the lack of the compass is worth noting, as is the notoriously unpredictable weather in the Aegean). Make sure the Greek names on the map can be written correctly in English.

The picture of the Acropolis gives the opportunity of talking about Athens and the port of Peiraieus, and how the Acropolis and the Parthenon can still be seen by the traveller arriving at the port by sea (Pausanias reported that in his day one could see the spear on the famous statue of Athene Promakhos glinting in the sun).

Cassette

Section 1A–C (*Text* pp. 3–8) is recorded with melodic accent on the *Speaking Greek* cassette, Side 1.

Commentary

Section 1A: p. 3, para. 1

Read the English introduction in the *Text* p. 3, referring students to the map for place-names. If asked by students, comment on the use of the definite article with place-names on the map. (If not, wait until τὸ πλοῖον and ask what τό means, then explain that it is used with place-names also.) Ask students to read aloud the whole of Section 1A in Greek and give much help (see pp. 7, 10–11). Alert the students to the accidence to be met (present indicative; definite article) and construct two empty grids on the blackboard or transparency for overhead projector. If the students are using a morphology chart, ensure that the blackboard or transparency grids are identical with it. It may be best to give the full grid, leaving the genitive and dative to be filled in later.

Nouns (similarly articles, adjectives)

	s.			pl.		
	m.	*f.*	*n.*	*m.*	*f.*	*n.*
nom.						
acc.						
gen.						
dat.						

Verbs

		παύω	ὁράω	ποιέω
indicative	1	παύ-ω	ὁρῶ	ποιῶ
	2			
	3			
	1			
	2			
	3			
imperative	s.			
	pl.			

Similarly for εἰμί and οἶδα later.

These plain, simple grids are probably more effective than the morphology charts in the early stages: they emphasize clearly what is being learnt, and there is no danger of the student becoming lost or despondent at the sight of how much will have to be filled in! Fill in the forms and endings as they occur, *or* at the end of the section.

Now reread, sentence by sentence, and ask the students to translate, e.g.:

p. 3 line

1* **τὸ πλοῖον:** What is the meaning? (see picture). What part of the article is *τό*? Does Byzanti*um* give a gender clue to Latinists?

ἐστίν: (cf. *il est*; *est*). Fill this in on the grid (the students can add -ν ephelkustikon later; often they spot it themselves).

2   **ὁ:** elicit its number, case and gender and fill this in on the grid.

βαίνει: refer to the English introduction – what does H. do? Fill in -ει on the grid.

ἔπειτα: give this meaning at once.

3   **τέλος:** should follow from *ἔπειτα*; otherwise give the meaning.

ὁ κυβερνήτης: what functions does *ὁ* indicate? Guess the meaning from the English introduction, then explain some derivations – cybernetics; Lat. *gubernator* etc.

οἱ ναῦται: Latinists should guess this correctly; others may say 'crew'. Acknowledge this as nearly correct, then give the exact meaning (cf. nautical, astronaut, aeronaut etc.). Fill in *οἱ* on the grid.

4   **εἰσβαίνουσι:** elicit 'go into' – what person? Enter -ουσι on the grid.

5   **πλεῖ τὸ πλοῖον:** if 'the ship goes...' is given, ask for a more precise meaning. Point out the -ον ending, and the similarity of *πλοῖον/πλεῖ*.

In general, students may ignore noun endings for the moment. It is the article that indicates a noun's case. Hence if students ask about *Εὔβοιαν*, tell them it is accusative, but point out that the article indicates the case. *τάς*, *τόν* may be queried: if so, explain and enter on the grid.

Now reread the whole of Section 1A (first paragraph) in Greek and urge the students to ask about anything they do not understand. Mention *πρός* and *εἰς* at the end – it helps with Section 1A (second paragraph) to have them clearly differentiated in meaning.

Section 1A (second paragraph)

Ask the students to read the paragraph in Greek and then begin translation.

p. 3 line

8   **μέν...δέ:** ignore this to start with, then, when the whole sentence has been translated, try to elicit the idea of a change of subject. If that fails,

---

* All references are to line numbers of *RG*.

explain the idiom. Mention 'on the one hand…on the other' as a literal, but forbidden, translation. Establish βλέπει as the verb in the second clause, then πρός as 'towards' τὴν γῆν. Hence Sd. is doing something towards something.

γῆν: cf. geography, geology – explain the literal meanings, then βλέπει should fit in.

τήν should be entered on the grid.

9 If punctuation has not been mentioned before, read the sentence with the intonation of a question, and ask about ; Establish Sd. as subject; if the students cannot translate, give them τί = what? Draw attention to ὁρᾷ. What person? Draw attention to the iota subscript (sometimes printed as an adscript) and its connection with the -ει ending. For ὁράω, cf. panorama, diorama, cyclorama.

10 ἀκρόπολιν: note acro- as in acronym, acrostic, acrobat (acro-+βαίνω); for -πολις cf. politics etc.

τόν: enter on the grid.

11 ὁρῶσιν: stress the ending – what person? Note the similarity with -ουσιν.

14 ἐξαίφνης will probably have to be given, but ἀκούουσιν can be guessed via derivations (acoustic etc.); ψόφον will then easily be deduced.

Again, reread the passage encouraging questions about uncertainties. Refer to the grids so far filled in (the complete singular of the definite article can be shown by reference to εἰς+accusative which gives the accusative neuter in lines 2, 3 and 4).

Two points to stress are the importance of the definite article as indicating the cases of nouns, and the verb inflections. Filling in grids must be seen as the recording of clues met during reading. Always ask students to tell you precisely what any new form is before it is entered on the grid.

N.B.: if the students have learnt Latin, it may be assumed that they all know what a subject and an object are. Do not assume this if they have learnt a modern language by oral, 'active' methods. For non-Latinists, note that the verb inflections mean that subject pronouns may be omitted. At the same time stress that inflections of both noun and verb mean that greater flexibility in word order is possible, and in Greek freely used. If the lessons of Section 1A are firmly fixed, 1B and C go at a lively pace. If the pace needs increasing, read the Greek yourself before the students translate.

Section One B

Background

Clarity of air   1.6
κυβερνήτης   6.31, 34, 41, 45

Commentary

p. 4 line
4 δεῦρο ἐλθέ: 'acted' reading by the teacher, coupled with reference to the stage direction, should enable students to translate this correctly. Note the phrase carefully; ensure that they know which word means 'over here' and which 'come'. Treat ἐλθέ as a regular imperative (it has a regular imperative ending). Ensure that the students note the stem ἐλθ-; this will help with strong aorists in Section 6G.
5 ὁρῶ, ὁρᾷς: the inclusion of pronouns ἐγώ, σύ, should ensure that these are correctly translated. Enter these forms on the -άω grid: if the students have absorbed the idea of contraction in Section 1A, they should be able to deduce -εις from -ᾷς. Always ask them what the *ending* is; in this way attention is drawn to the stem. As soon as σύ is learnt, watch out for its being mistaken for οὐ.
12ff. καλός begins to appear. Fill in the endings on the grid as they occur, pointing out the similarities with the definite article. Some students may take in nouns simultaneously as early as this. Otherwise fill in καλός first and ἄνθρωπος/ἔργον later, reinforcing the endings.
καλός: cf. calligraphy, callisthenics. 'Kal-eido-scope' is a 'beautiful-shape/pattern-examiner'. But to express 'goodness' or 'badness', eu- and dys- are more common prefixes in English (and Greek) than kal- and kak-. At 15, try the word eulogy; and at 28, connect eido- with εἶδον ἰδ-. Frequent repetition of καλός in this section is introduced not just to practise morphology but to show how Greeks viewed their cities; a poet will refer to his city almost as though he were in love with it. (Sophocles' Kolonos was little more than a patch of laurel, shrubs and ivy on a stony hillside, but it still evoked a hauntingly beautiful ode – *O.C.* 668-719.) That the Acropolis and Parthenon are beautiful causes no surprise. Yet it would be an unusual voyager up the Thames who exclaimed 'How καλός is Rotherhithe Dock'; line 25 generally raises a laugh. Yet point out that the Acropolis and the

Parthenon are not just beautiful in themselves but also visible signs of prosperity and pride. The admiration of the dockyards is not unintelligible. In nineteenth-century Newcastle, for example, any visitor would have been shown straight to the Elswick docks as the heart of the town's prosperity; and if a local said 'Fine docks', he would be expressing a sentiment close to Sdenothemis' here.

This section is based on an anonymous comic fragment:

δέσποιν' ἁπασῶν πόντι' Ἀθηναίων πόλι,
ὡς μοι καλόν σου φαίνεται τὸ νεώριον,
ὡς καλὸς ὁ Παρθενῶν, καλὸς δ' ὁ Πειραεύς.
ἄλση δὲ τίς πω τοιάδ' ἔσχ' ἄλλη πόλις;
καὶ τοὐρανοῦ φῶς, φασίν, ἐστιν ἐν καλῷ.
(Edmonds, *Com. Adespot.* 340)

Mistress of all, dear city of the Athenians,
How fine your dockyard seems to me,
How fine the Parthenon, and fine the Peiraieus.
What other city ever had such groves as these?
And the light from heaven too they say is fine.

Cf. Plutarch and Demosthenes:

There was one measure above all which at once gave the greatest pleasure to the Athenians, adorned their city and created amazement among the rest of mankind, and which is today the sole testimony that the tales of the ancient power and glory of Greece are no mere fables. I mean, Pericles' construction of temples and public buildings.
(Plutarch, *Pericles* 12)

Once the Athenians possessed greater wealth than any other Greeks, but they spent it all for love of honour: they contributed from their own property and shirked no danger for the sake of glory. Because of this an immortal heritage comes down to the Athenian people: on the one hand the memory of their deeds, on the other the beauty of the memorials set up for them – the Propylaea, the Parthenon, the porticos, the docks.
(Demosthenes 22.76)

Interestingly, this is one of the *very* few places in Greek literature where the Parthenon is called by that name.

21 φρόντιζε: the φρεν- stem gives frenetic, frenzied, phrenology, frantic. Phrenology combines φρεν- with the λεγ- / λογ- stem met in λέγεις (l. 28), the root of numerous -logy compounds. Note here the common ε → ο change in Greek (as in English, cf. foot → feet).

28 ἰδού: treat as an oddity, cf. *ecce!* or Lo! Ensure that the ἰδ- stem is highlighted (for εἶδον later) (ἰδ- was originally Ϝιδ-, hence *video*; digamma was possibly sounded but not written, in fifth-century Athens). Cf. ἔργον/ Ϝέργον = work (German *Werke*) (ε → ο again).

Section One C

Commentary

p. 5 line

1 **ὁλκάδας:** this may give the English word 'hulk'.
   ἐμπόρια: cf. emporium.

5 If students notice the singular verb with the neuter plural subject, this should be explained; otherwise it can be passed over for the moment.

6 **φίλοι:** cf. all the philo- and phile- words; note Philadelphia, the city of brotherly love.

9 **πόθεν:** refer to the stage direction which follows and ask what the question must have been. Mention the -θεν suffix, comparing πό-θεν and κάτω-θεν 'where from?', 'below-from'. For κάτω (κατά) cf. cathode, with its opposite, anode (ἀνά in Section 1E), being routes (ὁδοί) up and down.

Discussion

By the end of Section 1C, the present indicative and second person imperatives have been met; not all -άω forms have been encountered, but enough to summarize rules for contraction (e.g. α+ο/ω = ω; α+other vowels = α; iota becomes subscript). The definite article is complete but for the accusative masculine plural, and this can be added. If two hours' teaching per week is available, Section 1C can be reached by the end of the first week (excluding time spent on alphabet practice). All the major linguistic points of Section 1 have been met. This is a good time to ask students to learn the regular verb endings and the nominative and accusative (with genitive and dative, if you wish) of the definite article. It may be worth revising nouns, the definite article and adjectives by constructing a comparative grid as follows:

		s.			*pl.*	
nom.	ὁ	καλός	ἄνθρωπος	οἱ	καλοί	ἄνθρωποι
acc.	τόν	καλόν	ἄνθρωπον	τούς	καλούς	ἀνθρώπους
m. gen.				*	*	*
dat.						

nom.	ἡ	καλή	†	αἱ	καλαί	
acc.	τήν	καλήν		τάς	καλάς	
f. gen.				*	*	*
dat.						

nom.	τό	καλόν	ἔργον	τά	καλά	ἔργα
acc.	τό	καλόν	ἔργον	τά	καλά	ἔργα
n. gen.				*	*	*
dat.						

* Genitive plural to be added in Section 2, the genitive singular in Section 7, the dative in Section 8.

† Feminine nouns to be added in Section 2.

Section One D

Grammar

-έω contractions (enough occur to provide simple rules for contraction: ε+ε = ει; ε+ο = ου; ε+ long vowel or diphthong = ε disappears). These contractions are particularly helpful when third declension nouns are met. Note that the first and second persons plural of the present indicative do not occur, neither does the singular imperative. In general in Section 1D watch out for tricky word order.

Discussion

Section 1D introduces the fraud and this can be elicited from the students. The captain and Dikaiopolis go down into the hold and find Hegestratos hacking away at the hull. What should be in the hold? If the hold is full, how can H. be hacking away at the hull? That is, the hold must be empty/low. Why attempt sabotage? Here help may be necessary. Students may be groping towards the idea of an insurance fraud but be reluctant to suggest it in the context of the ancient world. Why might a modern ship-owner/captain scuttle a vessel?

Section ID–G is a good target to aim for in week 2. Its content is self-contained and its accidence light (vocabulary, however, is heavy).

Commentary

p. 5 line

26, 37; p. 6 line 14: not 'o Hegestratos', a common error. This introduces an important principle – that, when the structure of a sentence has been misunderstood, it should be tackled word by word (or phrase by phrase) *in the order in which it comes*, the teacher commenting, or demanding comment, on case, form etc. as each phrase is tackled. So – p. 5 l. 25: κάτω δέ – 'and below'; τόν – indicates object; 'Ηγέστρατον – 'Hegestratos' (hold and wait); ὁρῶσιν – 'they see', probably 'they see Hegestratos' – is there a subject?; ὅ – subject; τε – there's another one too; κυβερνήτης καὶ οἱ ναῦται – problem solved. Now translate the whole sentence. This is an important and constructive analytical technique to be used on all occasions when a sentence causes difficulty, and encourages students to 'hold' problems until they can be solved – an important skill. Challenge students to carry out this exercise in class on difficult sentences.

p. 6 line

14 πέλεκυν: cf. pelican, probably so called from its action in eating, a slow, dipping motion.

15 ἄνθρωπος: as well as mentioning 'man = mankind', note the derogatory usage. With complimentary adjectives, ἀνήρ is used; cf. *homo scelestus* but *vir optimus*.

16 καταδύει: stressing the κατα- element should give the meaning.

23 ῥίπτω ἐμαυτόν: students may need help in deducing what is going on in the picture! Once the meaning is established, give the literal meaning (σεαυτόν, ἑαυτούς occur later).

p. 7 line

4 ποῖ: refer back to πόθεν, after establishing ποῖ as an interrogative.

6 λέμβος: Greek 'lifeboats' were towed behind the vessel.

7 σῷζε: stress the σω- stem (several other examples of this stem occur soon). Draw a Christian fish and explain the acronym: ΙΧΘΥΣ ('Ιησοῦς Χριστὸς

Θεοῦ Υἰὸς Σωτήρ). It may help to fix the σω- stem as 'save'. Cf. creo*sote* ('flesh-preserver').

σεαυτόν: compare with ἐμαυτόν.

Section One F

Background

Value of human life 3.25–6
Friends and enemies 3.1–2, 13–14

Commentary

p. 7 line

17 ἑαυτούς: should pose no problem if ἐμαυτόν, σεαυτόν have already been mentioned.

23 This is a good moment to review ποῦ, ποῖ, πόθεν.

25 ἀποθνήσκω: accept 'drown' (a frequent guess), but add 'die' as the more correct meaning.

31 κακοί: cf. cacophony/euphony.

Discussion

This section is a useful introduction to some Greek moral values. A Greek tended to judge a man's worth by his value to the community, not by any inherent, automatic worth in the eyes of God. In the speech which is the source for this passage, the speaker says the men met an evil end *as they deserved*. He says this because he expected the jury to respond favourably to that judgement. It is unlikely that in a modern court of law such a thing would be said in quite that way.

Section One G

Background

Sacrifice 2.28
Prayers 2.34; 7.11

Commentary

p. 7 line

38 σῶον: what part of speech? Where has σω- stem occurred? *ΙΧΘΥΣ*...

39 περισκοπῶ: περι- (perimeter, periphery)+-scope suffix in English (microscope, telescope etc.) will elicit the exact meaning better than the direct derivation 'periscope'. Cf. kal-eido-scope = 'beautiful shape/pattern-examiner'.

ἀκριβῶς: note -ως as the usual ending for adverbs e.g. σαφῶς (cf. the English adverbial ending -ly).

p. 8 line

22 σωτηρία: establish the correct part of speech, pointing if necessary to the definite article. Refer again to the σω- stem.

33 σιώπα: expressive reading or guessing from the stage direction should elicit the meaning.

34 ἐν κινδύνῳ: if we are σῶοι, what are we *not* in?

Vocabulary

The longer vocabulary on p. 17 of *GVE* should be taken at this point and it is worth going through the list with students. It can be done as an oral test with students being asked to write down words they have forgotten (some may recognize words written on the blackboard even though the sound of them is puzzling). Stress Greek–English, NOT English–Greek.

Discussion

The form of Dikaiopolis' prayer is common to many religions, and typical of pagan Greek religion. There is first a form of address which identifies the proper god (essential in religions where there are many to choose from, each with their own sphere of interests: cf. Roman Catholic or Greek Orthodox saints); often a safety clause is added of the type 'and any other gods who may be listening and are interested'. Second, there is a review of the god's past services. Third, there is a brief statement of the problem, and fourth, there is a reason why the god should answer favourably. Here the tit-for-tat principle is strongly in evidence in Greek religion, where gods are regarded as powerful beings who are immortal and care for men only in so far as men acknowledge (= νομίζω) their power.

Exercises

The number of exercises done depends upon the time available and the ability of the students. Use exercises to reinforce grammar if needed, but if the students seem justifiably confident, do not feel guilty about omitting exercises – apart from the Test Exercises.

Note: There is a very useful Appendix on p. 207, where all the *regular* nouns, verbs and adjectives to be learnt are listed by section. These can be used when the teacher decides that a supplementary exercise is needed.

Supplementary exercises

Some teachers have felt that the exercises in RG are rather difficult, and would welcome more simple practice before they are tackled. The best form of oral or written practice is probably the 'transformation' exercise – i.e. changing one form of the Greek word into another and asking for the translation (if possible); e.g. give a series of nominative singulars and ask for them to be changed into accusative plurals; some first person singulars for changing into second person plurals, and so on. More challenging, and no less important, is the 'expansion' exercise – e.g. add the appropriate form of the definite article to certain suitable words. By consulting the lists in the Appendix, the teacher can construct such exercises very quickly, and put them on the board for the students. The teacher can thus check that students understand the basic forms and constructions, in preparation for the full exercises – or for carrying on with the reading. Using these lists also helps drill the vocabulary.

A *vital* principle – *always begin supplementary exercises with very simple examples indeed.*

Examples

1. Supplementary transformation exercises

> If ὁ κυβερνήτης ἀναβαίνει means 'the captain comes up', what would οἱ κυβερνῆται ἀναβαίνουσι mean?
> If ὁ ναύτης ῥίπτει ἑαυτόν means 'the sailor throws himself', what would οἱ ναῦται ῥίπτουσιν ἑαυτούς mean?
> If ἐγὼ βοηθῶ means 'I run to help', what would σὺ βοηθεῖς mean?
> If ἆρα οὐχ ὁρᾷς τὸν Παρθενῶνα; means 'Don't you (s.) see the Parthenon?', what would ἆρα οὐχ ὁρᾶτε τὸν Παρθενῶνα; mean?

2. Supplementary substitution exercises

> If τὸ πλοῖον πλεῖ πρὸς τὰς 'Aθήνας means 'the boat sails towards Athens', how would you say in Greek:
> (1) τὸ πλοῖον πλεῖ towards Chios
> (2) τὸ πλοῖον πλεῖ towards Euboia
> (3) τὸ πλοῖον πλεῖ towards Peiraieus
> (4) τὸ πλοῖον πλεῖ towards Byzantium?

3. Supplementary expansion exercises

> If φεῦγε means 'flee!', how would you say in Greek:
> (1) You φεῦγε!
> (2) You φεῦγε too!

Vocabulary learning

A constant check *must* be kept on this. It is suggested that students learn the lists from passages *already* translated as the first part of their home preparation before translating ahead for the next class. A short, routine review of the vocabulary before the start of every class is important to establish.

Test Exercise

The Test Exercises are essential and it is worth explaining that they are meant to be tackled unseen. If they cannot be translated in class (which is best), they should be set as written exercises, with careful instructions to the students to note and learn anything which they have to look up.

Note: The methodology outlined above – students reading aloud and translating, the teacher eliciting from the students the grammar, which is inserted on a grid or in the morphology charts (always in comparison with forms already met) – *will now no longer be outlined in detail for each section.* New grammar and its important features are noted but this methodology is now taken for granted. Teachers will of course make their own modifications.

Section One H

Background

> Homer   HI 1; 7.1; P 10–12
> Socrates   7.29–31

Arguing and the power of words 7.24
τέχνη 7.64–5
στρατηγός 5.29–31
War 6.1–8

Grammar

Accidence for 1H–J: present indicative of εἰμί and οἶδα. Most forms can be deduced by pupils, then entered on grids.
Neuter plural of adjectives
τε...καί
A group with a sound grasp of 1A–G can tackle this in a one-hour session.

Commentary

p. 9 line
8 ἐρωτᾷ: can be deduced from ποῦ following.
εἰσίν: emphasize the -σιν ending denoting the third person plural.
9 σαφῶς: ask for the part of speech.
νύξ = Latin *nox*, cf. nocturnal.
11 ὁμηρίζει: establish the part of speech. Ask if a well-known person is recognizable in the verb-stem.
12 παίζει: the meaning can be elicited by reference to παιδ- derivations, e.g. paediatric, encyclopaedia. A παῖς (boy *or* girl) needs *training*; hence παιδεύω = train, cf. pedagogue, orthopaedic. παίζω = play, 'joke' may be elicited at length from all this, and the effort is worth while.
13 μαθητάς: cf. polymath, mathematics.
15 ἐσμέν: parts of εἰμί, οἶδα are generally introduced with pronouns on their first appearance. Note that the plurals have -μεν, -τε, -σι(ν), like regular verbs. Warning: the plural of οἶδα does not appear in the text but is used in the Test Exercise. Forms can be deduced from the stem ἰσ-, and these *must* be learnt before the Test Exercise is set.
21 For the rhapsode's Homeric extracts, give the vocabulary; there is little point in attempting guesses. οἴνοπα = οἶνος + ὄψ = 'wine-faced', οἶνος was originally Ϝοῖνος, hence Latin *vinum*, English 'wine'.
23 δῆλον: cf. psychedelic – 'revealing the soul'.
26 μελαίνῃ: cf. melanine, the substance in the skin which aids sun-tan; melanite, the chemical which brings up the black in photographic negatives.
28 μῶρος: cf. moron.
37 πολλά: enlarge on the numerous poly- compounds.
γιγνώσκω (cf. Latin *cognosco*): cf. gnostic, agnostic (negative a-), gnome

(a being full of wise thoughts). Try to fix γιγνώσκω (γνο-, γνω-) as firmly as possible before γίγνομαι is met in Section 2A.

39 ἀπαίδευτος: here, if not before, the relationship of παιδ- stems can be explained. Make sure the a- prefix showing a negative is known – cf. agnostic, asymmetrical, asphalt ('non-slip' ἀ+σφάλλω, ἀσφαλής).

p. 10 line

3 πολεμικά: cf. polemic, -ical.

ἔργα: cf. erg (unit of work), energy, ergonomics.

4 στρατηγικά: cf. strategy, -egic.

7 ἔμπειρος: explain empirical knowledge as knowledge gained from experience.

16 τέχνη: cf. technique, technical.

21 ἄριστος: cf. aristocracy. Perhaps anticipate ideas about νόμος and φύσις by discussing the notion that noble birth = superiority.

32 Note the use of Socrates as a verb – 'You're Socrateasing me'; compare Cratinos' usage Εὐριπιδαριστοφανίζω (Cratinos fr. 307).

35 Note παῖδες from the παιδ- root.

Discussion

The rhapsode's claims sound ridiculous, but try to use the episode to discuss the enormous authority accorded to Homer and the still persistent feeling that reading a book by a hallowed expert transfers some of that hallowed expertise to the reader. How far can this be taken?

Section Two A

Background

Persia and the Persian Wars   HI 12–20 (esp. 18 – Salamis); P 2–6
Rhetoric   7.17

Grammar

Present indicative active -όω
Present indicative and imperative middle -ομαι, -άομαι, -έομαι, βοή, ἀπορία, τόλμα, ναύτης (nom., acc.)
Genitive plurals meaning 'of'

Uses of the definite article
More prepositions (παρά, ἐπί, διά + accusative)

It is probably best to treat the middle endings as something separate. If παύω and παύομαι are both met, there are likely to be questions about the distinctions between them and these questions are not answered in the Course until Section 5. If an interim explanation is required, it is possible to call the middle 'a sort of reflexive'. It is, however, essential to stress that many verbs have a middle form only, cf. deponent verbs in Latin. The contracted forms of middle verbs should cause no problems if the rules for contraction have been assimilated.

If time is short, it is possible to pass over the -όω contractions; only a handful of verbs are common, and they seldom present difficulties of recognition. Future prose-writers will of course need the rules.

As for first declension nouns the full rules for the occurrence of -α- or -η- will again only be needed by those who wish to do a substantial amount of English–Greek translation.

Set up a grid as follows, revising or reviewing the active forms in class and writing them in before reading the text and eliciting the middle:

1	παύω	παύομαι	ποιέω	ποιέομαι	ὁράω	θεάομαι
2						
3						
	etc.					

Discussion

There is a great temptation to spend too much time on the background. Some comment upon the invasion of Xerxes is essential – refer to the map – and upon the difference between the two narratives: the vague generalizations and high rhetoric of the rhapsode (based on Lysias' *Epitaph* written 150 years after the event), and the 'facts' of the captain (though his account contains few solid facts about the battle). He describes events from the viewpoint of the individual without any concept of overall strategy – the same, indeed, is true of the accounts given by Aeschylus and Herodotus, on which the captain's account is based.

Commentary

p. 11 line

15 βραδέως: ask for the part of speech.
ἔρχεται: ensure that the students distinguish the stem, and the ending.

Then elicit the equivalent form of παύομαι (παύ-εται) and write it on the grid (if this verb is used as a pattern).

17 ἀλλήλους: translate this, and fix the meaning by waiting for παρά in l. 18 and showing that παρ' ἄλληλα (γράμματα = lines) gives 'parallel'.

ἡδέως: ask for the part of speech; cf. hedonist.

διαλέγονται: ensure the stem and ending are correctly split (this is not so difficult, since λέγω has already been met). Use 'dialogue' to work towards the correct translation; comment again upon the vowel change λεγ-/λογ- (cf. p. 20, on p. 4.21).

19 διέρχεται: cf. 'I'll *go through* the main points again.'

20 γίγνεται may have to be given, as also τὰ Μηδικά. Persia had been a province of Media; the rise of Cyrus and the growth of Persia led to the overthrow of the Median Empire. The Greeks still used Medes/Persians almost synonymously – compare the way the Persians in Aeschylus' *Persai* and elsewhere used 'Ionians' for Greeks.

21 μάχονται: use the picture to prompt guesses;

τολμῶσι: usually guessed as 'do'; accept, and modify it.

22 ὁπόσοι πίπτουσιν: ask what you would want to know about a battle, e.g. Who won? The right questions may guide students towards the idea of casualties.

p. 12 line

2 ῥητορικά: elicit 'rhetorical' and establish the exact meaning in English.

4 Note carefully τὰ περὶ Σαλαμῖνα (πράγματα) as a very common idiom.

5 νῆσος: What was Salamis? Locate -νησ- in some names, e.g. Peloponn*ese*, Dodekan*ese*, Poly*nesia*, Mela*nesia* etc.

8 ἡμετέραν: ask for the part of speech (ἡμ- stem).

τόλμαν: refer back to p. 11.21.

10 βάρβαρος: anyone who could not speak Greek and seemed therefore to utter nonsense-noises (bar-bar).

12 ἴσασιν: the third person plural of οἶδα first appears in the text here; it should be familiar from the Test Exercise.

14 ποίει: review and reinforce the difference between this and ποιεῖ here.

κάλλιστον: try to take the meaning on from καλός: does -ιστ- suggest something? (ἄριστος, μάλιστα).

Section Two B

Background

Balanced, Gorgianic style 7.19
Use of μέν...δέ 7.9
Sacrifice 2.28ff.
Supplication 2.36
ὕβρις 3.15

Commentary

p. 12 line

23 Much needs to be given here (except Θεά, cf. theology – noting, however, the feminine ending). The invocation to the Muse, goddess of memory, was to ensure the poet got right the facts relating to adventures long ago (it is nothing to do with 'inspiration' in our sense). It became a long-lasting poetic convention. It is worth giving the students the opening lines of the *Iliad* both for comparison, and for first acquaintance with the rhythm of the Homeric hexameter.

26 ἀποροῦσι: ἀπορέω is always hard to translate. Once the idea of 'not know what to do' (with no direct English equivalent) is established, point out that this is a very useful verb. (N.B. ἀ + πορ- = 'no resources' is at the root of it.)

φοβοῦνται: cf. claustrophobia, hydrophobia, agoraphobia etc.

p. 13 line

1–8 Many words are here which have been met before but not yet learnt (e.g. κίνδυνος, θυσία, εὔχομαι) – mostly from p. 8. Refer back to find the meanings.

8 ἀγαθόν...ἐλευθερία: this use of the neuter = 'a good thing' is very common.

11 ὅσαι: cf. ὁπόσοι (p. 11.22).

12 ἱκετεῖαι: will need explanation, supplication not being a modern concept. The central idea is that the suppliant formally puts himself or herself at the mercy of the god and thereby sets up a relationship which obliges the god to offer something in return, e.g. protection, victory etc.

15 πατρίδα: elicit the idea of 'father', and 'fatherland' should follow.

17 ὕβριν: not 'pride' but (i) violence, aggression and (ii) intentional humiliation.

πλῆθος: cf. plethora.

Section Two C

Background

Herodotus and history   7.33–4
Aeschylus' *Persians*   7.38, 46
Religion and patriotism   2.47; 4.82
ἀγών and competition   3.1–2

Commentary

p. 13 line

26 οὐδὲν λέγει: explain the literal meaning and give an appropriate idiom, e.g. 'He is talking rubbish!'

34 ψευδῆ: cf. pseudonym and the numerous pseud- compounds.

36 Σαλαμινομάχης: elicit the meaning from the elements. Note the pride in the epithet, cf. *Μαραθωνομάχης* (p. 93.19).

40 ἡσυχίαν ἔχω: the vocabulary translates this as 'keep quiet'. Add *not* 'keep silent', but more 'take things easy, settle down, calm down, keep a low profile' etc.

p. 14 line

20 ἔνθα καὶ ἔνθα: it is best simply to give the meaning.

21 ἅμα ἕῳ: this can be deduced by reference to *νύξ* earlier.

22 σάλπιγξ: see the picture. Salpinx is also used as an anatomical term for a tube, e.g. Eustachian and Fallopian.

ἠχεῖ: tell students to transliterate the first person singular of this verb and watch their surprise!

πετρῶν: some may know that Peter means 'rock' or 'stone', so they may easily guess this (refer to Matthew 16.18 if they do not). Mention also petrify, petrology etc., and perhaps add that petrol (*πετρός + oleum*) also derives from it (as being found in subterranean deposits of rock).

25 Aeschylus, *Persai* 402–5. Show students the original text.

27 γυναῖκας: cf. gynaecology.

ἀγών: cf. protagonist, agony (the final struggle before death).

Section Two D

Background

Interventions of the gods   2.6–8
Sea-battles   6.31ff.
Salamis   6.37
Greek unity   1.1, HI 16, 29
Greek στάσις   HI 39, 72; 3.14
Use of past to throw light on present   7.25

Commentary

p. 14 line

33   θεᾶται: ask what you do in a theatre (cf. audience – *audio*). Discuss the different design of modern theatres.

35   φαίνεται: prompt the meaning via 'phenomenon'.

p. 15 line

2   κόσμῳ: cosmos = the ordered state of the universe; cosmetic = something which produces an ordered state of the face. The opposite of κόσμος is χάος (= void).

τάξιν: cf. taxidermy (= arranging, not stuffing, skins). For derm- cf. hypodermic, pachyderm.

5   οἱ μέν...οἱ δέ: stress as 'some...others' – one of the few points not picked up in *GVE*.

16   μεταβολή: cf. metabolism and other μετα- compounds indicating change (metathesis, metamorphosis etc.).

17   ὁμονοοῦσιν: elicit by contrast with φίλοι, then explain the constituents, viz. ὁμο- and νοῦς, cf. homeopathy, homogenous, homonym etc. Homosexuals are not necessarily men!

18   μισοῦσιν: cf. misogynist; explore the μισο- root further.

Supplementary exercises

Transformation exercises from active to middle and back, singular to plural and so on, are useful. It is also worth giving the feminine definite article a thorough revision with the new feminine nouns, so an expansion exercise here will help, as well as transformations of the definite article + noun. Work on, e.g., ἡ ἀπορία, ὁ ναύτης especially.

When you are dealing with the present tense, any verb from the learning lists will be suitable, whether regular or not. There is a list of irregular verbs by section on p. 214 of these *Notes*.

Section Three A

Background

    Source of this incident   1.24
    Peloponnesian War   HI 33–56
    Beacon fires   1.16

Grammar

    λιμήν, ναῦς, Ζεύς, οὗτος, ἐκεῖνος, ἐγώ, σύ, πολύς, μέγας (nom., acc.)
    Ellipse of εἰμί
    Negatives

The basic pattern of the third declension and the introduction of οὗτος are the two most vital points. It may be best to treat third declension nouns less fully than the morphology charts suggest and work towards a table such as this:

| | *s.* | | *pl.* | |
	m.f.	*n.*	*m.f.*	*n.*
nom.	★	★	-ες -εις (-εες)	-α -η (-εα)
acc.	-α -η (-εα)	★	-ας -εις	-α -η (-εα)
gen.	-ος -ους (-εος)	-ος -ους (-εος)	-ων -ων	-ων -ων
dat.	-ι -ει	-ι -ει	-σι(ν) -εσι(ν)	-σι(ν) -εσι(ν)

Lay out the empty grid *in full* on the board at this point, but fill in only the forms met, leaving gaps for the genitive and dative to come (Sections 7 and 8). This table covers almost all the forms met (but students doing English–Greek will need more detail).

In Section 3A–E, concentrate on 3a nouns, i.e. those ending in ★, -α (-ος, -ι), -ες, -ας, (-ων, -σι(ν)). (i) Emphasize the stem change from the nominative to accusative, and alert them to ἀνήρ, ἀνδρ- and similar changes; (ii) point out that, quite often, a *long* vowel in the nominative will be *short* in the stem, e.g. λιμήν, λιμέν-.

οὗτος needs a separate table. The endings are much the same as in the definite article. A good stem mnemonic is οὗτ- τουτ-, αὐτ- ταυτ-. Those doing English–Greek will need to be told that οὗτος ᾤ is normal Greek. Two omissions should be added here – ὅδε, ὁδί (though these are glossed in the Vocabulary at the back of *GVE*).

μέγας, πολύς are also dealt with here. If learnt in the form μέγας (μεγάλ-), πολύς (πολλ-), all parts are easily recognizable. (N.B. πολλά has already been learnt in Section 1.1.)

Commentary

p. 16 line

29 τὰ πυρά: cf. pyrotechnics, pyromania etc., and note (a) the neuter plural – it is necessary to point it out here, as ἡ πυρά appears in Section 4; (b) the use of fire beacons for rapid communication throughout the ages, from the Trojan Wars until very recent times.

37 δηλοῖ may cause trouble.

Section Three B

Background

Ships and hoplites 6.31ff.
Manning triremes 6.42–4
Slaves in battle 6.17

Commentary

p. 17 line

9 ἄνδρες: cf. android, androgynous.

14 μέγας: cf. megaphone, megalomaniac etc.

26 τροπωτῆρα: a leather thong attaching the oar to the thole-pin (acting as a rowlock); the rower provided his own.

27 ὑπηρέσιον: a cushion, possibly tallowed underneath for comfort when sliding back and forth (see Dionysos' complaints in *Frogs* 221f.). Polos is an armed soldier (ἐπιβάτης). There would have been about ten of these on the trireme, usually 'crack' troops, plus four archers; they fought on deck. Protarkhos is a rower. There were three banks of oars: the θρανίτης on the top bench had possibly the longest oar and the highest pay, the ζυγίτης was on the middle bench, and the θαλαμίτης on the lowest, with the shortest oar and the lowest rate of pay.

Section Three C

Background

Spartan history   HI 6, 10–11; 19; 22–4, 29
The legend of Sparta   P 7–9
Periclean policy in war   HI 38–9
Pericles as στρατηγός   5.29-33
Athenian sea-power and history   HI 15; 5.78ff.; 6.33
Trierarchs   5.71–2; 6.41–8

Commentary

p. 18 line
20 Note the idiom: in English 'I feel fear', but in Greek 'fear holds me'; it, not you, is in control.
21 For the rhapsode as στρατηγός, cf. Section 1H-J.
25 Fears of Spartan brutality: perhaps read from Thucydides II.67.
30 μιμνήσκομαι: stress μνη- root; cf. mnemonic.
33 ἐκκλησίᾳ: later used for a Christian assembly, hence ecclesiastical, French *église*. It means 'called out'.
35 Pericles' speech: Pericles advocated sea-power, which made him popular with sailors; farmers viewed him differently – see on p. 24.25, p. 93.14.
36 κρατοῦσι: point to the -cracy suffix in autocracy, democracy, aristocracy, plutocracy etc.
40 γεωργοί: explain the two elements: γῆ + ἔργον (Farmer George).

p. 19 line
29 Imagine the confusion when a fleet had to be launched at night; crewmen had to reach the ships from all parts of the city.

Section Three D

Background

κελευστής 6.31, 45
Competition to get ship ready 6.44–5
Houses 1.7, 35–7, cf. 4.26
Deme-names 4.16

Commentary

p. 20 line
8 κελευστής: from κελεύω, because he gave time (= orders) to the rowers.
13 Watch the accent on ζήτει – cf. ζητεῖ.
This is a good place to review imperatives.
20 The knocking scene is based closely upon several such in Aristophanes.
37 Name and deme are normal methods of identification.

Section Three E

Background

Libations 2.29
Journeys 2.33; 6.45

Commentary

p. 21 line
20 On prayers cf. p. 8.25.
22 πάλιν: cf. palinode, palindrome. Give an example of a palindrome.

Thucydides VI.31–2 (around which this section of *RG* is based) gives further details on preparations for putting out to sea. It makes excellent background reading.

RG has now covered the basic essentials, i.e. present active and middle, and first, second and third declension nominative and accusative nouns and adjectives. Hence this is an important point at which to ensure that these fundamental points are firmly fixed. Also review οὗτος very carefully. Note that there is a full contraction table in *GVE* p. 280.

The next sections (4–6) are heavily loaded with new accidence and syntax: if the foundation of Sections 1–3 is really firm, then the challenge of Sections 4–6 is more easily met.

Supplementary exercises

Transformation exercises on type 3a nouns are very important, as are expansion exercises using the definite article, especially with οὗτος and ἐκεῖνος, since such exercises combine type 3 nouns with type 1/2 adjectives. Be warned: οὗτος always causes trouble!

Section Four A

Background

Walls of Athens   HI 24; 1.23, 30–3
Farmer's lot   1.9, 13; 4.50–2
Sea-power   6.2, 8; HI 23
Periclean policy   HI 36
Beginnings of empire   HI 27; 5.78ff.
Plague and suffering   HI 36; 2.7; Thucydides and plague   7.34; 4.81; unpredictability of gods   2.6–7

Grammar

πρᾶγμα, πλῆθος, πόλις, πρέσβυς, ἄστυ; εὔφρων, τίς, τις, οὐδείς; ὤν (nom., acc.)
Present participle active and middle (nom., acc.)
Verbs taking participles
βασιλεύς (nom., acc.)
Adjectives translated as adverbs
Elision and crasis

The participle is crucial, first of εἰμί, then of the active and middle generally. Since participles are extremely common in Greek, and have such a wide range of usages, it is essential that their forms are firmly fixed at this point.

Set up a grid setting definite article+λιμήν, and definite article+τόλμα against the new ὤν, οὖσα, ὄν participle forms, e.g.

nom.	ὁ λιμήν	ὤν	ἡ τόλμα	οὖσα	τὸ ὄν
acc.	τὸν λιμένα	ὄντα	τὴν τόλμαν	οὖσαν	τὸ ὄν
gen.					
dat.					

Plurals similarly.

Review and fill in the two known nouns, then prepare to fill in the participles as they are met. Apply the same principle to κακοδαίμων.

Middle participles are much easier: stress the comparison with καλός and point to the -μεν-, *the* sign of a middle participle.

Other new accidence includes a further range of third declension nouns (τεῖχος, πρᾶγμα, πόλις). Again, compare these with λιμήν, but point up their -ε- stems (giving, e.g. τείχους (-εος), τείχη (-εα)). This contraction of epsilon is a very important principle, already met with verbs, and is worth pointing out here.

Commentary

p. 24 line

18 Herakles was most commonly invoked in times of (suspected) danger, for he had been human too, and he was invincible. See further E. R. Dodds, *The Ancient Concept of Progress* (O.U.P., 1973) 154.

21 δαίμων: a good starting-point for comment on Greek religious thought. Our derivation word 'demon' is 'black', since we tend to view the world in the light of the Christian dualism of white/black. δαίμων in Greek is simply a god; the gods themselves were not good/bad, white/black – they were all a murky shade of grey. Here the idea of gods punishing mortals occurs, but stress that it is only an opinion offered. Most examples of divine punishment are of individual gods punishing individual mortals for specific offences against either them, their temples or their priests. This begs the question of whether there was any such thing as a concept of sin (the usual word ἁμάρτημα means nothing more than a bad shot – you try, but miss). Punishment as a result of 'sin' is elusive; Oedipus, for instance, was most dreadfully punished, yet the question 'Whose fault?' remains unanswerable, since all acted for what they thought was the best. Similarly, in Thucydides' account of the plague – on which Section 4A is based – the writer's underlying feeling that some force hostile to Athens is at work can be clearly felt, as it can explicitly here with the repetition of κακοδαίμων in the text. Recommend students to read Thucydides II.51–3 in translation.

23 Note the κακοδαίμων forms: ask the students to identify the cases and to say how they are formed.

24 γεωργός: cf. the synonym αὐτουργός for its implicit comment on Greek ideas (see *WA* 3.18 for the value Greeks placed on independence).

25 Pericles again: an anti-Pericles sentiment from the farmer. Read Thucydides II.13–17 on the hardships imposed upon farmers by the evacuation of Attica. Stress here the diversity of attitudes towards both Pericles and the Peloponnesian War: Pericles advanced the mercantile and imperial interests of Athens (hence his popularity with sailors), to some extent without regard for the domestic problems caused by the War (hence Dikaiopolis' objections, vociferously given when he reaches the Assembly). Cf. on p. 18.35, p. 93.14.

29 φησί: treat this as an oddity; there is no need for a full explanation (which is given in Section 6D–F).

34–5 ῥήτωρ...πιθανός: outstanding individual orators like Pericles could keep the confidence of the Assembly (which was composed in theory of all adult male citizens) over a period of many years, lending some consistency to policy. The question as to how many attended is thorny: probably those from outlying areas seldom came. Discuss how unrepresentative local political parties or trade union branches can be: those with the greatest interest attend, but their views may not be typical.

37 Euboia: perhaps we now know what Dikaiopolis was doing there, back in the first passage of the Course.

38ff. Many more examples of ὤν–οὖσα–ὄν occur. Ask students to identify what part they are, entering them on the grid, and varying translations according to context ('when/since/as' etc.). Stress the variety of possibilities after the literal translation 'being' in each case. Note the possible confusion (implicit always with the verb 'to be') between 'Being a farmer, he...' and 'the farmer, being miserable, ...'.

40 οὔσας: students may need help to establish the feminine stem. The neuter does not appear though it can be deduced from κακοδαῖμον (23); as all neuter plurals end in -α (except those which end in -η which are contracted from -εα), the plural can also be entered.

p. 25 line

20–1 ὀλοφύρομαι...τὸν ἐμὸν υἱόν: note the emotional involvement there and cf. Herodotus I.87: 'No man is so stupid as to prefer war to peace, for in war fathers bury sons and in peace sons bury fathers'. In Plato's *Hippias Major* the Greek ideal is expressed as 'To live in health and wealth, bury one's own parents properly and be buried by one's own children'. The worst thing was 'to bury one's own children'. Cf. further Herodotus – Solon's choice of Tellos as the happiest of mortals – for a translation, see *Text*, p. 158. Once again note the pragmatism of Greek thought: one produces children and looks after them on the assumption that they will return the compliment when one is old and possibly unable to look after oneself or earn one's own living. πάλιν γὰρ αὖθις παῖς ὁ γηράσκων ἀνήρ (Sophocles, frag. 434).

Section Four B

Background

Death and burial   4.77–82
ὕβρις   3.15
Need to respect the gods   2.40; 4.13, 81
Human obligations   2.25–6
Pessimism about gods   2.22–3
The gods reciprocate   2.3; 2.24

Commentary

p. 25 line
34   ΔΟΥΛΟΣ: give the meaning.
βαρύς: cf. baritone, barometer, isobar.
35   νεκρός: cf. necrophilia, necromancy.
   φέρω: cf. (Latin) *fero* – Lucifer, Christopher.

p. 26 line
2   'νθρωπε: note the aphaeresis (converse of elision) and the derogatory usage, cf. p. 6.15.
3   Comment briefly on the exclamatory genitive; there are several examples in this section.
13   σέβομαι: link this with ἀσέβειας (8). Also note the derivation Sebastian and Σεβαστός, the Greek name for/translation of Augustus.
14   νόμους: cf. taxonomy, agronomy, nomothetic. This is the first mention of a concept which will become important later.

Cf. Aeschylus, *Seven against Thebes* 77: 'A city that prospers honours its gods.'

17 ὥσπερ πρόβατα: cf. our idiom 'like flies'.

18 For disasters calling even the existence of the gods into question, refer to Thucydides II.51-3; cf. Euripides' *Antiope* fragment:

τρεῖς εἰσιν ἀρεταί, τὰς χρεών σ' ἀσκεῖν, τέκνον,
θεούς τε τιμᾶν τούς τε θρέψαντας γονεῖς,
νόμους τε κοινοὺς Ἑλλάδος· καὶ ταῦτα δρῶν
κάλλιστον ἕξεις στέφανον εὐκλείας ἀεί.

20 If the gods honour piety, why do the pious die alongside the impious? Read Theognis 373-82; cf. Euripides' *Skuriai* fragment:

φεῦ τῶν βροτείων ὡς ἀνώμαλοι τύχαι.
οἱ μὲν γὰρ εὖ πράσσουσι, τοῖς δὲ συμφοραὶ
σκληραὶ πάρεισιν εὐσεβοῦσιν εἰς θεούς,
καὶ πάντ' ἀκριβῶς κἀπὶ φροντίδων βίον
οὕτω δικαίως ζῶσιν αἰσχύνης ἄτερ.

21 μήτηρ: cf. maternal, metropolis.

πατήρ: cf. paternal, patrimony, patronymic.

22 ἀδελφός: cf. Philadelphia, Christadelphians. The ἀ- prefix here is not 'negative' but indicates 'together-ness', i.e. 'together in the womb' (δελφύς). Cf. ἄλοχος (in bed with), and ἄκοιτις (lying with), both = 'wife'.

26 ἐφήμεροι: cf. ephemeral; explain the meaning from the elements. The young man himself is to be envisaged as in the incipient stages of the plague, hence his scepticism even in the face of a death that was regarded as a merciful release, cf. Aeschylus' fragment:

ζόης πονηρᾶς θάνατος αἱρετώτερος.
τὸ μὴ γενέσθαι δ' ἐστὶν ἢ πεφυκέναι
κρεῖσσον κακῶς πάσχοντα.

26-8 Pindar, *Pythian* 8.135. Have a text of the original available – even more laconic and desperate than the version in the text here. σκιά + οὐρά (= tail) gives us 'squirrel'.

33 βίον: cf. biology, macrobiotic. Also amphibious.

Section Four C

Background

Altar of Twelve Gods   1.28
Supplication   2.36–7
Travelling   1.14
The Eleven   5.36–7
ὑπηρέτης   4.64
κῆρυξ   5.39–40
Sanctuary   2.38
Responsibility for suppliants   2.25

Commentary

p. 27 line

32 λανθάνει: give the hackneyed translation 'escapes the notice of' to fix the basic idea of doing something unseen by or unbeknown to another.

τρέχων: even if students have not already been told that ὤν–οὖσα–ὄν provides endings for the active participles, extract this information from them, confirming it by προστρέχοντα in the next line. Enter this on the grid. (Note the suggested forms of translation in *GVE*, p. 55.)

33 ἄτοπον: ἀ- privative, τόπος – topical, so Utopia (= οὐ, τόπος – no (such) place). Carlyle (*Sartor Resartus*) uses 'Weissnichtwo', 'Don't knowhere'.

35 Why should the rhapsode suggest that he was δοῦλος? Could he not tell from his clothing? Possibly – but the 'Old Oligarch' (10–12) complains that in Athens it is no longer possible to tell a slave from a free man by clothing. Yet vase-painting, perhaps by convention, seems to differentiate. Most likely, the rhapsode is thinking of the number of runaway slaves during the War (as below on pp. 33–4): cf. Thucydides VII.75, hoplites carrying their own supplies because of the number of slaves deserting.

p. 28 line

28 ὁδοιπόρος: both roots are known so the meaning should be deduced.

φαίνεται: the verb has already been met: note that, where English uses an infinitive, Greek uses a participle.

30 ὀρθῶς: cf. orthodontic, orthodox, orthography etc.

32 πάσχει: note the variety of translations and explain that the sense is not so violent as the English 'suffer'. The basic meaning is 'have an experience'. The phrase 'Paschal Lamb' derives not from Greek, but from the Hebrew for 'Passover'.

33 ἱκετείαν: cf. p. 13.12. The mediaeval concept of 'sanctuary' may perhaps be familiar. Cf. children's games, where there is certain ground on which one cannot be 'had' or 'tagged'.

35 κῆρυξ: the herald of the original (Xenophon, *Hellenica* II.iii.54–6) was the herald of the Thirty Tyrants, conveying their orders for the arrest of Theramenes. Theramenes had taken refuge at the altar, from which he was dragged away bodily by Satyros.

36 ἕνδεκα: cf. hendecagon, hendecasyllabic. 'The Eleven' were chosen by lot, one from each tribe plus a secretary, to act as a kind of police-force – executing orders for arrest, for example, and looking after the prison (see on p. 30.3–4).

p. 29 line
7 φθάνει: another awkward word. Translate it literally first, and then adapt. See *GVE* 54 for suggested translations.

9–10 .The quotation may be found in context in the *Text* p. 178.35–6.

13 δυστυχής: dyslexia, dyspepsia, dysentery, muscular dystrophy (all invaluable Greek stems) will fix the idea that δυσ- indicates something unpleasant.

Section Four D

Background

Part-source of the story 2.37
πρεσβευτής (pl. πρέσβεις) 5.38, 41
Desire for peace 6.5

Commentary

p. 29 line
29 Herodotus reports the Aeginetans as doing exactly this, VI.91.

p. 30 line
3–4 πρὸς τοὺς ἄλλους Λακεδαιμονίους: viz. δεσμωτήριον, though note that this was never a place of punishment. It was used for those awaiting trial, or execution (e.g. Socrates).

21 νέμεσις μεγάλη: cf. nemesis in English, and cf. the Herodotus extract in *Text* p. 159.36.

προγόνους: Theognis 731-42 complains about inherited guilt – the guilty get off scot-free, the innocent descendants suffer. The text here envisages the ξένος as being one of the ambassadors killed (through inherited 'guilt') by Athenians in Herodotus VII.133-7.

26 ἀπορία: met only as 'at-a-loss-ness' so far. Explain the πορ- root as 'provisions', 'resources', and quote ἐμπόριον, 'place with provisions'. This helps both here and later.

27-8 The quotation from Solon (written in elegiacs (N.B. pentameter first), as is most of his gnomic poetry) underlines the theme of the chapter. On the breakdown of law and order leading to the questioning of conventional standards of morality generally, see Thucydides (as on p. 26.18ff.).

Supplementary exercises

Thorough revision of these nouns and participles is needed. Transform nouns from case to case, from singular to plural and from plural to singular; it is important to add the definite article or οὗτος ὁ to nouns so that students get an idea of the nouns' typical genders. To impress the idea of the definite article + participle = 'the people who', transform a series such as οὗτοί εἰσι → οὗτοι οἱ ὄντες as well as transforming cases, genders and number, and adding the appropriate forms of participle to nouns.

Section Five A

Background

Greek comedy 7.35-6; 53-63
Aristophanes and Pericles HI 37
Festivals 2.41-8
Coinage 4.61
Rich and poor 3.18
Horses 1.13
Alcibiades and horses 3.9
Women and marriage 4.23-31; and home life 4.32-6, 50-1; 'dangerous' women 3.19
Town and city 4.1-11; 1.21

Grammar

Imperfect indicative active and middle
Position of adjective

This is the first section in which real difficulties may occur; much new material is introduced and sentence structures are further developed. Students may need considerably more help with translation, and it often happens that the pace of reading slows down both here and in the next chapter. Supplementary exercises will certainly be needed to consolidate reliable recognition of vital stem changes, and practice must be given in working back from the forms of verb in the text to the form given in the lexicon. Check vocabulary thoroughly; there are many new words here.

As *Clouds* is the only source for this adapted text, try to add some material from the original (teachers are warmly recommended to the edition by K. J. Dover (O.U.P., 1968)). Students should also be encouraged to read a translation.

With all the problems, try to keep the students cheerful; the grammar is constantly revised in Sections 7–10, and if students can get over this hurdle, the way ahead will be much easier.

Cassette

Section 5E–F (*Text*, pp. 38–41) is recorded with melodic accent on the *Speaking Greek* cassette, end of Side 1; Section 5G–H (pp. 41–3), at the beginning of Side 2.

Commentary

p. 32 line
6 The opening sentence can be teased out: ὀλοφυρόμενος was learnt in Section 4D and most of the rest can be deduced from the English introduction.
7 ἱππομανής: cf. hippopotamus, hippodrome; mania and the various -maniac suffixes.
8 βαθέως: check that the part of speech is recognized. Cf. bathos, bathyscope, bathysphere etc.
ὕπνος: cf. hypnosis.
11 The first ten words are the first ten words of *Clouds*. It may be useful to have a copy of the original text open while reading all these sections: (a) to be aware of how close the text is to the original, and (b) to point out exact correspondences.

17 δάκνει τὰ χρέα: cf. χρήματα (6), then deduce the general sense of δάκνει ('annoy, get on the nerves' etc.). Then give the literal meaning 'bite' for future reference; the literal meaning occurs in Section 5E.

19 χρῆσται: the χρη- root again. (Illustrate the χρα/χρη- root (= need) between χράομαι, χρή, χρῆμα, χρήματα, χρήστης (see L.S.J.).)
Ask who is likely to be chasing him.

20 δίκην λαμβάνουσιν: the δικ- stem has been met in ἄδικος (p. 30.8), but it will need reinforcing. Put particular emphasis on the meaning of the δικ- stem; it is very heavily used both here and in Section 8.

22 Translate χθές = yesterday, and the past of εἰμί falls into place.

From this point the imperfect begins to appear: it is useful to revise the present active and middle endings and put these on the board ready for comparison with the imperfect endings.

Set up a comparative grid, revise and fill in the forms of παύω, then fill in the imperfect as it occurs. It is probably best to leave contractions till a little later since the augment preceded by prefix and new endings will demand much close attention.

	Pres. act.	*Imperf. act.*	*Pres. mid.*	*Imperf. mid.*
1	παύω	ἔπαυον	παύομαι	ἐπαυόμην
2	παύεις	ἔπαυες	παύῃ	ἐπαύου
3	παύει	ἔπαυε	παύεται	ἐπαύετο
	etc.	etc.	etc.	etc.

Stress the different endings for present and imperfect middles.

Pres. -μαι	*Imperf.* -μην
-σαι	-σο
-ται	-το
-μεθα	-μεθα
-σθε	-σθε
-ονται	-ντο

N.B. In the second person singular, intervocalic -σ- disappears and contraction takes place:

-ε(σ)αι → ῃ
-ε(σ)ο → ου

With augments, highlight four points during the reading: (i) the addition of ἐ-, (ii) the lengthening of initial vowels, (iii) the occasional lengthening of initial ἐ- to εἰ-, (iv) the augment nearly always replacing the final vowel of a prefix, e.g. διελέγετο.

p. 32 line

24, 25 ἐκάθευδον, ἐδίωκον: check the formation and ask for the corresponding παύω form; do the same with other imperfects as they occur.

p. 33 line

2 ὅλην τὴν νύκτα: cf. hologram, holocaust.

There is no need to mention the accusative of duration; it will be explained in Section 8A–E.

5 ὠνειροπόλει: use this to explain the lengthening of an initial short vowel to act as the augment, and cf. ἀ → ἠ (ἤκουε, line 8), and ἐ → ἠ.

6 αἴτιος: cf. aetiology.

7 διελέγετο: ask the students to explain the placing of the augment and develop the rule.

11 κεφαλήν: there are many medical derivations: encephalograph, encephalitis, hydrocephalitis, and the subdivisions dolichocephalic and brachycephalic according to the cephalic index.

The fact that Strepsiades was responsible for all his son's debts (Was Pheidippides a minor? There is no indication of his age) underlies the responsibility of the father in the Greek family. Judging from some of the sums quoted in *Clouds*, Strepsiades was certainly not impoverished – the family owned several horses, and his wife clearly came from a fairly wealthy family.

12 Quote in translation from the original Aristophanes text (*Clouds* lines 60–7) the quarrel about the name of the son. Strepsiades wanted his father's name, Pheidon, but his wife insisted on inserting a horse somewhere, hence Pheidippides.

p. 34 line

15 γάμους: cf. monogamy, bigamy, polygamy.

16 ἄγροικος: deduce the meaning from the ἀγρ- element (agriculture etc.), then the contrast with ἄστεως should give the meaning of the latter. Read the story of the wedding night (*Clouds* 49–52) to point the contrast. For the overtones of city life as against life in the country cf. *urbane, polite* (vs. *rustic, provincial*) in English.

Note that the second person singular and the first and second persons plural of the imperfect active do not occur; they can be supplied by comparison with the present verb endings. For the middle, the first and second persons singular and the second person plural do not occur; the second person plural can be taken from the present middle but the other two should be given.

Section Five B

Background

Olives 1.9, 20; 4.51, 57
Slaves 3.18; 4.62–6; slaves and war 4.10; cf. HI 51
Arguments as means to ends 7.17
Learning rhetoric 7.18–19

Commentary

p. 34 line

26 ἅπτε λυχνόν: λυχνόν – refer to the picture; ἅπτε – ask what the time was and how you lit the lamp. Note also the difficulties caused by darkness. Even battles had to stop at night, as night manoeuvres could be chaotic (Plataia; Thucydides III.34; Syracuse, *ibid.*, VII.44). Cf. the chaos in Peiraieus in Section 3.

28 Olives, the source of oil for lamps, were scarce during the war because of the annual Spartan invasions.

31 κλαῖε: ask for suggestions; make sure the accurate literal translation is known before idiomatic versions are approved. The verb recurs later (*Text* p. 129.38, derivative).

34 Why does war prevent the punishment of the slaves? The proximity of the Spartans during their annual invasions meant that slaves could easily desert to the enemy. What Strepsiades here laments is the fact that the war prevents him from treating his slaves as property for fear of their desertion. In his youth slaves were constrained through fear to remain loyal to their masters. This argument is not from *Clouds*.

ἀργούς: note the two elements: ἀ- privative + ἔργον.

Supplementary exercise

An important supplementary exercise is to make students work back from imperfects to the lexicon form. Begin with easy examples, e.g. ἐδίωκον, then progress to a contracted verb, e.g. ἐποιοῦμεν, add a verb with a prefix (very important), e.g. ἀπεχώρεις, then one which begins with a vowel and whose vowel lengthens to form the augment, e.g. ἠπόρεις. This is the moment to refer students to GVE pp. 335–6. Again, virtually *any* learnt verb will do for these exercises (NOT, however, ὁράω).

Section Five C–D

Grammar

Future indicative active and middle
Active/middle distinction
Indefinite words
Σωκράτης/τριήρης (nom., acc.)

This section introduces the future tense: αὔριον (20) should be given, then the tense becomes obvious. Elicit first the basic formation, leaving refinements (e.g. the lengthening of the stem vowel in contracted verbs) until later. -σω futures are easy enough, but note (a) those sigmas combining with consonants (write on the board γ, κ, χ+σ → ξ; π(τ), β, φ+σ → ψ; ττ/σσ+ σ → ξ; ζ/θ+σ → σ; (b) those which have middle forms (only ἀκούσομαι (p. 35.35) in Section 5C, so these may be left until Section 5D when the basic pattern will be more familiar); and (c) (most difficult to spot) the -εω futures, mainly for verbs with stems ending in λμνρ and -ίζω.

Make up a grid comparing the present tense with the future; also revise present epsilon-contract verbs for comparison with the future epsilon-contracts, e.g.

Pres. act.	Fut. act.	Pres. mid.	Fut. mid.	ε- contract	ε-contract future	
παύω	παύσω	παύομαι	παύσομαι	ποιῶ	διαφθερῶ	(cf. present διαφθείρω
παύεις	παύσεις	παύῃ	παύσῃ	ποιεῖς	διαφθερεῖς	διαφθείρεις
etc.	etc.	etc.	etc.	etc.	etc.	etc.)

The play proper begins here. Set the scene first with a description of the Greek theatre – the large circular orchestra (= dancing place), a low stage reached by steps from the orchestra and a building behind with door(s), windows and a flat roof. The plays were performed in daylight, so no lighting effects were possible – a problem in this play which is supposed to open at night when it is too dark for Strepsiades to read. Note how this affects the writing, for the characters have to announce the fact that it is pitch dark etc. (compare many similar devices in Shakespeare). How much scenery was incorporated is debatable: perhaps quote R. S. Glen, *Two Muses* (Macmillan, 1968) 77, which also contains an excellent translation): 'A modern audience at the *Elijah* of Mendelssohn does not think of the platform on which the performers stand as representing first Ahab's court and then Mount Carmel.' The parallel may not be exact, yet the point is still valid.

Commentary

p. 35 line

26 πείσομαι: consonant combinations may be collated as they occur, or left to the end of Section 5C and given all together, referring back to examples.

30 Note the change of oath from Poseidon (the god of horses) to Dionysos.

35 Comment upon the change to the middle in ἀκούσομαι only if students notice it.

Section Five D

Background

Socrates and sophists. 4.43–8; 7.20–31
Intellectuals and methods of arguing 7.1-19 (especially analogy 7.9; the world as 'soup' 7.13)
Importance of λόγος 5.19, 7.17, 24
Education 4.39ff.
Importance of leisure 4.49

Commentary

p. 36 line

26 Diminutives: Dover (*Clouds*, on line 92) calls them 'persuasive', i.e. the speaker is trying to gain a favour from another.

28 ψυχῶν: cf. psychology, psychiatrist, psychotherapy etc.

σοφῶν: cf. philosophy, sophomore. Note the high-flown style of the speech. Possibly Strepsiades is supposed to use tones of reverential awe, evoking an ironic response in the audience. As an ignorant man absurdly proud of the few half-digested facts he has acquired, Strepsiades is in some ways the prototype of Monsieur Jourdain in Molière's *Le Bourgeois Gentilhomme*; see especially Act II scene 4 (Jourdain and the Professor of Philosophy).

φροντιστήριον: the meaning can be extracted from φρόντιζε + selected English -ery words denoting a place of work (bakery, brewery etc.). All teachers will have their favourite translation: I rather favour 'reflectory' – cf. *-erium* in Latin, e.g. apodyterium (← Greek ἀπό, δύω, -ηριον).

29 μαθητής: the meaning should be elicited from the stem μαθ- (learnt with μανθάνω in Section 3C).

30 οὐρανός: Latin *Uranus* may help if students know him as the sky god.

πνιγεύς: refer to the picture. It was an oven heated by coals which were then removed to the outside and replaced by dough – see Dover on *Clouds* 96. Thus the point of the comparison is simply one of shape – any hemispherical object would do.

31 ἄνθρακες: cf. anthracite, anthrax.

32 The Sophists were the educators of a leisured and wealthy elite. Socrates often insisted that he was not a sophist, and there is no evidence that he ever took any money for his conversations. A vivid and amusing encounter with some sophists occurs in Plato, *Protagoras* 315c–316a.

35 μαθήσονται: now that the regular pattern for future verbs is fixed, those with middle forms may be commented upon here. This form should present no problems – the stem μαθ- has been not only learnt but revised six lines earlier! Refer back to ἀκούσομαι (p. 35.35).

37 λόγους: another meaning here – explain some of the possibilities, e.g. argument, story, an account, a word.

39 δίκαιον, ἄδικον: the δικ- root has already been mentioned (p. 32.20); reinforce it here.

p. 37 line

1 Strepsiades' motive: to win the lawsuits brought against him. Note what we might consider an amoral approach, typical of the Athenian legal system: one did not try to establish one's innocence, but to argue persuasively. The two might be the same, but the later fifth century manifested a dramatic growth of interest in the technique of persuasion, related of course to the development of the radical democracy, the Assembly and the law courts (cf. Sections 3C, 4A).

3 ὄνομα: cf. anonymous, synonym, pseudonym etc.

4 καλοί...κἀγαθοί: for the qualities indicating moral goodness, see K. J. Dover, *Greek Popular Morality* (Blackwell, 1974) 45.

6 ὠχρούς: ochre is pale yellow or brown. The students are pale because they are always indoors and are therefore unhealthy, unfit etc.

ἀνυποδήτους: explain by reference to the roots ἀν, ὑπό, δέω; the word here implies unkempt, scruffy. For more detail on epithets, see Dover, *Clouds* pp. xxxiii–iv.

15 διαφθερεῖ: this and ἐκβαλῶ (31) are the only examples of future tenses in -έω in this section. Beware of overlooking these – many common verbs have stems in -λ, -μ, -ν, -ρ, (and -ίζω), e.g. μένω, κτείνω, στέλλω, ἀγγέλλω (ὄλλυμι), etc.

21 εἰμι: εἰμι appears frequently in the next few lines: its meaning is clear from the context, but isolate and plot its morphology also. The second and third persons plural do not occur: note the stem shortening in the plural (cf. οἶδα – revise its forms by setting it side by side with εἰμι in a grid. See *GVE* pp. 281–2).

p. 38 line
10 If combinations of consonants have been explained at the end of Section 5C, use κόψω as the cue for revision – this will be needed for the weak aorist in Section 5E–F.

Supplementary exercises

Learning how to find the lexicon form is even more important with the future than with the imperfect, especially where consonant changes in the stem occur of the πράξω, ποιήσω, βαλῶ type. The list of regular verbs on pp. 212–13 should be especially useful here. Transformation exercises from present → future, future → present, and exercises in finding lexicon forms, starting with the easier ones and progressing to the epsilon-contract (say) will pay ample dividends, especially as weak aorists are just around the corner.

There is another advantage in spending a little time on simple exercises here. Since tenses come thick and fast, spreading the course a little so that one tense does not crowd in on the next is helpful.

Section Five E

Background

Physical speculation   7.7, 22
Mathematics and measurement   7.23
Thales   7.7

Grammar

Weak aorist active and middle
ὀφρῦς (nom., acc.)

Make a grid, which first revises present and future tenses, and then introduces the aorist, thus:

Pres. act.	Fut. act.	Aor. act.	Pres. mid.	Fut. mid.	Aor. mid.
παύω etc.	παύσω etc.	ἔπαυσα etc.	παύομαι etc.	παύσομαι etc.	ἐπαυσάμην etc.

Stress the -μην -σο -το endings of the middle, and cf. the imperfect.

Use the same method as for the imperfect, viz. stop at ἔκοψε (p. 38.18): ask what the augment indicates. Identify the person of the verb, explain the formation and ask what is the corresponding form of παύω. Only then enter the results on the grid. The first and second persons singular appear in the next two lines (no more until p. 39.30). If the formation of the singular is clearly explained, plural endings follow by comparison with the imperfect.

The middle is more difficult. Only the first and third persons singular appear (p. 38.26, 31). The second person singular was originally -σασο; 'intervocalic' σ drops → σαο; this contracts → σω (cf. imperfect originally -εσο → εο → ου).

Commentary

p. 38 line

38 The meanings of ψύλλα and ὀφρῦν obviously have to be given; δάκνει may be recalled (32.17). According to the scholiast, Khairephon had shaggy eyebrows, while Socrates was bald.

p. 39 line

14 Perhaps not the ideal refutation of the charge that the Greeks theorized well but failed to prove by experimentation. Yet the parody, to be humorous, must have had some foundation in fact. One need not be too explicit about how the experiment worked: as Dover says, one wouldn't have time to work it out in the theatre.

15 The Olympic crown was a wreath woven from the sacred olive tree at Olympia. Note the importance of athletics in Athenian education (see Plato, *Protagoras* 326b–d), and the emphasis the Just Argument places upon physical fitness (for a convenient summary, see Dover, *Clouds* pp. lixff.). The very name Plato derives from a wrestling nickname because of his broad (πλατύς) shoulders, and it was so universally used that his real name Aristokles seldom appears. Note also the importance now given to Plato's εὐρυθμία in dance and drama lessons; modern schools for disabled children in particular stress this in attempts to improve physical co-ordination.

37 Thales was the earliest of the Pre-Socratic philosophers who came from Miletos. Herodotus tells us of two of his exploits: subdividing the river Halys so that it became fordable (1.75), and predicting an eclipse of the sun (1.74) – though according to Herodotus he predicted merely the year of the eclipse. Plato, *Theaitetos* 174a tells the well-known story of how he was studying the stars so intently that he fell down a well. Hence Aristophanes uses him as a typical 'head-in-clouds' intellectual. (But for Thales' business acumen, see Aristotle, *Politics* 1259a3.) Only one of the various absurd researches is included in the text: refer to the others, reading them in translation if there is time.

Section Five F

Background

Intellectual achievement of fifth-century Athens   7.14, 21
Technical work   7.22
Peloponnesian War   HI 33ff.

Commentary

p. 40 line
4 Not a hostile question: 'What on earth are these creatures?' (Dover).
23 Herodotus v.49 describes how Aristagoras brought a map to Sparta hoping to enlist Spartan aid against Persia; he earlier (IV.36) refers to 'many people making maps'. If 'many' maps had been made, they certainly appear to have been still quite a novelty at Athens in the fifth century – but they must certainly have been known or Strepsiades' boorishness would not appear so comic.
27 **δικαστῶν**: explain the δικ- stem, + -της suffix (usually = agent, cf. κελευστής, κυβερνήτης etc.). δικασταί get fuller treatment in Sections 8 and 11–16.

The entrance of Socrates, swinging in a basket, must be one of the funniest in European comedy. The μηχανή must have been used here, probably swinging Socrates in the basket over the heads of Strepsiades and the student while they were talking. There is no reference in the text to the use of the μηχανή (but note 'Come down, Socratikins (or Socrateasy-weasy?)', and presumably he does so there or soon after). On the use of the μηχανή, read the sequence in Aristophanes' *Peace* 149–79 where Trygaios reprimands the μηχανή-operator for driving without due care and attention. Note also that the μηχανή was used in tragedy for gods or heroes only, so Socrates' appearance had an added effect for an Athenian audience.

Supplementary exercises

A pause here to revise present, future and aorist tenses is very important. Much very simple transformation work between the tenses (bring in the imperfect later on) is helpful: start with present → future and aorist; then future and aorist → present; then future → aorist and vice versa. Again, use the easiest verbs to start with.

Note: It is at this point that the concept of 'principal parts' *could* be introduced, and students should be asked to keep a list of the most important irregular verbs. The morphology charts contain such a list, and there is a list of irregular verbs learnt in Sections 1–5 on p. 214 of these *Notes*. Concentrate on regular principal parts for the moment (cf. *GVE* pp. 284ff.).

Section Five G

Grammar

Strong aorist indicative active and middle

Section 5G–H introduces the strong, or second, aorist: there should be no problem with the endings, which are already known, so make a comparison between present, imperfect and strong aorist, viz.:

Pres. act.	Imperf. act.	Str. aor. act.	Pres. mid.	Imperf. mid.	Str. aor. mid.
λαμβάνω	ἐλάμβανον	ἔλαβον	λαμβάνομαι	ἐλαμβανόμην	ἐλαβόμην

At some stage a common pattern of stem change between present and aorist may be pointed out, viz.:

λαμβάνω → ἔλαβον
μανθάνω → ἔμαθον
τυγχάνω → ἔτυχον

Warn students that the vocabulary does not distinguish weak or strong aorist stems. It is best to assume that an aorist stem is strong where it is given, and check with the irregular verb list in *GVE* pp. 284ff.

Stress that the distinction between weak and strong past tenses can be paralleled in English: past tenses are formed either by a regular suffix -d/ed, or by a change in the stem – either slight (I sit/sat) or strong (I go/went); in pronunciation only (read/read) or not at all (hit/hit). Mention also, when they occur, that three of the commonest (hence most irregular) stem changes have already been met: ἐλθ-, εἰπ-, ἰδ-.

Commentary

p. 41 line

14 Note the personal identification: name, father's name and deme. The deme Kikunna is unknown.

16 Socrates' words (his opening line in the original) are paratragic – again underlining, as did his entrance by μηχανή, his hyper-human status and pretensions.

22ff. Rehearses old material with the strong aorist inserted. Note especially ἤρου: the two ἐρ- stems usually cause confusion (they should not, because one always has active, the other middle endings – but they do!), although ἐρ- (fut. λέγω) does not occur until Section 8A, q.v. (note on p. 67.15).

35 δράω: cf. drama, drastic.

38 ἀεροβατῶ: cf. aerobatics. περιφρονῶ: explain περί + φρονῶ.

ἥλιον: cf. heliotrope, heliocentric, helium. Quite a number of irregular principal parts must be learnt from this point on. Ask students to write out a list of about twenty, with four columns and a fifth for meaning (excluding perfects; for these see *GVE* **165, 169-71**). This in itself is a useful revision exercise, and of course it is generally the most common verbs that are irregular. Other principal parts are then inserted as they occur in reading or in *GVE* (cf. the list of irregular verbs in *GVE* E.4; and the morphology charts).

p. 42 line

2 μετέωρα: cf. meteor, meteorology.

Section Five H

Background

Arguing from both sides of the case   7.26
Magic   2.18

Commentary

p. 42 line

16 ἕτερος: cf. heterosexual, heterogeneous, heterodox etc.

23 κατακλίνηθι: Students rarely comment upon this as an odd form: if they do, pass over it as an oddity to be explained later (an aorist passive imperative form). Derivations are mainly from the Latin -*clino*, e.g. recline, incline, clinic etc.

p. 43 line

2 Dover on *Clouds* 734 takes this as evidence of masturbation. Alternatively, less pruriently, Strepsiades could be merely protecting his vitals from the bed-bugs.

9 φαρμακίδα: cf. pharmacy.

κλέψω: cf. kleptomaniac.

18 In the original, Socrates approves of Strepsiades' plan.

Supplementary exercises

It is *essential* that students learn thoroughly the list of strong aorists on p. 75 of *GVE*. If they do not, there will be endless trouble and time-wasting. Full transformation drill between strong aorist, imperfect and present is very important, to fix the idea of stem change between aorist and present and the difference between aorist and imperfect. Build up exercises until lists of aorists (weak and strong) can reliably be changed into imperfects and vice versa.

Be aware also that *GVE* for this chapter covers other important details apart from the tense formations: the significance of the middle (*GVE* **65**) and indefinite and interrogative adverbs (*GVE* **66**).

Test Exercise

Note the mistake in paragraphing in the first impression (corr. 1981) – the mother's speech ends at ἱππομανίας. New accidence is very fully tested in this piece – go through translations carefully and immediately rectify weaknesses.

Section Six A–C

Grammar

Present infinitive active and middle
δεῖ
Comparative and superlative adjectives
ᾖα 'I went'

This is possibly the most taxing section to date: new accidence causes few problems, but sentence structure expands and syntax becomes more complex. In particular, the usage of participles extends. (Use the technique described for p. 5.26 to unravel complex sentences.) However, the grammatical points are heavily revised in Sections 7–10, with much slighter grammar loading. Once again, be encouraging: even if everything is not crystal clear after Section 6, repetitions in later sections rehearse the lessons of Section 6.

Cassette

Part of Section 6c (*Text*, p. 49.1–9) and all of 6d (pp. 49–50) are recorded with dynamic accent on the *Speaking Greek* cassette, Side 1 (part of W. S. Allen's talk, 'The sounds of Greek'). All of Section 6a–c (pp. 45–9) is recorded with melodic accent on Side 2.

By listening to both readings of Section 6c (p. 49.1–9), students can learn to differentiate between the two kinds of accent. ̄

Section Six A

Background

Rhetoric and speeches 7.16–19
Lawcourt practice 5.44–67 (especially 52)
Delphi and the oracle 2.12; 15–17

Commentary

p. 45 line
27 διαβάλλουσι: the meaning can be extracted by careful attention to the English introduction. Derivations (like diabolical, and devil via Latin *diabolus*, Italian *diavolo*) do not help much in getting at the meaning 'slander'.

29 δόξα: cf. orthodox, heterodox, paradox, doxology.

30 βούλομαι: help is needed with this phrase, as the infinitive occurs here for the first time.

33 ἴστε: better taken as an imperative than an indicative.

34 οὐδὲν ἄλλο ἤ: all but ἤ known – try to elicit the meaning.

36 εἰδέναι: the context should make the meaning clear. Note (a) εἰδ- is the stem of οἶδα (this is useful when the participle is met), (b) -ναι is an infinitive ending (cf. εἶναι, ἰέναι).

37 μάρτυρα: a martyr is one who witnesses to his belief.

40 Khairephon was introduced in Section 5, *Text* p. 37.7 etc. – though there he was hardly σφοδρός (47.1)! Point to the contrast in the two portraits of Socrates: despite Aristophanes' presentation, Socrates must have been generally regarded as a serious intellectual – indeed this is presumably precisely why Aristophanes chose him as his butt. He would certainly have been recognized (Aelian, *Var. Hist.* ii.13 preserves the story that at the first performance of *Clouds* the real Socrates stood up so that foreigners could recognize him – see Dover, *Clouds* p. xxxiii), and he was probably generally regarded as a great thinker. He appears to have had great faith in the oracle since Xenophon (*Anabasis* III.1.5) reports Socrates as advising him to consult an oracle before serving under Cyrus.

p. 47 line

3 The comparatives are well placed in the context, and ἤ has already occurred (p. 45.34) so there should be no problems. If the comparative is not translated correctly at first, read the sentence again stressing -τερ- and it should become clear.

4 Similarly with superlatives: if a reading stresses the -τατ- followed by ἀνθρώπων, there should be no difficulty. Point out that for reading purposes it is very nearly enough to know that -τερ- and -τατ- signify comparative and superlative forms of the adjective. Only irregular forms need to be added (*GVE* **76** (iii)). Those who have not done Latin will need to be alerted to *GVE* **76** (i).

5 ἰέναι: if the -ναι ending for an irregular infinitive has been noted (45.36), there will be no problems here.

7 ᾔει: the context may give the meaning, but note this carefully and plot its morphology during Section 6A–C (see *GVE* **77**).

8 μαντεύομαι: the two meanings, 'consult an oracle' (5) and 'receive an oracular response' (here), are initially somewhat confusing – explain the difficulty of translating something which is hardly conceived of in our language: the concept does not exist, so we have no vocabulary for it.

Many -mancy derivations exist: all have the meaning 'foretelling the future by means of' e.g. . . . ornithomancy (flight of birds); necromancy (spirits of the dead); catoptromancy (mirrors). That μάντις derives from μαίνομαι should come as no surprise. See E. R. Dodds, *The Greeks and the Irrational* (University of California Press, 1951), ch. 3, 'The Blessings of Madness', for a most stimulating discussion.

9 There are no serious grounds for doubting the authenticity of this oracle.

Section Six B

Background

Socrates' 'ignorance' 7.31
Inspiration and creativity 7.64–5
μάντις 2.19–20

Commentary

p. 47 line
21 ἠπόρουν: this may be difficult to recognize: check methods of finding the lexicon form, *GVE* p. 335.
24 δοκέω: translate δοκέω first time round as 'I seem to myself' and from that develop 'I think I am.' Translate δοκεῖ (impersonal) as 'it seems'.
29 . ἀποφαίνειν: the transitive sense 'make to appear' can be used to reinforce the note on the 'reflexive' aspect of the middle; *GVE* 65.
30 τῶν παρόντων: note the use of the article + participle as a noun, cf. *adstantes*.
35 ᾗα: refer back to line 7 (ᾗει) and/or the sentence structure of line 24.
36 'Socrates used to swear by the dog, the goose and the plane tree' (A. M. Adam – edition of *Apology* (C.U.P., 1914)).
κύων: cf. cynic (Cynic because Diogenes of Sinope, founder of Cynicism, acquired the nickname of 'the dog' since he rejected all conventions, tried to live on nothing, and generally behaved scandalously. See Diogenes Laertius VI.46, 69; Plutarch, *Moralia* 1044B).
40 φύσιν: another foretaste! What shade of meaning suits best here?

p. 48 line
19 On poets as inspired interpreters of the divine, cf. Aristophanes, *Frogs*, *passim*.

Section Six C

Background

Leisure and speculation   4.49, 52
The rich   3.18, 7.13
Early arguments over the gods   7.11, cf. 2.5
Questioning the gods   2.65–6
Death of Socrates   HI 59

Commentary

p. 48 line

33 πάθος: the stem παθ- was learnt with πάσχω; cf. pathos, pathology, osteopath, psychopath etc.
34 ταυτησί: final -ι was mentioned at *GVE* 33: Note, but this is the first occurrence in the *Text*. Notice it here – it is very common in Aristophanes.
36 σχολήν: suggest that school is what you do in your leisure time! i.e. time not consumed in working to keep body and soul together.
38 ὑβρισταί: refer back to ὕβρις earlier in the *Text* (p. 13.17).

p. 49 line

4 ἔχω+ inf. means approximately 'I am able'. Note this.
7 μή: this has occurred many times before, and is learnt in this section as 'don't'. If asked, explain that the indirect command retains the negative of the direct command.

Section Six D

Background

Words and arguments   7.24
Arguing on both sides of a case   7.26
Dissatisfaction with sophistic quibbles   4.47–8

Grammar

Weak aorist participle active and middle
Aspect
ἤδη, φημί, ἔφην

Weak aorist participles are introduced. Those unfamiliar with the concept of aspect should read the note in *GVE* 79. As so many other concepts are introduced in this section, it may be advisable to postpone a full explanation of aspect until Section 8F–G, where the aorist imperative will be met and the distinction must be made. After all, the English '-ing' can cover both 'aspects' satisfactorily, *pro tem.*

It is important to impress on students the different stems and endings to expect with present and aorist participles. Make a grid which revises the change from present indicative to present participle (active and middle); then plot the aorist indicative and wait for examples of the aorist participle in the *Text* before inserting them in the grid, e.g.

Pres. ind.	*Pres. part. act.*	*Pres. part. mid.*
παύω ⟶	παύων, -ουσα, -ον ⟶	παυόμενος, -η, -ον
Aor. ind.	*Aor. part. act.*	*Aor. part. mid.*
ἔπαυσα ⟶	παύσας, -σασα, -σαν ⟶	παυσάμενος, -η, -ον

The absence of the augment in participles should be elicited from students: an important point. Identify the form accurately, reconstruct the parallel form of παύω, and insert this in the grid.

Commentary

p. 49 line

29 Λύκειον – for the gymnasium and baths, see the map in the *Text* p. 61. The role of athletics in education has already been noticed (see above, on 39.15); mention also the exercise-ground where this discussion takes place as a meeting-place. Try to anticipate the trend of the argument here: tell students that the contention centres around the dual meaning of μανθάνω – 'I learn/I understand' – the distinction between 'clever' = 'capable of learning', and 'clever' = 'learned'. There are many other ironic passages in *Euthydemos*: a salutary reminder that Plato has a sense of humour!

31 προτρέποντες: τρέπομαι occurred in Section 4D; here there is an active, transitive sense.

35 φιλοσοφίαν καὶ ἀρετήν: stress the former as education, the latter as 'goodness' generally ('what is admirable in a person or a thing').

p. 50 line

7 ἀκούσας: this is the first aorist participle to occur – 'on hearing'. Identify the form accurately, construct the equivalent form of παύω and enter παύσας in the grid. It is pedagogically most instructive if they translate the form as if it were ἤκουσας.

9 ἀποκρινοῦμαι: it will probably be necessary to remind pupils that it must be future (verbs with stems ending in λ, μ, ν, ρ).

13 πότεροι: note that both Greek and Latin use 'whether...or' where English omits 'whether'.

14 ἀμαθεῖς: ἀ- privative + stem μαθ-.

15 ἐρώτημα: Identify the part of speech. What root can be recognized? Cf. other nouns in -μα, e.g. πρᾶγμα. For noun formation, see *GVE* p. 328.

16 ἀπορήσας: pay attention to the aspect – 'struck dumb' may be a good approximation. ἐρυθριῶντα (17) and γελάσας (19) are good aspectual examples.

40 ᾖστε: the past tense of οἶδα is introduced in this section, though only the first and second persons plural occur.

Supplementary exercises

Obviously the transformations should begin from the aorist indicative to the aorist participle and back again; but then from the present participle to the aorist participle and vice versa. Expand the participial forms by supplying previously learnt nouns in the nominative singular, and ask students to choose the participial form which is appropriate to each gender; then ask students to translate both noun and participle. Students should realize early that participles share functions with both verbs and adjectives.

Section Six G

Grammar

Strong aorist participle active and middle
αὐτός, ὁ αὐτός, αὐτόν
δύναμαι

Strong aorist participles are introduced in Section 6G–H, but if weak aorist participles have been assimilated well, strong aorists should cause no problems. Revise the strong aorist list on *GVE* p. 75 before beginning this section, stressing the stem change again. If the same type of grid as in 6D above (p. 63) comparing present with aorist is used, surprise and pleasure result as the endings of the strong aorist participle unfold – just like the present!

αὐτός is introduced in all three main senses: this must be covered separately (see *GVE* **86–9**), whereas δύναμαι should present no problem. What students find taxing here is the more complex sentence, which reduces reading speed considerably; but the gains in terms of understanding – particularly in wide-ranging use of participles – are enormous. Additionally, since it is a good story, it keeps the attention.

Background

Herodotus 7.33; P 1
νόμος/φύσις 7.28
Greek view of women (for comparison with Scythians) 2.9–10; 3.18–20; 4.22–36
For another perspective on alien women P 1

Commentary

p. 52 line

21ff. The introduction points again to the νόμος/φύσις distinction which is central to the story here. Herodotus is full of superb stories illustrating this distinction, including Dareios and the Indians (III.38), which ends with the Pindar quotation νόμος πάντων βασιλεύς or 'It all depends how you've been brought up'.

νόμος is cognate with νομίζω because Athenian law was quite simply what the majority of Athenians acknowledged.

37 εἰσπεσόντες: should be immediately recognized as a participle; break up into εἰς-, πεσ-, and ask of what verb πεσ- is the stem (this should have been learnt in Section 2B with πίπτω).

39 περιούσας: elicit the meaning via 'being', 'around', 'about', i.e. left over after the battle.

p. 53 line

22 ἀποβᾶσαι: ἀπό-, +βη-/βα- (the stem should have been learnt with βαίνω, Section 1A, *GVE* **17**).

23 ἱπποφόρβιον: the meaning is obvious when the next clause is translated.

26 ἀνεῖλον: the principal parts of αἱρέω are not learnt until Section 8H–J (*GVE* **123**); the stem ἑλ- may be known, but students always find this one of the most difficult Greek verbs to recognize, particularly in the unaugmented aorist forms of compounds. Add the aorist tense to the principal parts list (begun at the end of Section 5G: see on p. 41.38). Reinforce this when it reoccurs.

29 Students are alerted to the fact that αὐτός usages are coming; note the usages as they occur.

28–37 The whole paragraph is a good example of the wide-ranging usage of participles. Stop at the end of the paragraph and retranslate, stressing participial phrases each time with a literal '-ing' version, then with as wide a range of English phrases or clauses as possible. Greater fluency in translation results. Quiz the participles by giving students this paragraph with appropriate indicative verbs and καί substituted for the participles and ask them to transform the indicatives back into participles: e.g. ἔγνωσαν ταῦτα καί... (ἀπέπεμψαν) for γνόντες ταῦτα...

Section Six H

---

p. 54 line

33 ἐχρῆτο: give the meaning simply as 'make love to' – and encourage the link with χράομαι – 'I use' (cf. on p. 32.19).

35 τὸ αὐτὸ χωρίον: here the second usage of αὐτός occurs, which can be deduced from the context and added to the note on αὐτός. To complete the note, αὐτή (36) should be given to students (to discourage ideas that αὐτός in the nominative can mean 'this' or 'that').

p. 55 line

1 τὰ γενόμενα: notice this carefully – a very common phrase; it is also typical of many others.

5 Note the 'reversal of rôle' here: the Amazons take the men away from their homes, telling men what to do; the men are the subservient partners. Herodotus has fascinating records of matrilinear succession (I.11, 173; III. 150; IV.26, 147, 176).

10 ἔργα δὲ γυναιχεῖα: note how Herodotus reads Greek conventions into alien women's lives ...

12 ἁμάξαις: yet here he reverts to supposed alien ignorance of Greek conventions!

18–19 ἡμᾶς ἔχει φόβος τις μέγας: will probably be correctly translated as 'We have great fear', but pause to check the structure and cf. on p. 18.20.

21 Forms of ἵστημι begin to appear sporadically hereafter; stress the στα-stem as set up/stand; do nothing further until Section 11C when it is dealt with fully.

Supplementary exercises

Strong and weak aorist indicatives and participles should receive a final series of transformation exercises here. It is also worth setting a major vocabulary test at this point since the vocabulary of Sections 5 and 6 is so large and important.

Do not move forward until you are sure that the strong aorist list on p. 75 of *GVE* is known by heart, and that the principles of constructing the aorist are thoroughly understood; especially the problem of finding the lexicon form (see *GVE* pp. 284–9, where aorist stems are specially quoted in the principal part list). If this is done thoroughly, the rest of the Course becomes far easier for all concerned, and a really good reading speed can be achieved.

Test Exercise

The Test Exercise after Section 6F is particularly important as it is the first not based upon the text. This can present some problems but, as often with Plato, it is not so much the Greek as the thought that causes problems of comprehension. Read (and amplify if necessary) the English note which precedes the Test Exercise. Also note that, in addition to exercises covering individual points as met, there are some exercises at the end of *GVE* covering a variety of general points (pp. 94–5).

Section Seven A–C

Background

For the comic background, see the references in Section 5A
Aristophanes and politics   HI 37; 7.61ff.; and fantasy   7.59
Part-source of this scene   1.24
ἀγορά   1.27–9, 33–7
κυρία ἐκκλησία   5.10ff. (esp. 14)

Grammar

Genitive (all types) and usages
Irregular comparatives, and contracted comparatives
Present optative active and middle

ἄν + optative
ἀνίσταμαι, ἀπολέω, τί + participle, ἰέναι, ἰών, Περικλῆς

Not a section to linger over – the content is slight, accidence fairly light (all genitives occur, but plural genitives have been mentioned anyway, so there are only three or four endings to add to the grid). Summarize the genitive singular as:

1st decl.: -ης, -ας ⎫ cf. definite article
2nd decl.: -ου ⎭
3rd decl.: -ος/-ους (← -εος) (n.b. contraction)

The optative is the main new point; its accidence is simple and its only usage as yet is for the 'polite request'. Stress -οι- in the present, -αι- in the aorist, and -ει- in irregulars.

Commentary

p. 59

Genitives occur frequently here. All the important terminations can be found on this page alone. Of the usages (*GVE* 92) only comparisons are likely to cause problems. Names: try to elicit the ideas behind Euelpides and Peisetairos.

p. 59 line

22 ἀγοράν: cf. agoraphobia; note the frequency of -αγορας as a name termination.

23 ἀπιόντα: will be forgotten or confused with ὄντα. Revise both ὤν and ἰών here, and stress the importance of the difference.

24 κατιδών: despite the pointer in l. 23 and despite the fact that the ἰδ- stem was introduced in Section 1, this still causes difficulty. Reinforce firmly.

30 Note the use of the genitive: cf. 'take hold *of*'.

παῖς: slave – cf. the French expression 'Garçon!' = 'Waiter!'.

p. 60 line

23 ἕνεκα: note as 'postposition', cf. Latin *causa*.

25 τρέχω (δραμ-) learnt in section 3D, but it probably needs reiterating here.

κανοῦν: see the picture.

29 κύριος: has a wide range of meanings, usually involving some sense of 'power', 'ability', 'validity'. Cf. later usages (in the *Text* pp. 124.28, 129.17, 145.7). It became the 'Lord' in the phrase 'Lord Jesus Christ'.

30 κόρακα: can be recalled if you have already given the literal meaning of εἰς κόρακας.

33 ἀνιστάμεθα: elicit via ἀν-, στα-, -μεθα.

34 λέγοιτε: Ask what person of what verb. Establish the approximate meaning first and then explain that it is optative, used for a 'polite request' – and often hardly distinguishable from an ordinary future. (A fine example of this in Herodotus, *Text* p. 161.17–19.) Stress that -οι- is used in the present optative; -αι- in the weak aorist (still to be introduced) and -ει- in irregulars.
35 ἀκούοιμι: the person is fixed by ἐγώ. Pause here and ask students to fill in the other active endings (the third person plural must be given).
36 ἀπράγμονα: cf. Euripides, *Antiope* (fragment):

> ὅστις δὲ πράσσει πολλὰ μὴ πράσσειν πάρον,
> μῶρος, πάρον ζῆν ἡδέως ἀπράγμονα.

Section Seven B

Background

δικαστήρια   5.44ff.
Athenian litigiousness   5.63
Athenians and rhetoric   5.20–1
The 'new politicians'   HI 37
Importance of aristocrats   HI 7, 11, 37

Commentary

p. 61 line
25 ἡγεμών: cf. hegemony – also the name Hegestratos (Section 1), almost the opposite of Lysistrata.
30 The irregular comparative of μέγας occurs here – *GVE* **93**.
32 The first genitive of comparison occurs here – cf. the other type of comparison in l. 30; cf. Latin ablative of comparison.
34 There is little point in spending much time on the added -εστ- if the Course is being used to teach reading. Comparatives and superlatives are still shown by -τερ- and -τατ-.

p. 62 line
2 βαρέως φέρω: recall βαρύς (p. 25.34), cf. *aegre fero*. For an extended use of βαρύς, see the delightful aphorism in Sophocles' *Aletes*:

> ἀνὴρ γὰρ ὅστις ἥδεται λέγων ἀεὶ
> λέληθεν αὑτὸν τοῖς ξυνοῦσιν ὢν βαρύς.

With help (especially with λέληθεν) students can translate this.

3 The problems of dikasts have already been met (p. 40.27), and are dealt with more fully in the next section.

4 δικαστήριον: for '-ery' as a place of work cf. on p. 36.28.

9 κατεψηφίσαντο: this may be guessed from the κατ- element and the context alone. Stress the ψηφ- stem: it becomes vital in Section 8 (and later in the Neaira and Euergos sections). Cf. psephology.

10 ψευδομαρτυρίαν: both ψευδ- and μάρτυς are known.

13-15 This is taken almost verbatim from Aristophanes' *Birds* 39-41.

17 Refer to earlier discussions on Periclean policy (pp. 18.35ff., 24.25ff. and 92.9ff. later).

18 Note the double sense of ἡγοῦμαι = 'I lead' and 'I consider': cf. Latin *duco*.

25-7 See Aristophanes, *Knights* 304f. 'Attic' decl.

27 πλέως: explain only if asked. It is not actually -α- contract as explained in the vocabulary of 7C.

Section Seven C

Background

Attitudes to Pericles   HI 27, 5.33
Benefits of empire   5.90-1
Pericles' court-case   HI 36; 3.10; 5.31-2
Yearning for peace   6.5
Festivals   2.41-7
Pessimism   2.21-3

Commentary

p. 63 line

11 κλοπήν: The combined effects of the plague, the failure of peace overtures to the Spartans and Pericles' unsuccessful attempt to capture Epidauros were such as to make the Athenians look for a scapegoat (one danger of such radical democracy). Pericles was suspended from the post of στρατηγός and forced to submit his accounts for inspection. A jury of 501 found these accounts were five talents adrift (Thucydides II.59-65 for Pericles' defence). His conviction was secured by Kleon but, despite being found guilty and fined, he was very soon re-elected στρατηγός.

12 πονηρός: Peisetairos' view – not that of the electorate voting him back to power.

22 N.B. the philosophers' question – this again boils down to whether 'good' in any sense is relative or absolute: cf. the νόμος/φύσις controversy.

26ff. Some help may be needed – much can be elicited by questions.

30 βουλοίμην: this is the only middle optative in the text of this section. However, the optative can be recognized and students can deduce the other persons of the tense (some help may be needed with the second person singular).

33 κακὰ λέγειν: λέγω is apparently followed by a second accusative, but the phrase almost = κακολογεῖν + obj.

36 τόπον: see on p. 27.33. The name Νεφελοκοκκυγία does not occur in the text. Mention it, as it is used in the Test Exercise.

p. 64 line

2, 5–6 Quotations from *Odyssey* I.267; *Homeric Hymn* II.216–17. Note especially para. 100 in *GVE* – a very common type of phrase.

Section Eight A–E

Background

Lawcourts 1.35; 5.46–7; 3.2

Grammar

Dative (all types) and usages
ἐρωτάω, λανθάνω

All the most common forms of the dative occur in Section 8A. Note them as they occur; the definite article goes into its grid (which can do duty for both first and second declensions); the third declension goes into the summary grid (see the *Notes* on Section 3, *ad init.*).

If using morphology charts, enter datives met in Section A and leave students to fill in the rest themselves from *GVE*.

For simple recognition purposes, stress the -ι ending for all dative singulars (subscript in first and second declensions, but note the growing practice of printing it adscript); -ις or -σι(ν) in the plural.

Stress in particular that the dative plural present participle (-ουσι) resembles in spelling the third person plural of the present indicative. Add the 'irregular'

dative plurals χερσί (which should be entered in the full Vocabulary at the back of *GVE* (p. 352), since it occurs later on) and ἀνδράσι.
   D. M. MacDowell's edition of *Wasps* (O.U.P., 1971) is a useful aid throughout this section.

Discussion

A long section, with a very slow dramatic prologue which is essential as it sets up the plot. Here for the first time it may be advisable to translate a passage or two for the students provided that all examples of the dative in Section 8A–C are carefully noted. One way to speed the reading is simply to give any words not immediately recalled (rather than ask around or try derivations, etc.). If time is very short, most or all of Section 8C can be translated for the students since most dative forms have been met by then and the section needs much explanation.

Commentary

p. 66 line
13 χράομαι: met here in the sense of 'use'. Mention its ubiquity in such phrases as βοῇ χρῶμαι; suggest 'use a shout' as a literal, never-to-be-written version!

Section Eight B

Background

   Sacrifices   1.11; 2.28–33
   Homosexuality   3.21ff.

Commentary

p. 66 line
38 ἔγνω: no comment on this 'root' aorist unless students ask for it – it is treated in *GVE* **132**; the 'root' aorist paradigm for βαίνω is given at **126**.

p. 67 line
15 ἐρωτῶ: be alert for the usage of the stem ἐρ- (strong aorist of ἠρόμην) in this section. To avoid confusion, λέξω is used for the future of λέγω – but

be warned: the future stem ἐρ- is also to be learnt in this section (tucked away in *GVE* 106), though it is not used in the *Text* until p. 85.25.

19 φιλο + κύβος: cf. cube etc.

24 φιλο- + θυ-: φιλοθύτης and φιλόξενος would naturally both be compliments; they are used here simply for 'digs' at Nikostratos (not in our text) and Philoxenos.

Section Eight C

Background

φιληλιαστής 5.46–7

Commentary

Why was Philokleon's jury-mania regarded as so harmful/dangerous? One clue comes in Test Exercise 8 (from another section of *Wasps*): the old man complains to his fellow jurors that Bdelykleon won't allow him 'to serve as a dikast and do some evil'. It is no passion for justice that motivates him, but the power to do some harm. The same idea emerges in his last few words in our text: 'Pardon me, gods – I unwittingly acquitted someone.' The whole portrayal in Aristophanes is of power-mad, powerful yet irresponsible old men; powerless (or at any rate less powerful) physically, they seek power through another outlet.

p. 67 line

37 τῆς... ἡμέρας: expressions of time are covered in this section (*GVE* p. 114).

39 ἐραστής: ἔρως gives Eros, erotic; notice also pederasty (παιδ-, ἐραστής).

p. 68 line

1 Κημός: technically a wicker funnel inserted into the mouth of the voting urn to make the insertion of pebbles easier and more secret.

10 For the therapeutic effect of Korybantic rites, see Dodds, *The Greeks and the Irrational* 77–80.

13 'Kleon-lover', 'Kleon-loather': on Kleon see the 'Background' references for Section 8D.

Section Eight D

Background

Kleon   HI 37, 41-2, 5.21

Commentary

p. 69 line

15 λόγῳ...ἔργῳ: note the Greek love of contrasts.

20 κάπνη may be guessed from the stage directions; for ψοφεῖ, refer back to ψόφος (*Text* p. 3.14).

24 καπνός: elicit the meaning via κάπνη.

29 chimney-lids: some sort of cover to keep out the weather when the fire was not lit – see MacDowell on *Wasps* 147.

30 = *Wasps* 149 (perhaps note the complete iambic trimeter).

Section Eight E

Commentary

p. 69 line

40 νουμηνία: first day of the month was market day.

p. 70 line

22 ἡμίονος: see picture. A 'semi-donkey': the mule is technically the offspring of a male donkey and a mare.

23 πωλεῖν: cf. monopoly.

αὐτοῖς τοῖς κανθηλίοις: give the translation of the whole phrase.

25 δυναίμην: the -αι- based optative foreshadows the weak aorist middle optative (*GVE* **129**).

26–7 Variant forms of comparison occur side by side; useful for reinforcement.

32 The Odysseus story is probably familiar, but rehearse it here including the 'nobody' joke, which will help explain οὗτις (36). Sophocles in *Odysseus Akanthoplex*, like Homer, puns on the name Odysseus:

ὀρθῶς δ' Ὀδυσσεύς εἰμ' ἐπώνυμος κακοῖς.
πολλοὶ γὰρ ὠδύσαντο δυσσεβεῖς ἐμοί.

38 ἀπό, δραμ-, ἵππος: with help, all the components of this coinage can be recalled. 'Son of Fitzrunawayhorse' (MacDowell on 184–5).

p. 71
As mentioned in the *Text* p. 31, the words become ever closer to the original. Point this out by having the text of *Wasps* open during the rest of this section, showing the degree of similarity, e.g. *Text* p. 71.4–5 and *Wasps* 196.

p. 71 line
4 ὤθει: cf. osmosis, which may be thought of as 'suction'. However, the laws of physics do not recognize any such force as suction, which is always a driving force, viz. thrusting (ὠθέω).
7 λίθος: cf. monolith, megalith, photolithograph etc.
18–20 A complex sentence; help may be needed. If necessary, revert to the traditional 'find the subject, find the verb' here.

Section Eight F–G

Background
Pay for jury-service 5.47, 58

Grammar
Aorist infinitive active and middle
Aorist imperative active and middle (inc. εἰμί, εἶμι, οἶδα)
φέρω, ἔξεστι, δεινός, πᾶς

Revise the aorist indicative and participle and grid them, so that students can see how the infinitives and imperatives build on the aorist stem. For the -σον aorist imperative, Κύριε, ἐλέησον may help. Now is the time to discuss aspect (*GVE* **79**) if you did not do so in 6D–F. If you did, review it here.
The text now skips to *Wasps* c. 764.

Commentary

p. 72 line
2 δικάσαι: students will automatically translate this as an infinitive. Stop, look, and tabulate.
4 οἰκέταις: dative after δικάσαι (*not* after ἐξέσται).

9 κατάσκοπον: κατά, σκοπέω. Cf. various English -scope words, including the baffling stethoscope – used for *listening*. Note episcopal, from ἐπίσκοπος, the Christian Greek word for a bishop or 'overseer'.

11 ἐξέσται: it may be necessary to point out that this is a future tense. Revise the future of εἰμί here.

17 μισθόν: note one of Philocleon's highest priorities.

24 Mention that the principal parts of φέρω are coming, and are highly irregular; ἐξοίσω (25) and ἐξήνεγκον (29) can then be noted, pointing out the peculiarity of both strong and weak aorist endings on the ἐνεγκ- stem.

37 ἐσθίειν: can be given a similar treatment to φέρω.

Section Eight G

Background

Urns 5.60
κλεψύδρα 5.60

Commentary

p. 73 line
30 ἄκουσον: note this especially – it is always the most difficult form of the weak aorist to recognize.

37 Two voting urns, one for guilty and one for innocent. Jurors placed their pebbles in one or the other – cf. p. 78.40 and see MacDowell on *Wasps* 94 for further details.

p. 74 line
21 παῦσαι: distinguish this clearly from the aorist infinitive (παῦσαι occurs as the third person singular of the aorist optative in Section 9).

22 κυμβία: cymbals. The singular of this word occurs later (Section 16B).

30 ἀμίς – note the picture: when the pot is full, the case has lasted long enough! (See MacDowell on *Wasps* 858.)

31 κλεψύδρα: 'water-stealer'.

38 κατηγορέω: κατά+ἀγορ- ('speak against').

Section Eight H

Background

Coming to trial 5.55
Source of this scene 5.59–62

Commentary

p. 75 line

28 Third person imperatives: it is tempting to give them little more than a passing glance. In their simplest form, the endings are -τω/-ντων for all third person singular and plural imperatives active; -σθω/-σθων for middle. If they are treated cursorily here, draw attention to examples in the Test Exercise when setting it.

30 Note the use of φεύγων (and later διώκων, 39) in legal sense: defendant and plaintiff.

32 ἀκούσατ': This is nearly always taken as an indicative (particularly because of ἤδη), but use the mistake to emphasize again the need to notice the absence of the augment.

34 There is some evidence that Kleon may have intended prosecuting Lakhes, though why is uncertain. That Aristophanes intended *Kuon* v. *Labes* as a topical reference to *Kleon* v. *Lakhes* is made certain by the mention of *Kudathene* (Kleon's own deme). For further detail, see MacDowell on *Wasps* 240. This political aspect of the dog scene has been suppressed in the text.

36 καταφαγών: Greek idiom is 'eat down', cf. English 'eat up' 'gulp down'.

p. 76 line

16 This always causes trouble. Translate: 'This (dog) seems to me to be another Labes' (i.e. 'Grabber' – just as thievish as the first dog).

20 The dog's caper round the courtroom is not to be found in the original.

30 ἐλεῖν: here in the legal sense: 'convict'.

34 ἀκούσαντα: ask the reason for the accusative.

35 κυνῶν ... ἄνδρα: an intentional absurdity. See *Wasps* 923 (and MacDowell ad loc.).

36 μονοφαγίστατον: elicit μονο-, φαγ- and the superlative ending.

p. 77 line

5 ἐπίσταται + infinitive in the sense 'know how to' should be mentioned here – it recurs again soon (l. 25, and p. 79.3). Cf. English 'epistemology'.

Section Eight I

Background

Goat's milk/cheese   1.13
Witnesses and evidence   5.53

Commentary

p. 77 line
21 'Able to guard many sheep': note that (a) such a plea would be irrelevant in a modern court; yet establishing a good character – regardless of irrelevance – was normal (Section 12G suggests just such pleading); (b) the irrelevance is not quite so great as it seems at first. Cheese was made from sheep's milk (see Euripides, *Cyclops* 206f.) so guarding the sheep meant ensuring the source for more cheese! Modern scientific evidence indicates that Europeans have adapted to the digestion of cow's milk, which can be fatal to systems not accustomed to it. Note also the derivation of butter from βούτυρον = 'cow-cheese'.
24 εἰ...: note how Bdelukleon admits Labes may be guilty of the offence, but does not deserve to be condemned on these grounds. Contrast modern legal practice!
25 κιθαρίζειν: essential in Greek education (see Plato, *Protagoras* 325–6; cf. note on εὐρυθμία on p. 39.15). The phrase really means 'He hasn't had a good education.'
26 The shape of Greek cheese-graters is not apparent from illustration, but neither here nor in *Lysistrata* does that matter! (*Lysistrata* 231).

p. 78 line
3 Elicit κατέκνησας from τυρόκνησις – again cf. Greek 'grate down', English 'grate up'.
ἀμφοτέροις: cf. amphibian, amphitheatre, amphora.
9 I.e. Dog's work is indoors, less arduous than Labes' (see MacDowell on *Wasps* 970).
10 σιτία: cf. parasite, sitomania, sitophobia.
13 μηδέν: this use of the negative with a participle to indicate an 'if' clause may be mentioned here. It occurs a few times more where the idea can be reinforced.
18 The comic effect of mixing singular (σε, πάτερ) with plural (οἰκτίρατε,

and ἀπολύσατε in the next line as if to a massed jury) cannot easily or neatly be translated. Draw attention to it.

19 The puppies parody the typical parade of weeping dependent relatives in Athenian courts.

25 καταβάντος αὐτοῦ: not a genitive absolute, as it initially appears; καταδικάζουσιν + genitive.

Section Eight J

Background

Voting 5.60–1

Commentary

p. 78 line

34 ἀπεδάκρυσα: Philokleon blames his bursting into tears on the soup, rather than pity.

38 βελτίω = βελτίονα (as the τά indicates); revision of this form here does no harm.

40 ὑστέρῳ: viz. the acquittal urn. Juries filed past two urns, the nearer for condemnation, the further for acquittal, and deposited their pebbles in one. Cf. on p. 68.1; a fuller note in MacDowell on *Wasps* 94.

p. 79 line

3 Taken from Bdelykleon's defence (p. 77.25) – what MacDowell calls a 'boomerang joke'.

5 περίπατον: cf. peripatetic.

13 ἀγωνίζομαι: here almost in sense of settle a contest – 'What's the result of our trial, then?' (MacDowell).

15 Presumably there is comic business here in counting 'all' the one vote!

21 νυν: emphasize the force of unaccented νυν here: 'well, then'.

26 Note that πείσομαι may be from πάσχω or πείθομαι (here clearly the former, but use it to draw attention to *GVE* **127**).

Test Exercise

This Test Exercise is very important; it is a fresh piece and not an adaptation from the *Text*. Revise the third person imperatives before setting it.

Section Nine A

Background

Women 4.28–36 (esp. 31), 3.18–20 (and cf. on homosexuality 3.22); in mystery religions 2.58; in myth 2.10

Inconsistency of plot 7.59

The war (as it was when *Lysistrata* was produced) HI 52–3

Grammar

Aorist optative active and middle

δίδωμι, γιγνώσκω, ἀμελής, γλυκύς

Relative pronoun

The principles of comparative gridding suggest that the present active and middle indicative and optative should be revised, then the aorist indicative set up; for the relative pronoun, set up the definite article for comparison. γλυκύς and ἀμελής should be gridded against τριηρής (cf. Reference Grammar, GVE p. 270), and *active* participles against the first declension feminine forms.

(1) aor. opt.: it may be useful to teach -σαιμι, -σαις, -σαι etc. as normal, with -σειας, -σειε as alternatives. The former are much more easily formed from the present optative by reading -σαι- for -οι- throughout.

(2) δίδωμι: it is vital that διδο-/ δο- stems should be recognized; the forms are mostly straightforward. Note the shortening of the stem-vowel in the plural (δίδωμι → δίδομεν) as with εἶμι, οἶδα and φημί. Add τιθε-/ θε- as in GVE **131** Note (ii) (p. 136).

(3) Relative pronoun: there is little problem in explaining its formation, although it is surprising how hard students find it to spot when reading. Stop and check accurate understanding as each new form occurs; further reinforcement will be needed.

Discussion

Students seldom need much encouragement to read the whole play in translation. It is worth pointing out the central absurdity – how can the wives' sex-strike against the war work when their husbands are away all the time fighting?

David Daube, *Civil Disobedience in Antiquity* (Edinburgh University Press, 1972), referring to *Lysistrata* as a play 'which equals Shakespeare's *Tempest* in profundity and excels it in ambiguity', notes a modern parallel: 'At Birmingham in England, wives of striking motor car workers have recently been reported to have shut their husbands from the bedrooms in order to make them disgruntled and return to the factories.'

Cassette

Section 9C–E (*Text* pp. 83–8) is recorded with melodic accent on the *Speaking Greek* cassette, Side 2.

Commentary

p. 81 line

6 The first relative pronoun occurs in the stage direction and should be translated by students.

20 ἀπέχεσθαι: Ask which infinitive this is, and from what verb. What is the force of ἀπό-? Hence 'hold oneself away from'.

24 ἀφροδισίων: cf. Aphrodite, aphrodisiac.

25 οὕς: by this time seven forms of the relative pronoun have appeared. This is a convenient point to complete the grid and comment on usage, before the aorist optative is introduced.

30 ποιήσαιμι: this is usually correctly translated, on the assumption that it is some sort of optative. Try to elicit the -οι- to -σαι- change and add variants as they occur (ποιήσειας, l. 37; ποιήσειε, p. 82.2).

p. 82 line

6 ναὶ τὼ σιώ: there is no need to mention the dual. *GVE* gives this as 'Spartan dialect', referring to Castor and Pollux (twin brothers of Helen, sons of Zeus and/or Tyndareos by Leda. Tyndareos was king of Lakedaimon).

Section Nine B

Background

Treasury 1.34
Economics of empire 5.78ff., esp. 84–5

Commentary

p. 82 line

20   Triremes and silver – Athenian naval power first became prominent when Themistocles used the silver from Laureion to build up the fleet.

22   καταληψόμεθα: Daube, *Civil Disobedience*: 'the first sit-in in history'.

23   The Athenians set aside reserves early in the war which were kept in the Acropolis. The women intend to control the money-supply.

29   Note ἡ θεός – more common than ἡ θεά.

35   ὡς+ acc. = 'to', normally only with persons.

40   ἔγνω: only comment on this form if asked. A complete paradigm appears in *GVE* **132**.

p. 83 line

1   ᾤμωξε: 'she οἴμοι-d'.

4   Kinesias, and Paionides later: both κινέω and παίω are used by Aristophanes as slang terms for sexual intercourse.

6   συνοικεῖς: the regular word for man–wife cohabitation, not as in the modern English 'live with'.

6–7   φιλεῖν καὶ μὴ φιλεῖν: the meaning becomes apparent in the Kinesias–Myrrhine scene. Either anticipate this here, or leave it mysterious – 'to love, yet not to love'.

Section Nine C

Commentary

p. 83 line

18   σπασμός: It means 'erection'. Note also the phraseology: the erection is in control of *him* – cf. on p. 18.20.

23   If the φαλλός has been mentioned as customary in comedy, mention that here it was undoubtedly emphasized.

30   δώσουσι: 'grant' is closest to the meaning here.

p. 84 line

3   διὰ στόμα: the English idiom 'on her lips' catches the *double entendre* (*fellatio*).

4   There is erotic symbolism in giving an apple to the object of your desire; you hope he or she will take it. Note that Eve tempted Adam with an apple. Our custom is drinking to absent friends rather than eating.

8 Note the oath by Aphrodite.

17 What he had in his hand was probably his φαλλός.

27 ὑπάκουσον: the regular verb for 'answer the door'.

36 οἷον τὸ τεκεῖν: (*Lysistrata* 884): give the complete phrase. Neither the verb nor the usage of τό+ infinitive is known at this stage.

Section Nine D

Background

Purification 2.35
Male slaves caring for children 4.64

Commentary

p. 85 line

5ff. γλυκύς (cf. glucose, glycerin etc.) and ἀμελής are much used here to introduce the patterns. For reading purposes, note that the feminine of γλυκύς follows the first declension pattern.

19 βαδιῇ: cf. l. 21, βαδιοῦμαι. Since a number of -ιζω, future -έω, verbs appear in a little burst, together with a number with stems in -λ, -μ, -ν, -ρ, this is a good time to revise the ε-contract futures.

24 Note how Kinesias totally ignores the question, so Myrrhine begins the teasing...

25 ἐρῶ: the first occurrence. Use this to reinforce the point made earlier about two ἐρ- stems, but note that one always has active, the other middle, endings.

p. 86 line

2 Note the force of κατά in καταγέλαστε and the meaning can be elicited.

32 ἐκδύομαι: yet even by p. 88.13 she hasn't even taken her shoes off.

34 προσκεφάλαιον: πρός+ κεφαλή, then guess.

p. 87 line

22 στρόφιον: Refer to the picture to explain that the sash was worn below the breasts to give support.

35 ἡ ἄνθρωπος: derogatory here, as in the *Text* p. 6.15 etc. (but it is not always so; see p. 144 l. 3).

p. 88 line

2 Note the oath here – and the change from the goddess of sex to the goddess of chastity coming up at l. 13.

5 διατριβῆς: literally a 'wearing away': cf. the noun τρίβων, a threadbare cloak such as Socrates used to wear. Here it has sense of wearing/wasting away time, whence it is given as 'delay, procrastination'; the English derivative 'diatribe' comes from another sort of wearing away, that is, whittling down the reputation of another, hence a vicious piece of invective. Cf. tribadism.

13 A fine juxtaposition of two points already made – 'By Artemis (goddess of chastity), I'll take my shoes off!'

16 More positive than Aristophanes' βουλεύσομαι (951), but it gives a good ending here.

Refer to *GVE* **136** as many relative pronouns have occurred, but only a few in the form ὅσπερ or ὅστις. Note 'Revise...αὐτός' (*GVE* p. 140); it helps greatly with Exercises (b/c)3 and the Test Exercise to do so.

Test Exercise

Explain code-staffs and Aristophanes' deliberate phallic by-play.

Section Ten

Grammar

> Present and imperfect passive
> Genitive absolute
> Comparative adverbs and two-termination adjectives
> Optative of φημί.

Neither the present nor the imperfect passive (p. 92.7ff.) presents any problem to students who have done Latin, but those who have learnt modern languages by oral active methods usually have very hazy notions (if any at all) about the difference between active and passive. Explain the passive as being another way of articulating the active, and give plenty of easy English examples on the blackboard. Then write up five 'active' sentences (in English) for conversion into the passive.

Some students may have been taught that 'absolute' phrases (e.g. 'The day being clement, I had instructed my chauffeur to open my landaulette') are wrong in English – as they are in German. Encourage students to watch out for *noun + participle in genitive*. Translate 'with X-ing' or 'with X being-ed' as a first shot, then retranslate more smoothly.

Much of Section 10A–C is very close to Aristophanes; again, keep a text handy.

Section Ten A

Background

Solon, Kleisthenes and beginnings of democracy   HI 8, 11
Democracy   5.1–22
ἀγορά   1.29, 33–5; 2.40
Aristophanes and politics   7.60–2
κυρία ἐκκλησία   5.14, 77
σχοινίον   5.14–15
πρυτάνεις   5.10–12, 24
Countryman's love of his demos   1.21, 2.52
κῆρυξ   5.39
'Who wishes to speak?'   5.11
ῥήτωρ   5.19–21
Scythian archer   4.64; 5.14, 37
πρέσβεις   5.41–3
Persians   HI 12; P 2–6

Commentary

p. 90 line
7 κυρία ἐκκλησία: see on p. 60.29.
8 ἐρῆμος: cf. eremite, hermit: two-termination adjectives are dealt with in this section.

Pnyx: see the map on p. 61 and the drawing on p. 89.

11 σχοινίον [μεμιλτωμένον]: a rope with vermilion dye was swept across the agora to push people towards the Pnyx. The Assembly itself was proclaimed by a trumpet call; any citizen arriving with vermilion dye and therefore touched by the rope could be fined for late arrival at the Assembly. Aristophanes makes it fairly easy to dodge the rope!

14   Another farmer's lament is preserved in a fragment from Aristophanes' *Georgoi*:

εἰρήνη βαθύπλουτε καὶ ζευγάριον βοεικόν, εἰ
γάρ ποτ' ἐμοὶ παυσαμένῳ τοῦ πολέμου γένοιτο
σκάψαι κἀποκλάσαι τε καὶ λουσαμένῳ διελκύσαι
τῆς τρυγὸς ἄρτον λιπαρὸν καὶ ῥάφανον φέροντι.

17   Prytaneis: presidents, 'chairing' meetings of the Assembly. The ten tribes between them subdivided the year into ten parts, each tribe having a spell of providing these presidents.

21   καθάρματος: cf. catharsis: a purification ceremony, involving the sacrifice of pigs, whose blood was used to cleanse the area. This ceremony was performed before every meeting of both ἐκκλησία and βουλή.

22   Genitive absolutes occur only in stage directions in this section: it may be best to translate them with a brief explanation, leaving a more detailed treatment to Section 11 (where they are thoroughly revised).

24   Amphitheos claims to be a demigod, yet proceeds to claim travelling expenses!

p. 91 line

30   τοξόται: Scythian mercenaries, one of whose duties was keeping order in the ἐκκλησία. Here and elsewhere Aristophanes uses the nominative as a vocative.

38   In this line the herald summons envoys back from Persia to give their report. The incident is worth reading in translation, but in our text this episode is omitted and Dikaiopolis muses to himself.

Section Ten B

Background

Freedom and democracy   HI 11, 53, 55; 4.53; 7.14
Debate and democracy   5.5–7
Citizen power   5.9; HI 38
Trade and manufacture   4.53–61

Commentary

p. 92 line

3   ὀλ- and (and ἀπολ-, l. 4) should be stressed: the (ἀπ)ολ- stem is very commonly used.

5ff. Take these lines carefully: they lead to the first passive usage, and if students follow closely both sense and sentence structure, they will have translated the passive before they know they have done so! To avoid any confusion with the middle, all passives in the section are used either with ὑπό + genitive or the dative of instrument.

17 ἔστω: may have to be given – cf. English 'So be it.'

18 Periclean policy again – see on pp. 18.35, 24.25, and below on p. 93.14.

27 The horses and mules argument is from Plato, *Republic* 563. 'For although they are free, they are not completely free; the Law is set over them as their master.' Cf. Herodotus VII.104 = *WoH*, Herodotus, Section 23. The paradox there, as here, is that laws (= restrictions on personal freedom) are essential to preserve freedom.

29 ἐξισταμένοις: once more stress the στα- stem (especially to those deriving it from ἐπίσταμαι), and ask for the force of μή.

31–2 This is the first genitive absolute in the text. It is a useful check on how well the genitive absolutes in the stage directions were understood.

33 μοί: ethic dative '(and this is a matter of some concern) to me'.

Section Ten C

Background

Akharnians 1.22
Μαραθωνομάχαι HI 13
Peace 6.5
Festivals 2.52
City Dionysia 2.46–7

Commentary

p. 93 line

11 Explain here that Amphitheos has been to Sparta and back during the last six lines.

14 Akharnians: the eponymous chorus of the play – angry old men anxious to prosecute the war because of the destruction of their vineyards. Yet another reaction to the war: Dikaiopolis, a farmer, is anxious to get back to the farm by ending the war, whereas these farmers wish to continue it for vengeance.

19 Another proud epithet, cf. p. 13.36.

αἰσθόμενοι: because, as we shall see, peace treaties were presented as being

samples, perhaps in leather wineskins (but cf. picture on p. 93), hence giving
a pun on σπονδαί = 'treaty', = 'libation'. The Akharnians 'smelt'
(ὦσφροντο) the samples and so gave chase.
26 'sample bottles' – make sure no one thinks of glass jars!

p. 94 line
8 ὀξύτατα: the superlative adverb may need to be given here if it was not
explained thoroughly earlier. Use it to revise adverbs if it is mistranslated.
12 Rural Dionysia: held in the month Poseideon (roughly December).
The central feature was the phallos procession, to promote the fertility of
autumn-sown crops during the dormant period. In *Akharnians* Dikaiopolis
emerges from his house leading his family in a mini-procession of the Rural
Dionysia.
17 Immediately after this line, the chorus burst in with their exciting
trochaic–cretic–resolved cretic ode. Read the translation, then the original –
it is a very exciting chorus rhythmically.

Test Exercise

More explanation is needed before tackling this: (a) explain its context in the
play (Dikaiopolis has wrested from the angry chorus an agreement that they
should listen to his anti-war argument, and now proceeds to 'explain' its
origins); (b) Kleon had previously indicted Aristophanes for abusing the
Athenian people publicly when there were foreigners in the audience.

Sections Eleven to Thirteen

Grammar

Nearly all the most important accidence has occurred by now (aorist and
future passives, all perfect tenses, and all subjunctives are still to come in
Sections 11–13).
    Syntax now begins to be amplified and explained. It is worth asking
students to make a separate section of notes devoted to essential, basic syntax,
such as may be required for 'O'-level or advanced classes in Greek authors.
This can be completed as different constructions are met. A 'basic syntax'
might be as follows:

Syntax Summary

Indirect statement

	Met in
(a) ὅτι + indicative (may be optative after historic main verb – 12F)	Ch. 1 and later
(b) infinitive (change of subject in accusative)	11E
(c) participle (change of subject in accusative)	11H

Rule of thumb: (a) speech (except φημί); (b) thought (+ φημί); (c) knowledge. This is for guidance only, *not* a rule. N.B. tenses throughout are those of direct speech.

Indirect command

infinitive as English, negative μή as in direct commands.

Indirect questions

question word + indicative (may be optative after an historic main verb). The tense is that of the direct question.

Verbs of fearing

(a) infinitive where English uses an infinitive	*GVE* **182**
(b) past/present fear: μή + indicative	*GVE* **182**
(c) future fear: μή + subjunctive/optative (after a primary/historic main verb)	*GVE* **182; 194**

Indefinite clauses

ἄν + subjunctive in primary time; optative in historic time.	*GVE* **175; 187**

Temporal clauses

present/past – indicative; future = an indefinite clause.	*GVE* **176**
N.B. πρίν = 'before': infinitive (change of subject in accusative); 'until': use the temporal construction.	*GVE* **161; 198**

Purpose clauses   *Met in*
  (a) future participle;   *GVE* **160; 186**
  (b) ἵνα/ὡς/ὅπως + subjunctive/optative (according
      to sequence).

Result clauses
  (a) infinitive (negative μή);   *GVE* **200-2**
  (b) indicative (negative οὐ) – if occurrence of the
      result is stressed.

Conditional clauses...

  εἰ + optative/imperfect indicative/aorist indicative;   *GVE* **151-2; 162**
  ἄν in main clause, with optative/imperfect
  indicative/aorist indicative. See grid in Section 11G.

This is a suitable moment to point students towards the Reference Grammar
and Language Surveys in *GVE*. Particularly useful for *accidence* is Reference
Grammar A–G, and for *syntax* H–R. Language Surveys 4–6 are relevant to the
current work on subjunctives and optatives.

   This may also be a good point to move over to morphology charts if they
have not yet been used. Students can encourage themselves by filling in what
they know, and this acts as good revision of basic accidence before the
syntactical complexities of the rest of the Course.

Section Eleven A

Background

   Lawcourts 5.44–67; 3.16–17; HI 7; law v. lawless 7.17; courts and
      holidays 2.43
   On Apollodoros' history 4.70, and cf. 5.50–1; 6.40
   Decrees etc. in ἀγορά 1.35

Grammar

   Aorist passive
   ἵστημι, καθίστημι

Discussion

The Neaira prosecution was a complicated case; it is here considerably simplified. Further detail is most easily found in translation, either in the Bohn edition of Demosthenes vol. v (tr. C. R. Kennedy) or in the Loeb edition vol. vi (tr. A. T. Murray). The chapter on 'Oratory' in K. J. Dover, *Ancient Greek Literature* (Oxford, 1982) is excellent, and should be read by all. It contains a very lucid explanation of the importance of oratory in the ancient world. Also see N. R. E. Fisher, *Social Values in Classical Athens* (Dent, 1976), an excellent little book which translates and discusses large portions of *Neaira* and *Euergos* (Sections 15–16).

At the end of Section 10, ask students to read the introduction carefully (94–9); this is a complicated case needing some thorough preliminary work in order to get the most out of it.

NOTE: it is possible to cut this section further, if time presses. The main sections to cut (cut = translation or summary by the teacher) are those with the dialogue between dikasts, since (with one exception) no new accidence, syntax or facts of the case are introduced. However, the dikast dialogues very effectively reinforce accidence etc., and in this complicated case they are very helpful. Thus Section 11A, B and E may be 'cut' (Section 11E contains the first indirect statement using the infinitive, but this occurs frequently later); 11H may be also 'cut'. Section 12G must *not* be cut (it introduces the perfect middle and passive); 12C, D, H, I and 13C, D and F may all be cut, if necessary.

Commentary

p. 101 line

13 **κελεύοντος τοῦ κήρυκος**: if explanation of the genitive absolute has been postponed from Section 10, it should be given here.

κήρυκος: cf. the way in which citizens were summoned into the Assembly in Section 10. The dikasts have clearly already been selected when this scene opens.

14 **ἄλλος ἄλλον**: translate 'different' or 'one...another' when more than one ἄλλος occurs in a phrase.

16 **γραφήν**: generally anything written; here specifically 'indictment', cf. writ (in English used now only in a legal context). It used to be a past participle, until at least the last century. Cf. Fitzgerald's *Omar Khayyam*: 'The moving finger writes, and having writ moves on.'

17 **ἕτερος...ἕτερον**: if ἄλλος ἄλλον has been grasped, this should pose no problems.

20 ὄχλος: cf. ochlocracy.
23 ἐντεύξεσθαι: students should guess the meaning if they are guided towards the stem τυχ-; hence 'happen on', 'meet'.
διατρίβοντι: see on p. 88.5.
24 ἄπειρος: the opposite of ἔμπειρος.
25 ἐξέσται: this will probably be taken as ἔξεστι. Revise the future of εἰμί here; it does not occur in the text very often.

p. 102 line
1 χρῆμα: lit. 'what a (thing of a) crowd', i.e. χρῆμα is otiose in English.

Section Eleven B

Background

Meddling   5.63
Persuasion   4.44; 7.16–19

Commentary

p. 102 line
13 δίκη: a case was either referred to as a γραφή (usually containing charges that threatened the state), or as a δίκη (usually a more personal case) – cf. our criminal and civil actions. Note that even a charge of high treason would still be brought by a private citizen; the state had no officials whose duty it was to bring such cases, collect the evidence and conduct the prosecution. δίκη is used here as a general word for a trial.
14 πολυπράγμων: deduce this from the constituent parts. Apollodoros, son of a wealthy banker Pasion, was a prominent litigant. He appears in several surviving cases, including two by Demosthenes (perhaps the reason why this speech was preserved in the Demosthenic corpus).
15 διαφέρει: cf. Latin differo, whence 'differ'.
16 κοινός: the Koine was the common version of Greek used throughout the Greek-speaking world after the conquests of Alexander; it is the language used in the Septuagint and the New Testament; εὔνοια – εὖ + νοῦς; ἀγωνίζομαι – as for ἀγών, p. 14.27.

18 ὅρκος: cf. exorcism.

ἀπέδομεν: should be deduced from the stem -δο-.

20 εὐεργετεῖν: εὖ + ἔργον; κύριος – see on p. 60.29.

25 ὑπῆρξα (cf. l.31 ἀρχόμενοι) is worth analysing closely here. It will recur, and acts as a good test of whether students can work back to the lexicon form (see note on p. 103 l. 13).

27 Note that vengeance was a permissible reason for starting legal action. Cf. the reaction a modern lawyer would receive if he tried opening a case like that! Note also that all three possible openings for Apollodoros quote personal motives.

32 ὅπως + future indicative needs to be mentioned here as 'make sure that' (it is explained in the grammar for Section 11G).

33 προσέξεις τὸν νοῦν: deduce the meaning from the three ideas: 'hold – mind – towards'. Revise ἔχω, ἕξω/σχήσω, ἔσχον (σχ-).

Note the apparent informality – jurors pushing, shoving, chattering – as a contrast with the solemnity of modern procedure.

Section Eleven C

Background

Revenge 3.1–4; friends and enemies 3.13–14
Poverty 3.18; ἀτιμία 5.64–7, 3.12

Commentary

p. 103 line

8 γραφήν: note the prominence given to this word, underlining the fact that this is a 'criminal' case.

9 ἠδικήθην: elicit the past tense (augment), and ask what the corresponding form of παύω would be. Revise augmentation here if necessary (adding ἐ-, lengthening vowels etc.).

10 ἐσχάτος: cf. eschatology.

κατέστην: ἵστημι is dealt with in this section. The basic, all-purpose hint is to say that if ἵστημι has an object, it means 'place, set up'; if *not*, it means 'stand, be set up, set myself up'. This summary table may be useful:

Transitive	Intransitive
Pres. act. ἵστημι, 'I set up'	Pres. mid. ἵσταμαι, 'I am standing up (= setting myself)'
Fut. act. στήσω, 'I will set up'	Fut. mid. στήσομαι, 'I will stand up'
Imperf. act. ἵστην, 'I was setting up'	Imperf. mid. ἱστάμην, 'I was standing up'
Wk. aor. act. ἔστησα, 'I set up'*	Str. aor. act. ἔστην, 'I stood up'
Wk. aor. mid. ἐστησάμην, 'I set X up for myself'	← Wk. aor. mid. turns transitive ← strong drives out weak ←

Similarly:

καθίστημι εἰς, 'I put someone into a state'   καθίσταμαι εἰς, 'I get into a state'

* Given the commonness of the aorist emphasize the stem-difference between ἔστησα (στησ-) and ἔστην (στα-/στη-) and make *this* the starting-point for discussion.

There is nothing terribly difficult here; two further points should be made: (a) there is vowel shortening in the plural (as on Section 9, *ad init.*, δίδωμι), and (b) the aorist paradigm ἔστην shares endings with 'root'-aorist ἔβην (*GVE* 126). The future and weak aorist are absolutely regular. It pays to rehearse conjugations and to establish that the third person plural of the strong and weak aorist are identical (ἔστησαν).

p. 103 line

11 θυγατέρες: Why were daughters and wife at risk? Largely since one of the greatest causes of shame to an Athenian citizen father was to have daughters unmarried because he could not find an adequate dowry.

13 ὑπῆρξα may be found difficult to recognize: establish ὑπ- as a prefix to be ignored while finding the lexicon form; then point to -σα = weak aorist; de-augment to ἄρχω. This prepares for l. 20.

17 ἀτιμίας: if unable to pay a fine, Athenian citizens could lose their civil rights. This meant that they had no legal protection at all against assault, theft etc.: only the injured party could bring a δίκη, and he must be a citizen.

21ff. Note that it was laudable to harm one's enemies; contrast this with Christianity. The same sentiment occurs later in a Homer extract (*Text* p. 178.4–5).

Section Eleven D

Background

ἀτιμία   3.12; 5.64–7
ψήφισμα   5.48–51
κύριος of a family   4.16
προίξ   4.21
Family and women in general   4.12–38
State and religion   2.65–6
Marriage and property   4.4, 21

Discussion

p. 104: Explain the words in the English introduction: 'an illegal change in the law'. Note the 'catch-22' situation here: any change to existing laws must contradict existing laws and thus be illegal. Hence very many charges of γραφὴ παρανόμων are recorded. Anyone proposing a change in the law more or less put his head on the block (cf. Dikaiopolis literally doing so in *Akharnians*, and the unseen or sight passage, from Demosthenes (Test Exercise 13) on the Lokrian method of changing law).

Commentary

p. 104 line

24 Apollodoros had proposed that the ἐκκλησία should decide by a free vote whether the budget surplus should be devoted entirely to prosecuting the war against Philip, or split between that and state functions. This was accepted by the βουλή and due to be ratified by the ἐκκλησία when Stephanos charged him with illegality. His 'false witnesses' (l. 27) claimed that Apollodoros owed money to the Treasury and (in common fashion) made many other irrelevant charges against him. Whether true or false, they were enough to blacken Apollodoros' name and secure a conviction.

27 The size of fine (τίμημα) was fixed for certain offences; for others, e.g. the γραφὴ παρανόμων, it would vary according to the alleged seriousness of the offence. In this case, prosecutor proposed one penalty, defence another, and a straight vote decided the penalty imposed. The most celebrated instance of this was Socrates' trial: after conviction, Meletos demanded the death penalty, Socrates (after first suggesting that the appropriate 'penalty' was that he should be maintained at state expense as being invaluable to the community) suggested 30 μναῖ on securities of friends, Plato among them.

παρασχόμενος: σχ- as the aorist stem of ἔχω often causes trouble. Revision of the principal parts, with a clear distinction between εἶχον imperfect, and ἔσχον aorist, pays dividends here.

33 The explicit reason for fearing πενίαν is given here.

p. 105 line

1 Note the -ανδρ- contrasted with ἀνθρώπων (see on p. 6.15).

5 καταφρονεῖ: elicit from κατά (down) and φρονέω.

6 παρὰ νόμους/κατὰ νόμους: it is worth making a special note of these, as students regularly confuse them. The γραφὴ παρανόμων should help fix the meanings.

φάσκω: use the φα- stem from φημί to fix the meaning (cf. GVE p. 268, note on tenses). Students may need help with the accusative and infinitives here (to be learnt in Section 11E). Encourage a literal translation first ('I allege Stephanos *to be -ing*'), then make it more idiomatic. Alert students to the need for the English 'that', which does not occur in the Greek. They have, of course, been used to ὅτι.

8 Children were introduced at an early age to the 'phratries' (groups of families, a subdivision within the deme) and, at eighteen, to the demes, to be enrolled as full citizens. This was the only way in which a check was kept upon those who held full citizenship, and upon the fathers who had introduced them to the 'phratries' in the first place.

11 Note the 'inverted' ὅτι clause: this inversion (noun clause before main verb) is very common in oratory. It stresses an important fact/claim, and is frequent in *Neaira*.

13 ἐπιδεῖξαι: from the root δείκνυμι comes the noun δεῖγμα cf. paradigm.

Section Eleven E

Grammar

Accusative (nominative) and infinitive

If time is short, this section can be translated for the students, though indirect statement constructions with the infinitive must be highlighted while doing so (lines 23–4 contain a good example of the juxtaposition of an accusative + infinitive and a nominative + infinitive). If students are translating, insist that their translations are in the form '...that...'.

Commentary

p. 105 line

26 ἐλέχθη: this is usually deduced, but point out how λεγ- becomes λεχ- before a θ.

30 ἐκδοῦναι: the usual word for giving in marriage; note here because it recurs.

10, 31 Wherein lies the irreverence towards the gods? (a) in falsely claiming the paternity of Neaira's children, probably under oath, thus offending Zeus Horkios; (b) in the later incident with Theogenes (12E–F); (c) the betrayal of one's heritage: the land is given by its tutelary gods into the protection of its 'true' inhabitants (citizens), to be passed on to future citizens.

34 If ἐκδοῦναι has been carefully noted above, ἀν-εκ-δότους will fall into place.

38–9 The genitive absolute here may still need explanation – not many examples have been met so far.

Section Eleven F

Background

συνοικεῖν 4.24
Lysias 1.24, HI 57
Mysteries 2.53
Witnesses and evidence 5.53–4
Greek alphabet and writing 7.2–3, 15–16

Grammar

τίθημι

Discussion

The law quoted on p. 106 needs some comment.'If a ξένος lives with an ἀστή in any way at all. . .': this does not mean that a ξένος could not even be the lover of an ἀστή, or later that an ἀστός could not have a ξένη mistress (Pericles' Aspasia was a Milesian). 'Live with' = 'live as husband/wife', and the 'in any way at all' means 'in any way trying to pass off the relationship as a legitimate marriage'. That one-third of the man's property should go to the person securing the conviction was a clear incentive to sniff out any alien husband; but one-third of an alien wife's property would not (probably) amount to much, hence the fine in addition, since otherwise the ἀστός had little to lose (his wife enslaved, her property forfeit) in comparison with the ξένος (whose wife's property would legally be accounted his, so he would be enslaved and their joint property forfeit).

Laws were read out by a court official as the speaker requested them. There was no judge to guide the dikasts on whether the law was relevant (or even whether it existed!), though the relevance and genuineness here cannot be doubted. Speakers had a time limit for their speeches, but this excluded time used in reading laws, depositions or other evidence. Speakers thus had to 'clock-watch', as Apollodoros does a little later, saying 'if there is enough water left in the clock' (this does not, however, appear in our text).

Commentary

p. 106 line

31   Nikarete was a freedwoman and high-class 'madame'; Neaira was one of a batch of seven girls bought and trained by her, then subsequently sold.
35   **ἔθηκεν:** elicit the -θη- stem (several examples were used in Section 8); τίθημι is dealt with in this section.
36   **ἔδοξεν:** 'seem *good*' is a meaning often neglected, and needed here.

μυῆσαι: note Lysias' motive: when hiring Metaneira and paying for his session with her, he benefited her little, but Nikarete much. If he could get Metaneira to Athens for the Mysteries, his expenditure upon her could be personal remuneration for her.
37   **βουλομένῳ:** insist that this is assigned to its proper noun.

p. 107 line

27   **ἐπείσθη:** this may cause trouble (some confuse it with ἐπειδή). It is valuable to work this back into its lexicon form.
29   **ᾐσχύνετο:** since he would have 'shamed his wife', who, within the house, was, if not supreme, highly influential (cf. Section 16).
30   Note again the care for the old: his mother was living in the same house.
32–3   No precise indication is given of the age of Neaira at the time (nor have we any idea at what age prostitutes started work), but note how Apollodoros (a) conveys coarsely and bluntly that Neaira was already a prostitute and (b) uses the unqualified comparative νεωτέρα, 'rather young', with the implication that she was too young to be on the streets. Apollodoros

gives no reason for her presence in Athens – she merely came along with them, perhaps as a friend of Metaneira (she could have acted as a slave of Metaneira for the duration of the trip), perhaps to secure a portion of Metaneira's payment from Lysias in order to return it to Nikarete, their owner.

36 Evidence: this was merely read out in court by an official. There was no opportunity to cross-question those testifying, or any possibility of assessing whether it was all a pack of lies: the only constraint upon those giving evidence was the oath which they had to swear – and this was regarded as solemn and binding. Yet numerous cases cite 'false witnesses' – as indeed Apollodoros has already done – and while this citation may itself be false, instances must have occurred for the suggestion to carry any weight at all.

Section Eleven G

Background

  Solon   HI 8; 5.26–7
  Hippias   4.47
  Sophists   4.43–8; 7.20–1
  Evidence   7.27

Grammar

  Future remote unfulfilled condition
  Wishes for future
  ὅπως + future indicative
  Optative of εἰμί, εἶμι, οἶδα

This is one piece of dikast dialogue that must be read: conditionals are exercised here. Establish firmly the different usages of the optative:

  (i)   plain optative – a wish
  (ii)   optative + ἄν 'potential' = 'would, should, could, may, will'
  (iii)   optative + ἄν conditional (can be spotted by a preceding εἰ + optative)
  (iv)   indicative + ἄν conditional (spotted by a preceding εἰ + indicative)

Work towards a full conditional grid as follows:

	Open/fulfilled		Remote/unfulfilled	
referring to PRESENT time	εἰ+indic. indic.	'If I am now...' 'I am...'	εἰ+imperf. imperf.+ἄν	'If I were now...' 'I would be...'
PAST time	εἰ+indic. indic.	'If I did...' 'I did...'	εἰ+aor. aor.+ἄν (not until section 12C)	'If I had -ed' 'I would have...'
FUTURE time	(not until section 13)	'If I shall...' 'I shall...'	εἰ+opt. opt.+ἄν	'If I were to...' 'I would...'

It is perhaps interesting to add that Xenokleides the poet could not give evidence at the trial of Neaira because Xenokleides had been exiled – prosecutor, Stephanos!

Commentary

p. 108 line

24 καλύπτω new to students; it is synonymous with κρύπτω.

29 **εἴθε**: best given in the dated idiom 'Would that', 'If only' or the modern form 'I wish I could...'

p. 109 line

1 **μή**: as conditions occur in this chapter, reinforce the fact that a participle may stand for a protasis, retaining the negative (see on p. 78.13).

6 Hippias of Elis, celebrated in two dialogues by Plato, was famous as a mathematician, sophist and polymath; he collected the sayings of other philosophers, thereby laying claim to being called the father of doxography.

10 Solon was archon in 594 and the date of this trial was 340. Hence the two sentences do not refer to the same thing – there would have been *c.* one hundred and sixty-four archons since Solon!

25 ὅπως+ future indicative should be learnt here.

Section Eleven H

Background

Wives and parties   4.32, 37–8
Metics and ξένοι   4.67ff.

Grammar

Accusative and participle

Future passive

Discussion

Neaira is 'our only example (of a woman who) collected an ἔρανος – a loan raised by contributions collected from a group of friends of the debtor and lent to meet some extraordinary expense – from her former lovers in order to buy her freedom' (D. M. Schapps, *Economic Rights of Women in Ancient Greece* (Edinburgh University Press, 1979).

Phrynion was a son of Demon of Paiania who was a cousin of Demosthenes. This fact has been used to demonstrate (a) that the speech was by Demosthenes, because of the family interest, (b) that the speech was not by Demosthenes, because Phrynion is shown to be a pretty unpleasant piece of work.

Commentary

p. 110 line

22 Note that a man never took his wife to banquets. If he took any woman, she would be a ἑταίρα (cf. geisha girl: certainly not a street-touting prostitute in a 'high-society' symposium of the sort described in *Neaira*).

23 ἐκώμαζε: Apollodoros also claims that not only did Phrynion have intercourse with her in full view of the others, but, when Phrynion was under the table, so did others – including even the *slaves*.

28 At this point in the original text a definite date is given: 373–2 (N.B. some thirty years before the date of the trial). Megara: on the way back to Corinth, from which she was excluded under the terms of her sale by Eukrates and Timanoridas.

29 Megara was involved in the war between Athens and Sparta at this time: besides, the speaker adds, 'the Megarians were tight-fisted', so business was poor.

37 προΐσταται: 'set (him) up in front of' her, i.e. adopted him as her protector. A convenient point to refer back to ἵστημι, underlining the transitive and intransitive usages; add καθίστημι as before – it occurs in the first line of p. 111.

Section Eleven I

Background

> Phratries   2.50–1; 4.15–16
> Sycophants   5.63
> Polemarch   5.34–6
> Arbitration   5.55

Commentary

p. 111 line

9 ἄψεσθαι: in this place, if not before, the point can be made that the infinitive in indirect speech can have a temporal sense. It is obvious with future infinitives and it is also useful here because the future passive occurs in this section – the first example is a future infinitive passive in the next line.

10 If students are alerted to the fact that ἄψεσθαι and ἕξειν (9) are future, then εἰσαχθήσεσθαι will probably be correctly translated.

13 Three children: nothing is said in the speech about the two sons, nor is there any indication at what stage (or from whom!) Neaira acquired these. On illegitimacy: there is little evidence of social stigma, although of course children could never be full citizens. Pericles' son by Aspasia is exceptional. After the death of his two legitimate sons, Pericles jr was specially legitimated, and he was 'excessively afraid of the (slur) "son of a prostitute"' (Eupolis fr. 98).

16 Note how difficult it was to give a precise description of where one lived in both Greece and Rome, without the aid of street names and numbers.

18 ὡς…ἕξων: purpose, learnt in Section 12A.

20 συκοφαντίαν: as there was no official force to act for the state in maintaining law and order, litigious individuals tried to make a living by collecting as much evidence as they could against a person, then bringing him to trial in hopes of getting one-third of his property. Such individuals needed every scrap of information they could get (Apollodoros certainly would have needed a great deal), and lesser fry could pick up an ancillary income by selling damaging information. Eupolis, *Demes* 65ff. has an amusing scene with a sycophant threatening a man who has barleycorns in his beard because he had been drinking the Sacred Soup of the Eleusinian Mysteries (in this case the man paid up to avoid being exposed: the sycophant stood to gain either way if he had some information – blackmail, if the offender paid up, or payment from his enemy). See also Aristophanes' *Ploutos* 898–950.

23 ἀφαιρουμένου: a difficult expression – 'with Stephanos taking her away to legal freedom', meaning 'asserting her freedom according to the law'. When Phrynion had last seen Neaira, it was as a slave whom he had bought.

24 κατηγγύησεν: 'compelled Neaira to give securities before the πολέμαρχος' – similar in theory to the modern system of bail, but simpler in practice as the person 'on bail' had to present the 'bail' to the πολέμαρχος there and then, recovering it later if the case against him/her was not proven. Phrynion clearly intended taking Stephanos to court over the ownership of Neaira, and was not risking her running off again as she had done previously!

Arbitration: another practice very similar to today's, when, for instance, pay negotiations are submitted to the arbitration of three individuals, one representing either side and the third a mutually agreed 'neutral'.

Agreement: an extraordinary arrangement altogether. Note that (a) Neaira now becomes one of the very few women known to us who were not subject to the nearest male as her κύριος; (b) what had to be returned was property belonging to the οἶκος of Phrynion, excluding personal gifts to Neaira; (c) a slight variation exists between Apollodoros' reporting of the terms (as translated on p. 112) and the terms as read in court (not included here). In the latter, Neaira is to spend an equal number of days per month with both men. Requirements (d) and (e) would apparently have worked well for some while – evidence is adduced from three men who frequently dined with Phrynion, Stephanos and Neaira, all seeming on the best of terms.

What happens to Phrynion after this is unknown: he simply vanishes from the case!

GVE gives many useful exercises on various points of syntax and accidence here.

Test Exercise

This is very difficult; some of the following points may help:

(1) Read the note at the bottom of page 172 in GVE, stressing that all four were homosexuals;

(2) Mention again the 'oratorical inversion' (p. 105.11), adding that it is not confined to ὅτι clauses;

(3) Further help might include the possible meanings of participle phrases (including conditional) and a revision of relatives.

This is one Test Exercise which should be read carefully before it is set to try to anticipate likely difficulties.

Section Twelve A

Background

Divorce and dowry   4.24

Grammar

Aorist infinitive passive
Future participle
ὡς + future participle
πρίν + infinitive

Commentary

p. 114 line

17   Phano...Strybele: why change the name? Did the former sound more Athenian? No reason is offered by Apollodoros – see note at the end of 13 below for a hypothetical answer.

18   πρίν ... ἐλθεῖν: the usage of πρίν + infinitive ('πρίν + infin.' makes a memorable jingle) is picked up here. Note that where English often uses a participle ('before coming to Athens'), Greek always uses the infinitive. Stress the change of subject in the accusative, and link this with the accusative and infinitive of indirect statements.

21   Andocides, *Against Alcibiades* 14 tells how Alcibiades beat the system by sheer force. After obtaining an enormous dowry with his wife, he spent it on hiring prostitutes, who came to their house in crowds. When his wife expressed her dissatisfaction by going to the archon to petition for divorce, Alcibiades and friends swooped and forcibly carried her back home. The problem of enforcing the law – even express decrees of courts – was the responsibility of the individual. The theme is central to *Euergos* (Sections 15–16).

22   Note that because Neaira was a prostitute, Phano had learnt that kind of φύσις.

26   Yet another shade of meaning for κοσμίος – orderly conduct. Cf. on p. 15.2

27   Apollodoros remains scrupulously vague about how Phrastor discovered Phano was not Stephanos' daughter; her paternity is completely unknown. The original text adds that, at the time of his betrothal, Phrastor thought Phano was the daughter of Stephanos by his previous wife.

29 The aorist infinitive passive is new here. There should be no problem if -ναι is remembered as an infinitive ending (p. 45.36), and cf. εἰδέναι next line.

35 λαγχάνω: here in the legal sense of bringing a lawsuit against someone. For ἔλαχον, cf. ἔτυχον, ἔμαθον etc.

38 Note that while Stephanos' action is a δίκη, Phrastor can bring a γραφή on the grounds that Stephanos' offence was against the whole community.

p. 115 line
2 Why the reconciliation? If Phrastor was sure of his evidence, why did he not continue with the prosecution – he stood to gain one-third of Stephanos' property if successful? Certainty of evidence, however, would not necessarily be sufficient to secure conviction. One point that must repeatedly be stressed in these sections is that the verdict would depend not exclusively upon the facts, but upon what sort of impression the prosecutor could make upon the jury, by whatever means, however foul.

Section Twelve B

Background

Women's role 4.32ff.

Commentary

p. 115 line
17 διετέθη: revise the basic parts of τίθημι – future, aorist and aorist passive stems.
22 Note ὡς + future part, expressing purpose.
25 Patronising chauvinist piggery? Or merely pragmatic?!
32 Even this would not ensure Phano's son as heir. If objections were made about Phano's status, then the child (as non-Athenian) could not be an heir – and Phrastor would incur heavy penalties in addition.

Section Twelve C

Background

Citizenship 4.5–6
κύριος 4.15–16

Phratry   4.15–16; 2.50–1
Legitimacy   4.17–20
Oaths   2.27; 7.16

Grammar

Past unfulfilled conditions (see on 11G)
Emphasize ἄν + optative – 'would', 'should', 'would' (potential or
    conditional)
    ἄν + indicative – either as above, *or* 'would have' (conditional)
This should clear the way for ἄν + subjunctive, still to come

Commentary

p. 116 line
9   Phrastor takes a citizen wife without (it seems) redivorcing Phano. This
would have been quite in order if Phano were a proven alien, since his
previous 'marriage' to her would have been immediately invalidated.

11   ὅ: note the accent, showing that it is a relative pronoun.

12   τό + infinitive is actually to be learnt in Section 12D, but it can equally
well be noted here. Stress the accusative (marking a change of subject) +
infinitive. Cf. πρίν.

25   Swearing by solemn oaths: note that the greater the sanctity of the
objects by which one swore, the more solemn and binding the oath. Compare the story that Duke William of Normandy, after delivering Harold,
Earl of Wessex, from captivity, tempted him to promise support for William
as next king of England, having secretly filled the shrine at which the oath
was taken with all the bones of all the saints of Normandy. Harold blenched
visibly when he later saw them...

26   ἦ μήν: also emphasize the solemnity of the oath: 'Yea verily'. Six
members of the Brutid γένος submitted evidence that this refusal to take the
oath actually occurred; we may thus conclude that there was some doubt
about the paternity of Phano. Yet in England until the Compulsory Regis-
tration Act (1836) proof was always very difficult – and absolute proof of
paternity a very recent phenomenon. Phrastor's reluctance to swear a solemn
oath need therefore reflect little more than unwillingness to assert his absolute
certainty.

Section Twelve D

Grammar

This section summarizes what has gone before; no new grammar is introduced (τό + infinitive is to be noted here, but it has occurred previously). Rehearsal of the accusative and infinitive is very useful; insist on 'that' as the marker before every accusative + infinitive clause and insist on a clear distinction between indirect statement and τό + infinitive in this passage.

Discussion

Phano continued to bring in income for Stephanos: an extraordinary episode (not in the text) ensued. A former lover of Neaira, coming to Athens, went to see her; he found instead Phano, and became her lover. This man, Epainetos, was caught in bed with Phano by Stephanos, who immediately charged him with adultery. Instead of court action, they resorted to arbitration: the result was that Epainetos paid 1,000 drachmas εἰς ἔκδοσιν (a contribution to her dowry!), but Stephanos was to make her available to Epainetos whenever he was in town!

This episode immediately precedes that with Theogenes, making the latter yet more heinous.

Section Twelve E

Background

βασιλεὺς ἄρχων 5.36; 2.53
Gods in general   2.1-5
Offices of state   5.29-34
Purity of family   4.17-20
Piety and city   2.66
Marriage to Dionysos   2.56
Danger of defiance of gods   2.65

Grammar

Perfect indicative active

Commentary

p. 117 line

36 ἀναίδεια: the concept of αἰδώς becomes important later; it is worth mentioning the 'shame' concept here.

39 ἔλαχε: with the exception of the posts of the ten στρατηγοί and that of the ʽΕλληνοταμίαι (for which there was voting), all posts in the democracy were filled by lot.

βασιλεύς (sc. ἄρχων): one of the three senior ἄρχοντες. His duties, as chief religious official in the state, included superintending the Mysteries, the Lenaia festival and the torch race. As a legal official, he was responsible for the trial of all offences involving religion, and of homicide.

εὐγενής: cf. eugenics. Noble birth still conveyed some advantage, if no privilege.

πένης: Stephanos and Neaira were probably fairly affluent by this stage (if we may believe Apollodoros) and so could be quite useful to Theogenes.

p. 118 line

1 πάρεδρος (παρά + ἕδρα, cf. 'cathedral'): it is uncertain whether this was an official post, or simply refers to a personal aide.

6 ἔθη: cf. ethics; but the Greek word ἔθος was wide-ranging in meaning, including habit, custom, manners, i.e. general character.

8 ἄρρητα: a- privative + (ῥήτωρ) will give the meaning.

9 ξένη: the rites of the Mysteries could not be witnessed even by Athenian women – that a stranger should see them was sacrilege. Note that the wife of the βασιλεύς also had various religious duties (including administering the oath to various priestesses). Note further that, as the office of βασιλεύς, like most other priesthoods, was allotted annually, the 'secret' rites would have been known to (at least) several people.

The Anthesteria, celebrated on 11th–12th Anthesterion (end of February), was one of the major festivals of Dionysos. Its ritual was closely connected with wine (the first day was called πιθοιγία = opening of wine jars, the second χόες = jugs: all participants brought their own wine in jugs); its climax was the ἱερὸς γάμος between the wife of the βασιλεύς and Dionysos.

13 At this point a digression has been omitted: Apollodoros described the origin of the festival, stressing (a) that the wife of the king had to be a citizen, and a pure virgin at her wedding to the king; (b) that she administered the oath of chastity to the priestesses. Hence it was doubly sacrilegious for a prostitute's daughter to celebrate these mysteries.

Perfect tenses

First, revise οἶδα in all its forms (since it is a perfect of the non-extant εἴδω, of which εἶδον is the true aorist!). Then establish a grid revising the present and aorist active, middle and passive, and fill in the perfect, thus:

Pres. act.	*Aor. act.*	*Perf. act.*	*Pres. mid.*	*Aor. mid.*	*Perf. mid.*
παύω etc.	ἔπαυσα etc.	πέπαυκα etc.	παύομαι etc.	ἐπαυσάμην etc.	πέπαυμαι etc.

Pres. pass.	*Aor. pass.*	*Perf. pass.*
παύομαι etc.	ἐπαύσθην etc.	πέπαυμαι etc.

Reduplication of consonants must be stressed, and special note must be taken of reduplication by lengthening where a verb begins with a vowel, and reduplication by the addition of ἐ- in certain other cases. These are important when it comes to participles and infinitives (since it shows that they *cannot* be aorist indicative forms; aorists *never* have an augment in their participle, infinitive etc. forms).

Actually, little about the perfect is wholly new.

Consider:

(i)   reduplication in the stems of διδο-, δο-
(ii)   infinitives in -ναι with e.g. εἰδέναι
(iii)   participles in -ώς with εἰδώς
(iv)   participles in -μένος with e.g. present and aorist middle (but N.B. accent – a 'giveaway' for the perfect if final syllable short)
(v)   that the middle endings are just like the present
(vi)   that the active endings are virtually the same as the aorist active.

As for meaning, emphasize that the 'true' perfect = a present state arising from a past action. Then the fact that Phano/Stephanos 'has done...has despised...has sacrificed' stresses not just the impiety of the past action, but the inevitable miasma still tainting the city.

Section Twelve F

Background

Areopagus 5.26ff.

Grammar

Aorist optative passive
Optative in indirect speech
Future optative
These should all be handled with the minimum of fuss.

Commentary

p. 118 line

32 The Council of the Areopagus (not to be confused with the ordinary
βουλή, which met in the βουλευτήριον) consisted of ex-archons. Originally
it had large powers, but, as a result of the activities of Ephialtes and subsequently Pericles, its powers became very restricted. Its prestige, however,
remained: apart from trying cases of homicide, it also dealt with any crime
deemed to be a grave offence against the state.

34 Note the very common Greek practice of making the subject of an
indirect question the object of the main verb (e.g. Mark 1.24, 'I know thee,
who thou art'; *King Lear* 'I know you, who you are').

40 **εἰδείη:** a suitable point to revise the optative of οἶδα – it neatly paves
the way for the aorist optative passive.

p. 119 line

1 **ἐξαπατηθείη:** Revise the range of optative uses here: (i) plain optative
= wish; (ii) + ἄν = either potential or conditional (with optative or indicative in the latter case, εἰ being the clue); (iii) as here, in indirect speech.

4 **διοικέω:** for the οἰκ- stem, refer to the English derivative 'economics'
= 'laws of the οἶκος'.

5 **κηδεύω:** 'ally oneself by marriage'. Cf. the dramatic irony of Oedipus
calling Creon κήδευμα (*Oedipus Tyrannus* 85).

7 **τὴν ... ἄνθρωπον:** derogatory (see on p. 6.15), 'the female creature'.

10 **ἐλεήσασα:** cf. eleemosynary. 'The stout little milk girl dispensed one
pint of milk into Anna's jug, and spilt an eleemosynary supply on the step
for the cat' (Arnold Bennett, *Anna of the Five Towns*, ch. 2).

Section Twelve G

Background

Liturgies 5.71–2
Choruses 7.35
Competitions 3.1–4, 16

Grammar

Perfect indicative middle/passive
Perfect infinitive participle
Irregular perfects

See notes on perfect at 12E. Infinitive in -ναι and participles in -ώς -υῖα -ός and -μέν-ος -η -ον have been met before, as have middle passive endings in -μαι -σαι -ται etc. Utter a warning that reduplications *stay* in infinitives and participles (they do *not* augment; the perfect is *not* a past tense).

Commentary

p. 119 line

38 **καταπεφρονηκέναι**: will be read as an infinitive with no problem (cf. -ναι ending). Stress the retention of reduplication in all moods of the perfect.

p. 120 line

1 **πεπολίτευμαι**: perfect middle/passive – note (a) reduplication, (b) -μαι -σαι-ται endings, as for a present tense. Mention briefly the perfect participle + εἰσί(ν) as an alternative to the third person plural.

4 **λειτουργίας**: (cf. liturgy = a service of public worship). The λειτουργίαι were public duties performed by citizens, and included equipping/commanding a trireme, or paying for the training of a chorus to perform at one of the great dramatic festivals. Attitudes towards the spirit in which these duties were performed have changed during this century: for A. E. Zimmern, *The Greek Commonwealth* (Oxford, 1911) 290, they were done from nobility of intention; for V. Ehrenberg, *The Greek State* (Blackwell, 1960), ch. 4(*d*), they were a duty which later became a compulsory tax. Perhaps the motivation was a combination of Greek pride in the city (cf. p. 4.12ff.), and the fact that such service could be used as evidence of good character (as suggested here) in any litigation (as such, it could mean the difference between life or death!).

5 διαπεπράχθαι: easily recognized as an infinitive; stress again the retention of the duplication and ask what the infinitive ending is. That leaves the stem πραχ-. Ask what influence the θ could have had on the preceding consonant, and so back to πραγ-, ἔπραξα, πράσσω.

8 ἀποφαίνωσι: the subjunctive will be met in the next section. Don't mention it here unless questioned.

προγόνων: note the apparent concept of 'inherited civic worth', as though one might φύσει be a good citizen. The opposite concept was held equally strongly: if you could dig up any mud to throw at an opponent's parents or family, the muck would adhere also to descendants.

10 τετριηραρχηκότα: elicit the fact that this is a perfect participle; note that it has the same endings as εἰδώς. Mention again the retention of reduplication in all forms and stress once more the present state resulting from a past action ('having served as trierarch' = 'being a good citizen now').

Section Twelve H

Commentary

This may be translated by the teacher, if necessary: there is not much new accidence, and the material is a restatement of the evidence so far. Irregularities in the perfect are introduced: these are all in *GVE*.

p. 120 line

29 εἰσηγμένοι: apparently unreduplicated, but stress that the lengthened vowel = reduplication. Add a note on the accent -μένος to prepare for the tricky ὑβρισμένος to come.

33 εἴρηται: the ἐρ- stem of ἐρῶ may be identified.

36 πεφύκασι: 'Yet man is born unto trouble as the sparks fly upward' (Job 5.7); cf. ὡς ἔμφυτος μὲν πᾶσιν ἀνθρώποις κάκη (Euripides, *Bellerophon* fr.).

p. 121 line

8 ἠσεβηκυῖαν: the lengthened vowel = reduplication. Note that it is retained in the participle, giving a clear indication of a perfect. Give a reminder that the aorist drops the augment in such forms.

ὑβρισμένοι: the most difficult of perfects to spot – the long υ and the accent may be worth mentioning.

Note especially the irregular perfects in *GVE* **171** (γέγονα, τέθνηκα and βέβληκα may be added), as these alone are common enough to pose problems when they are met, particularly ἐζήτηκα, where the added ἐ- may be confused with the augment of ἐζήτησα.

Test Exercise

The first future optative occurs here (θεραπεύσοι, line 2). It causes no problems (even if notes **167–8** in *GVE* p. 185 have been ignored), but may be mentioned here to be entered (in the form παύσοι) on the morphology chart.

Section Thirteen A

Background

Creating citizens   4.5–6, 70
Citizen solidarity   1.1, 4.82

Discussion

An 'appeal to the heart' (English note): as will be seen, there is equally an appeal to the prejudices of the jurymen as well as the suggestion that they will have 'the wife' to contend with if they should acquit Neaira! '...no judge to warn the dikasts against such appeals', yet the impassioned plea is a permissible peroration, and 'Is this [sc. *Lady Chatterley's Lover*] a book that you would give your wife or servant to read?' is not so very far a cry from Apollodoros' appeal to the dikasts' consciences.

Grammar

Subjunctive
Indefinite with ἄν

Subjunctives: all one needs is a grid comparing the present active and middle with the subjunctive, and to stress the lengthened vowel (add that the aorist passive has the active subjunctive endings).

Indefinites: usually they are taught so that students are encouraged to translate them with the word 'ever'. This is misleading: it is better to teach students to translate indefinites *as indicatives*, and then to add subconsciously 'whenever that may be, it may never happen at all, but if/when it does, then...'. For example, 'If (ἐάν) it rains tomorrow (whenever that may be; it may not, but if it does), I shall not go out.'

Commentary

p. 122 line
34-5 ἦν ... πολῖτιν: may need careful sorting out.
35 Citizenship could be granted by popular vote to those whose contribution to the state was regarded as outstanding, but (as the original text emphasized) it was a rare occurrence, and had to be confirmed by over 6,000 citizens voting by secret ballot. The newly created citizen could not hold any priesthood or the office of archon, but provided he had legitimate offspring by a citizen woman, his heirs and successors held full citizen rights.
36ff. Here (and to a greater extent later) Apollodoros stresses Neaira's notoriety as a prostitute. Was prostitution really regarded with as much contempt as he seeks to apply? Most other writers seem to accept it as a way of life; some of Euripides' characters have harsh words to say about it (Elektra in *Elektra* 1060ff., Pasiphai in *Cretans* 6-8); but Apollodoros is whipping up passions, and by underlining her notoriety (and note the use of the perfect here: 'she has prostituted herself, and the results of those past actions are still felt') he is seeking to make her Athenian activities yet more heinous.
40-p. 123.22 Lit., 'And what fine thing will you claim to have done, to those asking, voting [i.e. if you vote] like this?' This causes trouble!

p. 123 line
23ff. Note the force of the argument: 'it was a private matter, but now I've done my duty in exposing it, you will be accounted by the gods as accessories after the fact if you don't punish the offenders'.

Section Thirteen B

Background

Protection of women 4.32-6; their dangerous habits 2.10, 3.19
Impiety a danger to the state 2.65
Tragedy and family chaos 7.40

Commentary

The whole of this section from p. 123.33 to p. 124.2 is a marvellous extended rhetorical question, reaching a superb climax in the incredulous 'we acquitted her!'.

p. 123 line

33 Note the contrast in appearance between the πολῖτις and the πόρνη in the illustration before starting 13B.

35 Subjunctives appear from here on; usually students translate them correctly, often without noticing any difference! Pause at some stage to fill in the subjunctive on the morphology charts, stressing that the subjunctive = the present indicative endings with the vowel lengthened.

p. 124 line

5 ἀνοήτοις: Is Apollodoros convincing here or not? Was Neaira ἀνόητος?

16 συνεπαινεῖς: the text envisages some cheers from jurors – such of course were common enough at trials, the dikasts feeling free to heckle as much as they liked. N.B. the frequency of μὴ θορυβεῖτε etc.

24 Would the acquittal of Neaira make it possible for prostitutes to marry as they pleased? In modern English law, it would certainly set a precedent to be cited by learned counsel in a subsequent trial. Would such precedent-setting have applied to ancient Athens? Apollodoros claims that it would.

28 Perhaps 'powerless' and 'empowered' could be used to translate ἄκυρος/κύριος here (see on 60.29).

31ff. μέλει occurs several times. Revise δεῖ and ἔξεστι at the same time.

Section Thirteen D

Background

Importance of οἶκος 4.12ff.
Jealousy of citizenship 4.4

Commentary

p. 125 line

3 ἀπορηθῇ: here in sense of poverty. N.B. the *active* subjunctive endings on the aorist passive stem.

5 προῖκα: metaphorical – the law safeguarding citizenship gives women an invaluable gift.

11 Strymodoros' interjection (invalid anyway – the possession of citizenship was a bonus on top of the dowry, regardless of physical appearance) is from the original: it is somewhat reminiscent of Herodotus 1.196 describing the Babylonian wife-market, where the beauties were paid for by their future husbands, and the money thus collected used for dowries for the uglies (cf. *WA* P1).

21 For prostitution to gain a dowry, see Herodotus 1.94 (in Lydia); 1.196 (in Babylon).

25 Note the close connection between citizenship, status and ritual.

Section Thirteen E

Background

Danger of female sexuality   3.18–20
Being   σώφρων 3.17

Commentary

p. 126 line

1 τρέφετε: cf. the high regard in which wives were held in Aristophanes' *Lysistrata*.

5 ἐπί (here and l. 17)+ genitive is difficult to translate: 'at' in the sense of concentrating upon or listening to.

9–10 εἰ Νέαιρα οὖσα: 'if it is the woman who is Neaira who...': i.e. 'Just look at her, and make up your mind' – cf. Philokleon accusing the dog, 75.38.

Section Thirteen F

Background

State pay   5.47

Commentary

p. 126 line

31 The imperative may need revision (cf. κύριε, ἐλέησον).

34 Jurors' pay had been introduced by Pericles and increased by Kleon.
35 Small coins were often kept in the mouth.

The English note on *Text* p. 127 should be read carefully. Encourage some attempts to suggest what Stephanos might have replied. Two almost certain suggestions are given in the note, viz. that Neaira was his mistress, and that Phano was his daughter by an earlier (legitimate) wife. The second, indeed, is hinted at in the speech (though not in our extract); Phrastor, before divorcing Phano for the first time, mentioned it as his assumption (see on p. 114.27). What then of the name Strybele? Stephanos' reply would clearly have had to account for the daughter Neaira (appears to have) had in Megara: the easiest reply is that Neaira did indeed have a daughter of that name, but she had disappeared and the idea that Phano was Strybele is a simple case of mistaken identity.

In fact, no conclusion can now be reached – nor could it have been in 440. The crucial point in the indictment is the parentage of Phano. Apollodoros adduces evidence of several who thought she was Neaira's daughter. Doubtless Stephanos produced quite as many who thought her to be Stephanos' legitimate daughter. Without modern scientific evidence (which alone could determine whether any offence had been committed), the question could not be settled.

Finally, stress that 'proof' in the modern sense is not what mattered. The verdict would be most likely to go in favour of the man who had most successfully appealed to the jurors' prejudices. Note that vengeance is still the main motivation; contrast the revolutionary attitude of Christianity: 'Ye have heard that it hath been said, An eye for an eye, and a tooth for a tooth: But I say unto you...whosoever shall smite thee on the right check, turn to him the other also' (Matthew 5.38–9).

Section Fourteen

Although the subject-matter of this section complements the excerpts from *Neaira*, the language is much harder and it may be worth postponing it until before or after Section 17.

Alkestis

This is the earliest play by Euripides to have survived intact. It was produced in 438 (his first, *Peliades*, was presented in 455) as the fourth play (the other three being *The Cretans*; *Alkmaion in Psophis*; *Telephos*), and it won second prize.

English introduction

p. 128: Only Alkestis could be found to die for Admetos. This usually provokes controversy, leading to the conclusion that Admetos must have been a very selfish man to have allowed her to do so – indeed, exactly that point is made in the play by his father, Pheres, Admetos countering by accusing Pheres of selfishness in not volunteering, and Pheres replying by suggesting that Admetos was selfish to expect him to volunteer!

Writers of later versions of the story clearly felt that the character of Admetos was the most unsatisfactory thing in the play: Alfieri (1798) makes Alkestis' death an oracular prediction, viz. fated rather than chosen, while in Browning's *Balaustion's Adventure* (1871) Alkestis herself freely volunteers to die for Admetos, who initially rejects the offer and accepts reluctantly later; and cf. T. S. Eliot, *The Cocktail Party*. All these authors interpreted the story with moral values of a later time. Would the Greeks have thought Admetos selfish? To some extent; but he was a king, he was head of his House (the House is an essential motif in the play), and he had to ensure its continuity. Alkestis was a foreigner, and the wife's role in the House was inferior to her husband's. See further A. M. Dale's warnings against seeing Greek tragedy too much in the light of characterization (introduction xxiv–xxv to A. M. Dale, *Euripides' Alcestis* (Oxford, 1954)).

Section Fourteen A

Background

Greek tragedy 7.35–52
Burial 4.77ff.

Grammar

Future perfect
Tragic usages and iambic trimeters

Commentary

p. 129 line

9 ἴστω … κατθανουμένη: a difficult opening sentence; it should first be established that ἴστω is from οἶδα, then that κατθανουμένη is a future participle.

10 Murray's Oxford Classical Text makes certain that ἡλίῳ μακρῷ are not taken together by printing a comma between the two words.

11 πῶς γάρ οὐ; as 'of course' has been familiar from Section 1 onwards. ἐναντίον has been learnt as a preposition (7C), but may have been forgotten: use it to deduce ἐναντιώσεται. The usage in Section 9D (*Text* p. 86.2) may be recalled!

12 A difficult line (Dale ad loc. even suggests obelizing), but the general sense 'What must a woman be like to surpass her?' can be elicited.

ὑπερβεβλημένην: establish that this is from ὑπερβάλλω, cf. the derivation hyperbole (as a figure of speech).

14 προτιμῶσ': isolate the τιμ- stem; emphasize elided -α.

ὑπερθανεῖν: isolate θαν-, then add ὑπέρ.

15–16 μέν … δέ: note the contrast: it becomes important later. See on p. 129.40.

17 It may be necessary to point out that ᾔσθεθ' = ᾔσθετο; note another meaning for κύριος, 'her appointed hour'.

18 λευκόν: complimentary, a sign of beauty for the Greeks: as most women would naturally be sun-tanned, white was regarded as beautiful.

19 ἐκ … ἐλοῦσα: the first example of tmesis, which should here be explained (cf. τέμνω). Tmesis may be known from 'post…quam' separation in Latin.

κεδρίνων: Priam's store-room was of cedar wood (*Iliad* XXIV.191–2), as the fragrant (εὐώδης, Homer) wood was thought to protect clothes from moth and damp. δόμων the 'home' of the clothes, probably a chest or cabinet.

21 Ἑστίας: the hearth was central to the home; it is, paradoxically, the House's survival that Alkestis' death may ensure (see above).

22 As θεράπων – θεράπαινα, so δεσπότης – δέσποινα.

23 πανύστατον: elicit from πᾶν and ὕστατον.

προσπίτνω: note πίτνω as very common poetic form of πίπτω.

24 ὀρφανεῦσαι: the obvious derivation does not point directly to the correct meaning here – 'to look after orphans'. The middle ὀρφανεύομαι means 'I am an orphan'.

τῷ μέν: look ahead to τῇ δέ to emphasize 'to my (son)…to my (daughter)…'.

25 ζυγόν: give the meaning; biologists may know zygomorphic, zygotes etc.

γενναῖον: root γεν-, cf. English noble = well-born and also = fine in character, morals etc. Homer (*Iliad* 11.714–15, xxiii.288f.) knew the son as Eumelos. The daughter's name was Perimele. Note again the underlying idea of the perpetuation of the House.

26 τεκοῦσα: in iambic trimeters the aorist participle feminine of τίκτω is commonly used as a noun (μήτηρ could stand only in the 1st, 3rd or 5th foot, whereas τεκοῦσ' could be used anywhere); hence it takes a dependent genitive (αὐτῶν).

27 θανεῖν: indirect command (hence also μηδ' in the previous line).

ἀώρους: ἀ-, ὥρα (cf. Latin *hora* meaning 'season'), hence 'unseasonably, untimely, premature'.

28 γῆ πατρῴᾳ: Alkestis herself came from Iolkos, where her father Pelias was king. Admetos had to win her by yoking a boar and a lion to a chariot, a feat he managed with the help of Apollo, then in servitude to him.

Note that living until death in one's native land was a constant pre-occupation – of females, one wonders, as much as of males? Cf. the plight of women depicted in Sophocles' *Tereus* (frag. 524N) in *The Oxford Book of Greek Verse* (Oxford, 1930) no. 337; or in Euripides' *Danae*:

γυνὴ γὰρ ἐξελθοῦσα πατρῴων δόμων
οὐ τῶν τεκόντων ἐστίν, ἀλλὰ τοῦ λέχους.

Section Fourteen B

---

p. 129 line

37 κἀξέστεψε: = καὶ ἐξέστεψε. A suppliant placed a garland upon an altar. If his request was granted he removed the garland, but left it if the request was refused. One line, omitted here, tells us that Alkestis cut myrtle shoots for each of the altars.

38 ἄκλαυτος, ἀστένακτος: both can be deduced by reference back to *Text*, p. 34.31 and p. 70.30 respectively.

40 λέχος: the crucial turning-point between her outward public self-control and her breakdown in the privacy of her own bedroom. Cf. Raskolnikov in Dostoyevsky's *Crime and Punishment*. Note especially the central feature of the bed: it was what originally yoked her to Admetos, and from it came the children, the continuity of the House.

p. 130 line

24 δή: emphasizes ἐνταῦθα, 'then indeed (though she had restrained herself earlier)'.

25–6 παρθένεια ... κορεύματα: tautologous, in that both the adjective and the noun have sense of 'maidenhood, virginity'.

26 Two difficult prepositional usages here: ἐκ + genitive for an agent is not uncommon ('from (the action of) this man'); περί + genitive to mean 'for whose sake' is unparalleled.

28 μόνην: 'you have destroyed me alone', viz. not Admetos, whose life has been spared because of her death. Some take this as: 'me alone (amongst all women)', viz. 'I am the only one to have made this supreme sacrifice.'

προδοῦναι: cf. the usage in the *Text* p. 131.16. Alkestis would have been betraying Admetos in the sense that refusal to die would have implied denying her position within the οἶκος as being less than her husband's. This is made explicit in

εἷς γ' ἀνὴρ κρείσσων γυναικῶν μυρίων ὁρᾶν φάος

(Euripides, *IA* 1394).

29 Probably 'some other woman', as Alkestis later extracts a promise from Admetos never to remarry. This too is relevant to the House motif, as her children will be guaranteed succession unless Admetos should take another wife and legitimize the inheritance of any issue therefrom.

Future perfect: mention briefly that some verbs have a future perfect (usually middle); that it has reduplication + future endings; that it is future with a perfect aspect (i.e. not the same tense as in Latin) – those three things alone need to be known.

29–30 Parodied in Aristophanes' *Knights* 1251–2 (Kleon saying farewell to his garland, symbol of his favoured position under Demos, now taken by the Sausage-Seller):

σὲ δ' ἄλλος τις λαβὼν κεκτήσεται
κλέπτης μὲν οὐκ ἂν μᾶλλον, εὐτυχὴς δ' ἴσως.

Note the use of μᾶλλον + adjective for comparative – this is common in tragedy because comparatives are difficult to fit into the metre.

Section Fourteen C

Background

Women, marriage and home   4.23ff.

Commentary

p. 130 line

37 κυνεῖ: actually the same verb as κύσαι (*Text* p. 86.28) but with a different meaning.

38 All three words will probably have to be given here: note the effect of a three-word line, imparting a ponderous quality.

40 προνωπής: the usual translation 'headlong' implies a haste which is not required here: Dale (ad loc.) takes the word to mean 'with head bowed'.

ἐκπεσοῦσα: not so much 'falling away', as 'rushing away', or 'tearing herself away from' (Dale).

p. 131 line

1 πολλά: not given in vocabulary as meaning 'often', though the adverbial usage (neuter plural) is very common.

8 κακός: the opposite of ἐσθλός above, here not 'morally vicious', but 'lowborn'.

11-12 Difficult: establish that 'he' (= Admetos) must be the subject (because of the masculine participle). Even when correctly translated, the sentence seems a truism – 'if he had died, he would have died' – and needs explanation, viz. that would have been an end of it, whereas by escaping death he will have...etc. οὗ ποτ'...κτλ. – Murray's reading in the Oxford Classical Text, where he explains 'quod aliquando – non oblitus erit', viz. οὐ λελήσεται as emphatic (perfect) litotes.

13 στενάζει: here followed by εἰ, 'grieves that', cf. θαυμάζω εἰ, 'I am amazed that'.

15 χεροῖν: duals are not explained until Section 17 (where only one example occurs – a verb), so this should be noted here. At most, only three noun/adjective endings need be noted: the article τῶ, τοῖν (from which the feminine ταῖν would follow), and -οντε for the singular of the participle.

16 προδοῦναι: ironically the same word as the servant quoted Alkestis as using (p. 130.28), here apparently meaning 'forsake, desert', as though Admetos wants to eat his cake and keep it!

17 νόσῳ: it is never made explicit from what (natural) cause Alkestis dies, one fact used by Verrall in his theory that Euripides meant us to suppose that she never actually died.

18 With the punctuation of the text (as Murray, Oxford Classical Text) ἄθλιον βάρος must be in apposition to the subject: 'she, exhausted, a pathetic weight in (literally of) his hands'. Others omit the comma, taking βάρος as a cognate accusative after παρειμένη: 'relaxed with regard to the pathetic weight of her hands', implying that she is now too feeble even to lift her hands, a known sign of utter exhaustion.

Much has been written about *Alkestis*, and students should be encouraged to read the whole play. A note of comparison: Philip II of Spain married his fourth wife, Anne of Austria, in successful pursuit of his twenty-five-year quest for a male heir (his son by his first wife, Maria of Portugal, was the homicidal lunatic Don Carlos). Once, when the king was critically ill, the pious queen prayed earnestly that she might die instead of so important a man as the king.

> evertere domos totas optantibus ipsis
> di faciles.

She died, Philip lived.

Section Fifteen

Several sections may be cut here too, if time presses. The dialogue (15A, B, C) can be omitted without loss of sense, though here again it is best translated to the class. If translated in this way, there is the opportunity to pick up the various bits of syntax that must be noted; if omitted entirely, these must be taught from *GVE*.

The dialogue is mainly adapted from Plato's *Phaidros*.

Section Fifteen A

Background

Liturgies 5.71-2
Trierarchies 5.71-2, 6.40-8
ἐξηγηταί 2.4, 25
Blood-guilt 2.35
Revenge 3.1-4, 12-13

Grammar

Pluperfect
μή + aorist subjunctive
φοβοῦμαι μή
-τέος verb-forms

Commentary

p. 135 line

18   τὴν ... ὁδόν: note a cognate/internal accusative after βαδίζων (not the direct object).

21   ἀθύμως ἔχοντι: can be elicited; mention that an adverb + ἔχω = an adjective + εἰμί; ἀ- (privative); θυμ- (cf. πρόθυμος), therefore 'be dispirited'.

25   Note the agora as the 'city centre' where all business was transacted.

29   ἐξηγηταί: it is best merely to transliterate and refer to the explanation opposite (*Text* p. 134).

30   κάθαρσις: cf. catharsis.

   ταφῆς: cf. cenotaph.

33   ἐπεποιήκει: ask for suggestions about the tense (there is only one left!), and then deal with its formation.

34   χωρίον: learnt in Section 5G, here to be relearnt with a slightly different meaning.

36   ἀπελευθέρα: deduce this from ἀπό and ἐλεύθερος.

38   ἐπεπόνθη: πέπονθα was mentioned with the irregular perfects in *GVE* **171**, though it has not occurred in the *Text*. Elicit tense by drawing attention to augment and reduplication.

Section Fifteen B

Background

   Climate   1.5–6

Commentary

p. 136 line

3   μή + aorist subjunctive for prohibitions is introduced here: mention this as an 'aorist aspect' alternative to μή + present imperative – cf. Latin *ne* + perfect subjunctive.

5   -τέος/τέον verb-forms: it is often enough to explain these as 'sort of gerundive' implying obligation.

8   διέξει: = διέξειμι second person singular (future).

10   ἀπολέσω: will probably be taken as future, which it cannot be. Hence (a) refer back to the principal parts of (ἀπ)όλλυμι (future = ἀπολῶ), (b) discuss and establish that fears for the future after a primary main verb take μή + subjunctive.

19 'suitable for those walking to...'. It will probably be necessary to say something about the form πορευομένοις, frequently translated 'by walking'. Suggest adding τοῖς in front of it, and that may help to show the adjectival force.

20 πνῖγος: unlikely to be remembered from Section 5D (picture, *Text* p. 36). The πνιγ- stem implies the stifling quality of heat, not the heat itself.

25 εἴσομαι: the future of οἶδα has not been met before, and must be noted. Add this to the principal part list. Contrast with ἔσομαι, future of εἰμί.

Section Fifteen C

Background

Enmity 3.13
Trierarch 6.41
στάσις HI 73
Ship's gear 6.42

Discussion

The case which occupies the rest of Sections 15 and 16 is not as complex as that against Neaira, but as less English comment is given in the text, the following notes may prove helpful.

The plaintiff (nowhere named in the original, another speech spuriously attributed to Demosthenes; the name Aristarkhos is a γενναῖον ψεῦδος) is bringing an action for false witness against Mnesiboulos and Euergos, brother-in-law and brother of Theophemos. Section 15 deals with the antecedents to this false witness, as follows:

(1) Theophemos, the outgoing trierarch, refused to hand over the ship's gear.
(2) The plaintiff, the succeeding trierarch, obtained an order first from the jury court, and then from the βουλή, ordering Theophemos to hand it over.
(3) Theophemos still refused; the plaintiff called witnesses and tried to seize some of Theophemos' property as security, which led to a fight.
(4) The plaintiff brought a successful charge of assault against Theophemos; the gear must have been handed over (the plaintiff sailed away at this

point), and according to the plaintiff private injuries were to be assessed later.

(5) At the assessment of private injuries, Theophemos secured a conviction against the plaintiff, who was left with a heavy fine to pay.

According to the plaintiff, the conviction was secured by the false evidence of Euergos and Mnesiboulos, whom he now prosecutes for false witness. In the mean time, further charges can be brought against the unholy trio; the plaintiff, owing a fine to Theophemos and asserting his promise to pay, has been pre-empted by them, in that they visited his farm and collared whatever they could lay hands on, in the process injuring a freedwoman so badly that she died.

The charge of murdering the old woman has been discounted by the ἐξηγηταί, (a) because the plaintiff did not witness the beating-up, (b) because he could secure no witnesses apart from his wife and children, and (c) since she was no relative, why should he bother? But their advice does contain the recommendation that he should try to get his own back somehow – precisely as he is now doing. The actual charge of false witness plays an important part in the original, but is hardly mentioned at all in our extracts (it makes a fleeting appearance in Section 15H). Our extracts concentrate upon the action, and on generally blackening the characters first of Theophemos (who has little to do with the present case), then of Euergos and Mnesiboulos; a great deal is made of the fact that they are (the prosecutor claims) responsible for the murder of the old woman. Once more, it was more important to convince the jury that the defendant(s) were undesirable citizens than to establish their guilt in a particular crime. Nearly all the material here presented would be discounted by a modern lawcourt as being irrelevant to the charge as brought, viz. perjury.

Grammar

Accusative absolute
ὡς + superlative

Commentary

p. 136 line

37 μάθῃς: it is worth checking that this is not taken as an aorist passive.
38 The people and βουλή had been wronged by Theophemos – but how relevant is this here?

p. 137 line

3 δέον: note that impersonal verbs, used absolutely, are *accusative* absolutes. Revise genitive absolutes at the same time here.

8 ἀποστέλλειν: cf. ἀπόστολος, 'apostle'.

12 πρίασθαι: will need to be noted in the list of irregular verbs (see ὠνέομαι, *GVE* p. 289 and morphology charts).

15–16 ὅς ἄν...: note the indefinite construction and revise. Indefinites using the optative come shortly (15E). Similarly ᾧ ἂν δυνώμεθα...in *Text*, p. 138.1.

p. 138 line

1 Note ἵνα+subjunctive to express purpose here. It is used with the optative in secondary sequence in Section 15D, and is there explained in the grammar (but 15D has no subjunctive examples of the construction, so it must be stressed here).

Section Fifteen D

Background

βουλή HI 8; 5.15–16, 23ff.
Evidence 5.52–4
ὑπηρέτης 4.64

Grammar

ἵνα+subjunctive/optative

Commentary

p. 138 line

17 Note that the βουλή was the body responsible for ensuring that laws were enforced.

22 κοινή: i.e. had they made division of their inheritance, or did they share it between them without splitting it up?

εἴη: note the optative in secondary sequence. Prepare to contrast the optative in secondary sequence in indirect speech (where meaning is not affected) with the plain optative used in place of ἄν+subjunctive with indefinites, in secondary sequence (e.g. at Section 15E, *Text* p. 138.38).

Section Fifteen E

Background

Self-help in law 5.48, 62

Grammar

Indefinite in secondary sequence

Commentary

p. 138 line
35 ἡ ἄνθρωπος: not derogatory here (cf. p. 6.15, p. 87.35).
36 καταλαβών: cf. the contradiction inherent in the English 'Finding him not at home...'.

p. 139 line
5 Note the importance of having independent witnesses – cf. the modern practice in motoring accidents; the first priority is to take particulars of witnesses! Isaios 3.19 recommends taking your most reliable friends along with you on any such occasion to ensure that you have some witnesses.

ἴδοι: note a vital distinction between two possible meanings: 'if he were to see' or 'if ever he saw'/'if he saw (we do not know if he was likely to, but if he did...)'. The key lies in the *main verb*: if there is an ἄν with the main verb, then the clause is conditional; if not, it is indefinite.
6–7 A string of genitive absolutes; it is important to locate the noun first of all.
10 ἐνέχυρα: cf. on p. 111.24. Here Aristarkhos threatens to take property to the value of the σκεύη as security for the transference of the σκεύη.

Section Fifteen F

Background

Protection of women   4.35 (and source)
Self-help in law   5.48

Grammar

Perfect optative
ἁλίσκομαι

Commentary

p. 139 line

24 ἐπεπύσμην: elicit the stem -πυ-, which may give the essential clue.

γεγαμηκὼς εἴη: linked in text, so students should be able to tell how the perfect optative middle and passive are formed.

Note the importance of the wife within the home. Had there been a wife within the house, Aristarkhos would not have entered, the wife being almost sacrosanct in her own territory. This contrast with the behaviour of the others must be emphasized at, e.g. *Text* p. 144.1ff.

27 Revise aorist passives here, and related future passives. Note those verbs which do not show -θ- in the aorist passive, e.g. συνεκόπην (cf. ἐμάνην, ἐστάλην, ἐγράφην etc.).

31 Note once again the 'self-help' attitude: the βουλή wanted Theophemos arrested, but it was Aristarkhos who was ordered to secure him.

ἀλῶναι: ἁλίσκομαι. The principal parts occur here and should be noted. Compare the aorist with γιγνώσκω – ἔγνων (ἑάλων, ἁλ-).

38 Why did Aristarkhos settle for one-twentieth of the fine he could have imposed? Presumably to conclude the matter – he was required as trierarch to sail with the fleet against some recalcitrant allies; as the date of this speech is *c.* 336, the allies concerned must have been some of those who defected from Athens as the power of Philip grew. This particular fine was punitive, imposed because Theophemos had not handed over the gear promptly and had ignored the decree. Private damages were not dealt with here; they were to be submitted to arbitration after Aristarkhos had returned from the expedition.

Section Fifteen G

Background

Climate   1.5–6
Site   1.20

Grammar

First person orders ('let us...')
ἕως ἄν

Commentary

p. 140 line

9 πλέον: pleonasm.

10 The jussive subjunctive appears here; it should pose no problems – cf. Latin. French and German, as well as English, use the subjunctive for third person commands: 'honi soit qui mal y pense', 'Gott sei Dank', 'so be it'.

11 ἕως ἄν may be treated in the same way as other clauses using ἄν + subjunctive, or a plain optative in secondary sequence, i.e. that 'until' in these circumstances carries the idea that we do not know if or when it will happen at all. Insist that 'whenever that may be' is added as a rider to these clauses when they are translated.

18 ποά: *poaceae* is the biological term for the family which includes grasses.

25 διέκειτο: note the idiomatic usage: διάκειμαι + adverb.

Section Fifteen H

Background

Slaves giving evidence   5.54
Banking   4.60, 65, 70

Grammar

φοβοῦμαι μή + optative

Commentary

p. 141 line

4 A quotation from Herodotos v.97 (the Ionian Revolt was 'the beginning of evils for Greeks and foreigners'), itself a modified quotation from Homer (*Iliad* v.63) used also by Thucydides (II.12.3).

6 αἰκείας: Theophemos retaliates by a counter-charge of assault. Note (a) the 'he started it' approach (cf. Section 11c); (b) Aristarkhos' belief that innocence would ensure acquittal; (c) the importance of witnesses – here there appears to have been only one real witness (the old woman), and she was withheld by Theophemos; and (d) that only here do we come to incidents relevant to the present trial, which students may have forgotten is an accusation against Euergos and Mnesiboulos for false witness.

14–15 'A few days later': the plaintiff in the original adds a further point in his favour by saying the delay was caused in defraying expenses met as a trierarch – while he was performing his λειτουργία (see on p. 120.4).

16 τράπεζαν: still the modern Greek word for bank. Cf. 'the tables of the money-changers' in the Temple at Jerusalem (Matthew 21.12; Mark 11.15; John 2.15).

17 ἀντί: beware: many instinctively translate this 'before' or 'against' rather than 'instead of'.

There is something very odd going on here: why, if the plaintiff had volunteered to pay the fine in full, did Theophemos and the others swoop on the farm? (Theophemos will probably 'reply' that he *did not* volunteer.) Further, when this plundering and pillaging had taken place, even if the ἐξηγηταί ruled against prosecution for murder, why did the plaintiff not sue for criminal assault/damage etc. and settle instead for a case of false witness? Because the penalty was higher?

Test Exercise

Further detail is needed before this exercise is set. Details of the trierarchy may have been given before, but the following must be known here:

(1) The trierarchy was a λειτουργία involving equipping and commanding a trireme for one year (later six months); the crew were paid by the state.

(2) Ship's gear was provided by the state, and had to be returned with an inventory at the end of a term of office. But a wealthy trierarch could equip the ship from his own resources – an incentive which might secure him the best officers, for although crews were predetermined (they had to know which ship to report to, viz. the one in which they had practised), officers were not, and efficient ὑπηρεσίαι (petty officers, probably ten in number), κελευστής (boatswain) and πρῳρεύς would increase efficiency generally.

(3) Apart from the additional kudos a trierarch might acquire from having a most efficient ship, there was a prize for the first ship manned and ready for action after the alarm had been given.

Section Sixteen

Discussion

In view of what was said at the end of the notes to Section 15, it will come as no surprise that the whole of Section 16 is quite irrelevant to the case; the false testimony of Euergos and Mnesiboulos is not so much as mentioned. The whole thing is designed merely to show what nasty people they were.

Grammar

The most important points of accidence and syntax are respectively ἵημι and result clauses. Indefinite temporals (including πρίν) are completed here, together with a full range of optative usages in secondary sequence. Deliberatives complete the syntax.

If pressed for time, translate Sections 16c and D for the students, highlighting essential features.

Section Sixteen A

Background

Houses   1.7, 35–7; farming   1.9–13
Sheep   1.13
Slaves and slavery   4.62–6
Slaves and population   4.10–11
Slave jobs   4.51–2
Seclusion of women   4.32ff.

Grammar

ἕως + optative
(ἀφ) ἵημι

Commentary

p. 143 line
27   Insist that the significance of ἕως + optative is appreciated.
28   μαλακά: most sheep had long, tough and shaggy wool; those with

shorter and softer wool provided much more profitable fleeces which were ideal for fine cloth.

31 διάκονος: cf. deacon, from the Christian Greek usage of this word. In classical times it meant attendant, valet – a servant clearly considered here reliable enough not to drop a valuable pitcher borrowed from a friend.

32 ᾐτημένην: analyse this out very carefully as the perfect participle passive of αἰτέω. Work here may help prepare the way for ᾖξαν (ᾄσσω) at l. 35.

ληφθέντων: there is useful revision of the genitive absolute here.

33 ἐπεισελθόντες: note ἐπι- compounds often with the sense of 'attack'. The sheep had been taken from the fields; the χωρίον comprised the farmhouse and the area immediately surrounding – all that is visible in the illustration on *Text* p. 142.

40 Insist on 'whatever they wanted' for ἃ βούλοιντο (as elsewhere in the passages to come).

p. 144 line
4ff. Note this digression upon the old slave: she had been loyal, therefore freed. When widowed, she had returned to the son of her former owner, who treated her almost like an aged mother whom one was duty-bound to protect and support (note especially ἀναγκαῖον, 7). The episode is as irrelevant – to us – as the whole of this section to the case actually being tried, but would have appeared far differently to the original jury: the slave-woman (who is in fact the one murdered in this attack) is here established as almost a second mother – an interesting comment on some family's public attitudes towards slaves.

At this point various forms of ἵημι begin to be introduced. It may be useful to revise all the stems of the -μι verbs met to date, and show how ἵημι fits neatly into the pattern, e.g.

δίδωμι	διδο- δο-	διδου- δου-	διδω- δω-
τίθημι	τιθε- θε-	τιθει- θει-	τιθη- θη-
ἵημι	ἱε- ἑ-	ἱει- εἱ-	ἱη- ἡ-
ἵστημι	ἱστα- στα-	ἱστη- στη-	

As the above table clearly shows, comparison with τίθημι is very instructive.

10 The other female slaves kept clear – contrast the involvement of the γραῦς, still as loyal as ever. The whole presentation is 'see what a nice man I am in contrast to these murderous thugs'.

11   πύργος: slaves' quarters on the upper floor, called a πύργος because it did not cover the whole of the ground floor.

In the whole of this episode, note the offence against property in bursting in upon the womenfolk when the man of the house was absent – contrast the plaintiff himself earlier (see on p. 139.24).

Section Sixteen B

Background

Female rights in the home   4.32–3
κύριος of the house   4.35

Grammar

ἕως + indicative
πρὶν ἄν + subjunctive, πρίν + optative
διατίθημι, διάκειμαι

Commentary

p. 144 line

24   Property in the dowry: see on 114.21.

Note the wife's absolute refusal to be cowed by this incursion into her own territory. She knows her rights and insists that they leave *her* property alone. Cf. l. 27: Greek women *could* be informed of their husband's business deals. They were, therefore, not *necessarily*, in certain circumstances, as helpless or ignorant as they are sometimes represented.

26   Note the neighbour's propriety – he merely knocked on the door and passed on his message, not entering.

27   Presumably he told his wife, on leaving, where he was going and for what purpose.

28   It may be necessary to clarify that τὸν ἄνδρα refers to the husband.

32   κυμβίον: the plural has been met before in Section 8G (*Text* p. 74.22).

34   οὕτω(ς) ... ὥστε clauses begin here. Translate 'so...that' and prepare for the usage with the infinitive 'so as to' (p. 145.26).

35   ὕφαιμοι: elicit from ὑπό and αἷμα, cf. haemoglobin, haemorrhage etc.

βραχίονες: cf. the medical and biological terms brachiotomy, brachiopod. Also French *bras*.

καρποί: zoologists use *carpus* (the Latin form) for wrist; also carpal (of bones).

37 τράχηλος: cf. trachea.

38 στῆθος: cf. stethoscope etc. Note that the basis of most medical words is Greek.

p. 145 line

7 Once more the proprieties are underlined: one does not enter a house unless its κύριος is present. Hagnophilos is even more circumspect: he does not even enter the χωρίον but observes from the land of neighbour Anthemion.

11 οἰκέτης: here to be taken as 'house-slave' rather than 'member of household': Euergos and Mnesiboulos might have taken a slave (as they had the παῖς διάκονος), but drew the line at abducting a (citizen) son.

11–12 Why ἕως with indicative? Stress that the indicative shows that it actually happened. Compare this with indefinite usages.

(We are told that the testimony of Hermogenes was given here, but it is not included in our mss. of the speech.)

Section Sixteen C

Background

Travel   1.14
Doctors   4.72–6; 7.10, 14, 25
λιθόκοπος   7.64–5

Grammar

ὥστε + indicative/infinitive
Numerals

Commentary

p. 145 line

25 There is no need to mention the oddity of πρίν (before, until) + indicative/indefinite construction (after a negative main verb) unless specifically asked about it.

26 Cf. on p. 144.34 above.

31-2   Insist on 'whomever' for ὃν βούλοιντο.

34-5   καὶ αὐτός: 'that he himself also'. αὐτός may need revision here.

38 χρεία: here in its basic sense of 'necessity' (χρή) – met earlier (Section 5A) as 'debt' (see on p. 32.17, 19).

p. 146 line

22   One stipulation made by Theophemos is omitted in this text: he demanded that the plaintiff should release him and his friends from all claims, including that of false witness. On those terms, he would restore the stolen property.

ἡρπασμένα: revise perfect participles middle and passive, as there are some more to come.

Section Sixteen D

Background

ἐξηγηταί   2.35
purification   2.35, 4.80; family and murder   5.48

Grammar

Aorist passive imperative
Middles with passive forms in aorist

Commentary

p. 147 line

15   Note the inadmissibility of evidence from wives or children.

17   The βασιλεύς (ἄρχων) was responsible for murder trials.

18   The old woman was neither family nor slave: the law assigned the duty of prosecution to relatives or masters, and nobody else. Even in murder cases, the prosecution had to be brought by a relation of the deceased.

19   Duties at the funerals of those who had died a violent death included carrying a spear in front of the funeral procession (representing the pursuit of the murderer), reading a proclamation at the graveside which laid the murderer under an interdict to keep away from the tomb and all sacred places, planting the spear near the tomb (to keep the murderer at bay), and watching over it and the tomb for three days.

Section Sixteen E

Background

Friends and enemies   3.2, 13
Climate   1.5–6

Grammar

Deliberative
χράομαι
Correlatives

Discussion

It is worth taking some care with this section, as it revises most of the subjunctive and optative usages encountered in Sections 15 and 16. If students have a good grasp of these, they are well prepared for Sections 17–19.

From the final sections of the speech (not included in our text), it becomes clear that the three men still possess what they have taken of the plaintiff's property at the time of the trial, holding on to it in the hope of dissuading him from the suit of false witness. How much time elapsed between the seizure of property and the case we do not know (χθές (147.5) is not from the original, and gives a false sense of 'swift justice').

Section Seventeen

Background

νόμος/φύσις   7.28
Sophists and civilization   7.25
Myths   2.9–11; 7.6
Greek speculation   7.8

Grammar

Deliberative in secondary sequence
ἄτε + participle
Duals

Commentary

p. 150 line

29 Note the fairy-tale opening: 'Once upon a time...'.

θνητὰ γένη, as becomes clear, include animals as well as mankind.

30 τυποῦσιν: from τύπος, a blow – perhaps 'shaped', as the process is vague.

31 Note the double chiasmus here and in the next line (γῆς ἔνδον, ἐκ γῆς καὶ πυρός... πυρὶ καὶ γῇ).

The whole section is full of poetic turns of phrase, unlike Plato's normal style. This may be an effort to imitate Protagoras' style.

31-2 τῶν ὅσα... κεράννυται: 'whatever of things are mixed with fire and earth...', viz. air and water. Fire is the most rarefied, earth the most dense – air and water must be a mixture of them in different proportions. Most of Plato's contemporary physicists believed there were four elements, from which everything else was composed.

34-5 A reversal of roles; Epimetheus (Aftersight) is to distribute qualities, Prometheus (Foresight) is to inspect.

36-7 Note the changing patterns of construction in these four clauses – the τοῖς μέν...τοὺς δέ...τοὺς δέ...τοῖς δέ – the two outer clauses containing abstract expressions (ἰσχύν, ἄοπλον φύσιν), the two inner more concrete.

38-40 Once again note the word-balancing – the inverted relative clauses, the former abstract, the latter directly descriptive; the usage of τῷδε αὐτῷ (for the more usual αὐτῷ τουτῷ) to make the juxtaposition αὐτῷ αὐτά.

p. 151 line

9 'devised means of escape from mutual destruction' – another very poetic phrase.

10 ὥρας: as on 129.27.

11 στερεοῖς: cf. stereophonic; stereophonic sound is 'solid' in the sense that it appears to surround the listener rather than be directed at him from one source. δέρμα is used by biologists: cf. also hypodermic, pachyderm, dermatitis etc. Note the variation again (ἱκανοῖς...δυνατοῖς); ἀμῦναι needs to be supplied in the second clause, and two different verbs found in English to translate its meanings 'protect against (cold)' and 'withstand (heat)'.

14 N.B. ὁπλή – nothing to do with ὅπλον, -α.

15-16 Variations again: τοῖς μέν...ἄλλοις δέ...τοῖς δέ...ἔστι δ' οἷς.

15 ἐξεπόριζε: the basic root is the -πορ- as in ἀπορία, familiar from Section 2 onwards. Many biological terms here (botany, dendro- compounds including rhododendron). Plato's distinctions are now designated by the terms herbivorous and carnivorous.

17 ὀλιγογονίαν: may be elicited from the roots ὀλιγο- and -γον- (from -γεν-). The same 'balance in nature' argument is presented by Herodotus (III.108) pointing out that animals preyed upon reproduce quickly and in large numbers.

27 οὐ πάνυ: litotes or meiosis.

28 ἄλογα: 'brute beasts that have no understanding' (The Book of Common Prayer: Form of the Solemnization of Matrimony); 'a beast that wants discourse of reason' (*Hamlet* 1.2.150).

29 χρήσαιτο: an indirect deliberative – explain only if it is necessary.

35 Athene possessed 'the gift of skill in the arts', Hephaistos had fire. Athene does not figure in the traditional version, e.g. Aeschylus, *Prometheus Vinctus* 252–4; she is necessary to Protagoras' argument here, since skill is central to his thesis.

36–7 γενέσθαι must be taken both absolutely and with χρησίμην: 'it was impossible without fire for anyone (τῳ = τινι) to have this skill or for it to be useful'.

39 παρά... Διί: for the purposes of his argument, Protagoras treats 'political skill' as though it were a concrete object.

ἀκρόπολιν: the gods' Olympian, mountain-top dwelling envisaged as a citadel of a Greek city.

40 οὐκέτι ἐνεχώρει εἰσελθεῖν: οὐκέτι here not 'not yet' but 'not now' – Prometheus had not yet been punished, so presumably here the reason Protagoras is giving is that there was no time for him to find a way into the acropolis to steal political skill for men.

p. 152 line

1 φυλακαί: *Prometheus Vinctus* names these as Kratos and Bia. This ends the 'digression' begun at 151.38, and εἰς δέ κτλ. reverts to the narrative of the theft – this needs mentioning as students sometimes see two sets of theft involved here.

2 ἐφιλοτεχνείτην: the one dual ending in this section. If noun/adjective endings in dual have already been mentioned (see on *Text* p. 131.15), it can here be explained that -τον/-την, -σθον/-σθην indicate active, middle and passive duals.

3 As before, Hephaistos' specific skill is with fire while Athene is concerned with technical skill generally (see above on 151.35).

5 δι': 'through' in the sense of 'thanks to'.

6 κλοπῆς δίκη: the charge is mentioned here, not the punishment; *Prometheus Vinctus* gives punishment without reference to a 'trial', as Zeus is there a new upstart tyrant, actively opposing human progress and survival which is achievable through Forethought. Cf. Sophocles, *Hipponous* fr.

> σωτηρίας γὰρ φάρμακ' οὐχὶ πανταχοῦ
> βλέψαι πάρεστιν, ἐν δὲ τῇ προμηθίᾳ.

14 μοίρας: the skill of fire and the technical skill to use it were divine (θείας) prerogatives.

14–15 διά... συγγένειαν: rejected by several editors (a) because there was no 'kinship' between men and gods in this version (except in so far as men were products of the gods – if this interpretation of the words were adopted, then all the ἄλογα would be 'kin' of the gods); (b) the singular 'god' is odd – it cannot be monotheistic, nor has any single god been mentioned as the 'parent' of man.

15 Man conceptualizes his gods as human in shape: cf. Xenophanes fr. 15:

> ἀλλ' εἰ χεῖρας εἶχον βόες ἵπποι τε ἠὲ λέοντες
> ἢ γράψαι χείρεσσι καὶ ἔργα τελεῖν ἅπερ ἄνδρες
> ἵπποι μέν θ' ἵπποισι, βόες δέ τε βουσὶν ὁμοίας
> καί κε θεῶν ἰδέας ἔγραφον καὶ σώματ' ἐποίουν
> τοιαῦθ' οἷόν περ καὐτοὶ δέμας εἶχον ἕκαστοι.

Voltaire: 'If God created man in his own image, man has certainly returned the compliment.' Cf. *WA* 7.6–13.

16 The articulation of speech – fundamental difference between men and ἄλογα.

19 σποράδην: the vocabulary in *GVE* may appear self-contradictory – the meaning is perhaps better explained as 'in scattered groups', i.e. sporadically.

20 Early man was undoubtedly a frequent victim of prehistoric beasts. Cave paintings illustrate the hunts, but casualties must have been high.

21 δημιουργική: technical skills in various crafts and sciences were regarded as part of Athene's demesne – cf. *Odyssey* VI.232–4 (see *Text* p. 179.28–30).

23 πολιτικήν: i.e. grouping together into (24) πόλεις, a necessary preliminary to subdividing into groups of armed men for fighting. The whole concept of this early grouping into cities is explored by Thucydides in his opening chapters.

25 ὅτ': useful to note that ὅτι never elides, so ὅτ' must always be ὅτε.

ἠδίκουν: the 'freedom of individual' motif again (see on p. 92.27). Protagoras, like Rousseau later, saw early men as naturally aggressive, selfishly destroying each other until learning to submit to what Rousseau termed a

'Social Contract', whereby the individual surrenders his rights to the state, itself to be an embodiment of majority opinion. Cf. also Solon in many fragments – including *Text* p. 30.27–8.

35 Note the different Zeus here from the νέος ταγός of *Prometheus Vinctus*.

36 αἰδώς, δίκη: two crucial concepts, which must be explained. The former ('respect for others', GVE) entails fear (as in Plato, *Euthyphro* 12c) – men behave well through fear of what others may think of them if they don't. E. R. Dodds in *The Greeks and the Irrational* explored the nature of this 'shame-culture', and it is everywhere apparent in Homer – the heroes must not 'lose face'.

δίκη is a more abstract quality – hence Plato's quest for an absolute form of Justice. The two terms are comparable with modern ethical theorists' teleontological (viz. what will happen if you do not conform) and deontological (viz. what you feel you ought to do) approaches to the problem.

36–7 πόλεων κόσμοι τε καὶ δεσμοὶ φιλίας: chiasmus – a poetic turn of phrase again.

40 Note the φύσις concept underlying this: some men are born with, for instance, medical skill. The Spartans did have hereditary professions (e.g. heralds – but then so are the Earls Marshal of England, and so were the Constables of France). The Egyptians had seven classes – priests, warriors, cowherds, swineherds, tradesmen, interpreters and pilots (Herodotus II.164),

p. 153 line

20 μή: shows generic nature of the participial phrase.

21 κτείνειν: poetic again, as ἀποκτείνειν is the regular prose usage. If 'all must have a share in' δίκη and αἰδώς, how is it that there are any left to be killed for not having a share? That is not what Protagoras says – he says that any who are incapable of having that sense must be executed.

27 ἰέναι: cf. our 'go the way of'.

28 αὕτη...: note the asyndeton, and the Q.E.D. ending to this part of the argument – *all* have the potential for developing political skill. Protagoras goes on to describe how Athenian education was aimed, from earliest childhood, at developing this potential. Yet he had in his audience two powerful arguments against either hereditary or environmental education in statesmanship – the two sons of Pericles. The introduction to *Protagoras* is contained in *IR*.

Section Eighteen: Herodotus

The introduction to the Penguin translation by A. R. Burn is good and accessible; W. G. Forrest's introduction to the abridged translation of H. G. Rawlinson (New York, 1963) is even better. The relevant sections in M. Grant, *The Ancient Historians* (Weidenfeld and Nicolson, 1970) are excellent; see also chapter 6 in K. J. Dover, *Ancient Greek Literature* (Oxford, 1980).

Ask students to read the introduction (pp. 155–6) and translation of 1.29–33 (pp. 157–9) before starting this section, drawing attention to Solon's view of life, in particular the 'Count no man happy before he dies' motif.

Section Eighteen A

Background

ὕβρις   3.15
Dreams   2.13–14

Grammar

Herodotus' dialect
Accusative of respect
οὐ φημί

Commentary

p. 159 line
36   μετά + noun + participle: a favourite idiom of Herodotus, cf. *ab urbe condita*.

νέμεσις: cf. on 30.21. For the ideas, cross-refer also to the translation (*Text* p. 158.34–6). It is the antithesis of the moral approach – the god considers not the merit or otherwise of the individual, but merely how he (the god) can keep happiness as a divine monopoly (*WA* 2.22–3). Cf. Zeus (*Iliad* XXIV.527ff.) giving no man unmixed happiness; the 'jealous god' idea was attacked by Plato (*Phaidros* 247a): ὁ φθόνος ἔξω τοῦ θείου χοροῦ ἵσταται.

38   ὀλβιώτατον: note the emphatic position.

αὐτίκα: note the immediacy of retribution for Croesus' proud thoughts.

οἱ = αὐτῷ should be carefully noted (this recurs several times here and in Homer).

ἐπέστη: the dream is almost a physical manifestation (cf. Athene, *Text* p. 171.14) and so 'stands over' the dreamer. For a fuller account of dreams and attitudes to them, see Dodds, *The Greeks and the Irrational* 105–22. Oneiromancy was ubiquitous in antiquity. But contrast Artabanos' modern-sounding explanation of dreams as no more than a confused jumble of the previous day's events and thoughts (Herodotus VII.16b).

39 μελλόντων: μέλλω is used frequently in Herodotus (and elsewhere) to imply a sense of 'fate' or 'destiny'.

40 διέφθαρτο: perhaps 'handicapped'; note the derivation (διαφθείρω).

p. 160 line

1 κωφός: explained by Hesychius οὔτε λαλῶν οὔτε ἀκούων, viz. deaf and dumb. Note the inherent attitude: because of his defect he was (almost) 'a write-off' - the underlying feeling of διέφθαρτο. Herodotus later (1.85) completes the story of this dumb son (nowhere named): an oracle predicted that his first words would be uttered on a day of sorrow. This was fulfilled when Cyrus captured Sardis. A Persian soldier was about to attack Croesus when the dumb son suddenly shouted 'Don't kill Croesus!' (whom Cyrus had ordered to be captured alive), and thereafter spoke normally for the rest of his life.

ὁ … ἕτερος: literally 'the other by far the first of his contemporaries in all respects'.

2 Atys: a doom-laden name, very close to ἄτη. Note also ὦν = οὖν - this can be very confusing unless it is explained. Note also in ll. 2–3(a) the order of words (object – verb – indirect object – subject) and the varying emphasis it gives to each component of the sentence, while the whole still flows smoothly; (b) the extra emphasis given since the direct object of the main verb is also the direct object of the subordinate clause; cf. on p. 118.34.

3 ἀπολέει: 'that Croesus would lose him'.

βληθέντα: the first use of βάλλω in the sense of 'hit'.

αἰχμῇ σιδηρέῃ: elicit this from the English note.

4 ἑωυτῷ λόγον ἔδωκε: can be worked out from a literal translation; καταρρωδήσας must be given.

5 ἄγεται: elsewhere used of bridegroom or bride's father 'marrying' a girl.

ἐωθότα κτλ.: 'and him (acc. s. = the son) (though) being accustomed to lead the Lydians in battle, Croesus (subj.) no longer sent on missions of this sort'.

στρατηγέειν: the first very obvious absence of contraction; mention this as an Ionic variation.

6 πρῆγμα: another Ionic variation: -η- for -α- is very common.

ἀκόντια: zoologists may know acontium as a cord-like organ in a sea anemone flicked out when the animal is disturbed. Even so, give the meaning 'javelin'.

7 τοῖσι: note (a) the form of the dative plural; (b) the use of the article for a relative pronoun. These few notes on the Ionic dialect make Homer easier on first encounter.

8 θαλάμους: simple 'chamber', not necessarily 'bed-chamber' (Herodotus uses this word only three times, only once as bed-chamber).

9 συννέω: will have to be given.

μή τί κτλ.: 'lest anything hanging over him (οἱ) should fall on the child.'

Section Eighteen B

Background

Purification   2.35, 4.80
νόμος   P1; 7.28
ἀτιμία   3.12; 5.62–7

Commentary

p. 160 line

19 ἔχοντος κτλ.: '(with) the child having in hand his (οἱ) marriage'.

ἀπικνέεται: note the absence of rough breathing and of contraction.

20 ἐχόμενος: probably passive in sense – 'held by', 'hemmed in by'. The idea is difficult to bring across neatly in English. Because guilty of accidental homicide, the victim is limited in his participation in ordinary human activities. In that sense he is 'held in by' his fate but, of course, a more terrible sense is to emerge.

Phrygia: a province of Lydia, probably conquered by Croesus' father Alyattes – although Aeschylus (*Persai* 770) makes the ghost of Dareios claim the conquest for Cyrus.

21 γενεῇ, γένεος: note the anaphora.

22 καθαρσίου: the adjective is used here (with 'rite' understood), the object of *ἐπικυρέω*.

24 κάθαρσις: the earliest reference to this custom seems to be in the Epic Cycle. According to Proclus (*Chrestomathia* ii) Achilles killed Thersites and had to be purified of blood-guilt. In Apollonios Rhodios (ιv.693ff.), Circe performs the Zeus-ordained ritual by slitting the throat of a sucking-pig, allowing the blood to pour over the hands of the guilty and praying throughout to Zeus Katharsios. On catharsis generally: Dodds, *The Greeks and the Irrational* 35ff., 153ff.

25 ὁκόθεν: note the Ionic use of κ for π in question words and indefinites. Note also that Croesus asks no questions until after the purification: it was a religious obligation to grant catharsis to any stranger. Circe (*see above*) also asked no questions.

26 ἐπίστιος: the suppliant presented himself to the hearth, and was under the protection of Zeus Epistios (as in Section 18F).

27 ἐγένεο: now the oddities of second person singular middles fall into place!

ἀμείβετο: a word very frequent in Homer (mainly as ἀπαμείβομαι). Note absence of augment, but tense marked as past by personal ending in -ετο.

28 Early Kings of Phrygia were called alternately Midas and Gordius; the first Midas was the golden touch/asses' ears Midas.

29 Note (a) the postponement of the name, (b) the tragic significance of Adrastos (elicit from students via ἀ- privative, δρα(μ)- from τρέχω): he cannot escape.

30 ἐξεληλαμένος: will need to be given (a) because the derivation is not obvious, and (more importantly) (b) ἐλαύνω (ἐλα-) is one very common verb not yet learnt.

31 ἀνδρῶν...φίλων: Phrygia was subject to Lydia (as on l. 20), but clearly retained some autonomy (hence its own royal family); this accounts for 'friendship' between the families.

33 ἐν ἡμετέρου: cf. English 'at the doctor's/dentist's/Jones's' (abode understood).

Section Eighteen C

Commentary

p. 161 line

7 Mysian Olympos – see the map (*Text* p. 157).

ὑὸς χρῆμα... μέγα: note (a) συὸς μέγιστον χρῆμα in Sophocles' *Meleager*; (b) χρῆμα is otiose, as in the *Text* p. 33.11.

8 ἔργα: here anything that is the fruit of human labour – cultivated land, farm buildings etc.

διαφθείρεσκε: note (a) the absence of an augment, (b) iterative forms in -σκ-, with ποιέεσκον (l. 9).

15 ὡς ἄν: a common Ionic idiom for expressing purpose.

16 ἔπεα: note the 'personal appearance' idea of the dream (as on p. 159.38).

17 παιδός: note the emphatic position (and the singular: the κωφός is ignored).

18-19 The juxtaposition of ἄν+ optative/future indicative has already been noted (see on p. 60.34).

Section Eighteen D

Background

    Public eye   3.5–7
    Envy   3.9–11
    Persuasion and psychology   7.25
    Power of argument   7.17

Commentary

p. 161 line

32–3 ἔς τε πολέμους ... εὐδοκιμέειν: the whole clause is epexegetical of τὰ κάλλιστα, hence the apparent lack of agreement in the participle: 'the finest and noblest deeds were once ours (that we should), going to wars, ... etc.'

34 ἀποκληίσας ἔχεις: the usage of the aorist participle+ ἔχω for a past tense is very common in Herodotus; many modern European languages, including Greek, form their past tenses in this way.

    παριδών: not here (as usually in Attic) 'overlook', but simply 'notice'.

35 'with what eyes': cf. the devastating irony of *Oedipus Tyrannus* 1371-2.

    ἀγορά: Herodotus is reading Greek customs into Lydia, cf. on p. 55.10, 12. Notice the ἀνάπεισον (l. 39) – another Greek custom, the love of debate/ argument, which is not appropriate within the context of Eastern autocracy.

39–40 ἀμείβεται Κροῖσος: asyndeton, recurring increasingly as the tension mounts.

p. 162 line

2 ἐπιστᾶσα: even ὄψις 'stands over' one, cf. on p. 159.38.

3 πρός: 'with a view to', 'in consideration of'.

4 παραλαμβανόμενα: 'undertakings', 'enterprises' generally.

5 εἴ κως: the obsolescent English 'if perchance' corresponds most exactly, otherwise paraphrase 'to see if I could by some means...'.

διακλέψαι: 'steal you (sc. from Fate) for my own lifetime'.

7 Cf. earlier comments (on p. 160.1) on the handicapped son as a write-off.

9 τὸ δέ: with both μανθάνεις (as direct object) and λέληθε as an accusative of respect.

10 φής: exceptional students may spot that Ionic omits iota subscript...

13 ὀδόντος: cf. orthodontist, odontograph (used in engineering for laying out gear-teeth).

χρῆν: ἄν is regularly omitted in an apodosis with χρῆ; it is already virtually potential.

14 νῦν δέ: 'but now, as it is'. A constant feature of tragedy, as of this story, is the *almost* completely accurate analysis of past events being, very reasonably, applied to the present – with appalling results. Hence the frequency of νῦν δέ in Greek. Cf. *WA* 7.34.

16 ἔστι τῇ: *GVE* gives this as 'it is the case that', but the meaning is perhaps vaguer – cf. the very common ἔστι τις (cf. ἔστιν οἷς, *Text* p. 151.16) for 'someone', which would make ἔστι τῇ mean 'somehow', 'in some way' – almost as though Croesus himself was only half-convinced.

Section Eighteen E

Background

Reciprocity in human relations   2.28–9; 3.5, 13

Commentary

p. 162 line

27 εἴπας: note that εἶπον has a variant weak aorist form εἶπα, always used in the second person.

30 ὑποδεξάμενος ἔχω: ἔχω + aorist participle for a past tense: cf. on p. 161.34.

33 ἐπὶ δηλήσι φανέωσι: note (a) ἐπί + dative 'with a view to', (b) φανέωσι is aorist subjunctive *passive* (for aorist middle), not active, as it initially appears.

34 τοι: almost otiose immediately after σέ, cf. English 'I'll have you know that you ought...'

ἀπολαμπρυνέαι: note that -ε- indicates the future tense.

37 κεχρημένον: the perfect has a present sense, '(a man who) has met with (such bad luck)'.

39 πάρα accented on the first syllable = πάρεστι.

40 ὀφείλω...χρηστοῖσι: note the inherent tragic irony. Adrastos, as *everyone* in this story, behaves with absolute propriety, consideration and logic: the very fact that they act like this engenders the tragedy.

p. 163 line

1 Note how, as the climax approaches, the elements of the sentence have become shorter: 'I am ready to do this,/ and your son,/ whom you order me to guard,/ unharmed,/ thanks to his guardian,/ you may expect to return to you.' Herodotus' normal λέξις εἰρομένη breaks into shorter segments to build up to the climax.

Section Eighteen F

Background

Zeus' roles   2.8, 37, 40
ξένια   2.25, 36; 3.14; 4.67
Injustice of the gods   2.24–6
Human responsibility   3.25–6
Herodotus and history   7.33

Commentary

p. 163 line

11 Notice carefully the structure and build-up of the climactic sentence: from here until φήμην there are self-contained word-units of not more than about six words – the narrative then reverts immediately to Herodotus' more flowing normal style as life generally goes on, regardless of the tragedy of Atys. The devastating effectiveness of this can scarcely be brought across in English.

13 ἐσηκόντιζον: recall ἀκόντια (*Text* p. 160.6) and see the illustration.

13–14 Notice the triple build-up of participles followed by two short main clauses in parataxis, the lesser before the greater. Note further the ξεῖνος...

Κροίσου emphasis at the beginning and end of the sentence (as opposed to, e.g., using proper names 'Adrastos...Atys' in these places, which would lack the tragic effect); point also to the tragic irony of mentioning once again at this point καθαρθεὶς τὸν φόνον when another φόνος is about to occur; the emphasis given by underlining the tragic name Adrastos; and chiasmus in two main clauses. The whole sentence is a marvel of construction.

15ff. Note (as above) how the sentence continues short-clause pattern, then from ἔθεε δέ τις reverts to greater flow and movement.

16 ἀγγελέων: a future participle as shown by the single -λ- and -ε-. Observe how Herodotus 'throws away' the climax, because there was no doubt it would happen.

p. 164 line

2 μᾶλλόν τι: 'all the more', a common usage in Herodotus.

3 τόν: note (a) the definite article used as the relative pronoun again; (b) the suppression of the antecedent.

4 Δία καθάρσιον: Zeus is invoked here by three of his many epithets, as god of purification, hospitality and friendship, partly in reproach (δεινῶς ἐκάλεε) for allowing the tragedy to occur, and partly to summon assistance for vengeance upon the perpetrator. There is a terrible irony here: Croesus had fulfilled scrupulously his obligations to Zeus under each of these headings, yet had received no mercy. Croesus, of course, does not understand the real reason for his 'punishment' (see *Text* p. 159.38).

5 πεπονθὼς εἴη: the optative may either be indefinite or in oratio obliqua after a historic main verb.

7 Note the juxtaposition of ξεῖνον φονέα, both objects of their respective clauses.

ἐλάνθανε: the indicative is retained here, cf. εὑρήκοι (l. 8), with no significant change in meaning – both were causes assigned by Croesus himself and could be optative.

8 φύλακα ... πολεμιώτατον: antithesis by opposite means here, the contrasting words at the beginning and end of the clause (cf. on l. 7).

9 Again note the word order: in both clauses there is emphasis at the beginning and end. First there is the dramatic entry (παρῆσαν), with νεκρόν at the end of the clause; ὄπισθε follows (almost out of the picture in contrast with 'there they were'), then finally comes φονεύς.

10 Adrastos – unnamed here – dominates the sentence; once again note its construction carefully. στάς gives him dramatic prominence; notice παρεδίδου, the main verb, in uncharacteristically unemphatic position and with imperfective aspect; προτείνων as in unconditional surrender;

ἐπικατασφάξαι displacing the participle for greater emphasis upon the violent word; λέγων, by zeugma, taking first a direct object then a noun clause, both emphasizing the double disaster that had befallen, and the perfect optative adding 'permanence'; it ends quite simply – and most effectively.

14 Adrastos is here, significantly, named for the first time since p. 163.14.

16 πᾶσαν ... δίκην: the mere admission of guilt with the offer of his life constituted all that could be required by Croesus – any more would have been vengeance, not Justice.

17 οὐ σύ ... αἴτιος: cf. *Iliad* III.164ff.

18 Note that here the gods are responsible because they forewarned, i.e. predestined in a Calvinistic sense.

20ff. Note the climactic build-up of the last sentence, with 'weighty' words towards the end; the repetition of φονεύς (the second time not literally, but in the same transferred sense as *Oedipus Tyrannus* 534 (Oedipus to Kreon), *Hekabe* 882 (Hekabe calling Polymestor 'my murderer' because he murdered her son Polydoros)); note too the contrast between Adrastos' earlier public outpouring and this calm stillness ('ἡσυχίη'); and above all the extraordinarily solemn dignity conveyed.

On completion of Section 18, take time to retranslate the whole section to the students: it gives an overall perspective of what may have been a struggle the first time through.

Supplementary exercises

A good way to revise vocabulary in this section is to ask students to provide Attic equivalents of many of the Ionic words, and then give their meaning, e.g. ἑωυτῷ Ionic/ἑαυτῷ Attic, 'to/for himself'.

Section Nineteen

To the note on *Text* p. 168, '(Homer's) sentences tend to be very straightforward grammatically', append the rider that his syntax often does not conform to what have so far been 'the rules', which can make translation tricky.

   The English introduction on *Text* p. 170 illustrates the problems of transliteration – Cyclopes and Kirke in the same line! It is an insoluble problem, made worse by the very familiarity of Latinized/Anglicized forms; Aiskhylos may seem grotesque, but νόμος πάντων βασιλεύς.

Section Nineteen A

Background

Homer 7.1
Use of Homer 7.4
Homer and the Greeks P 10–12
Homer's gods 2.59–64
Dreams 2.13–14
Display and reputation 3.1–4

Grammar

Homeric dialect, syntax and respelling
Homeric hexameters
Verse quantity

Cassette

Part of Section 19E (*Text* p. 176.8–20) and all of 19F (p. 178) are recorded with dynamic accent on the *Speaking Greek* cassette, Side 1 (part of W. S. Allen's talk, 'The sounds of Greek'). All of Section 19C–E (pp. 174–8) is recorded with melodic accent, Side 2. By listening to both recordings of Section 19E (p. 176.8-20), students can differentiate between the two accents.

Commentary

p. 170 line

34 ἔνθα: Odysseus is sleeping under a pair of olive bushes, having scooped out a hollow in the earth and covered himself with dead leaves (v.482–5).

πολύτλας: elicit from the stems and mention as a stock epithet in the *Odyssey*.

35 As mentioned in the English note (*Text* p. 167), gods and heroes mix easily; mention Athene as Odysseus' staunchest supporter, regularly appearing to help him.

36 Note the absence of augment – already met in Herodotus (p. 161.8) and very common in Homer. Note also the relaxed pace which is one of the delights of Homer – never in too much of a hurry to include 'irrelevant' background details. Compare Penelope crossing the threshold (*Odyssey*

XXI. 43–5) – even at that crucial stage Homer can devote some two and a half lines to a doorway! Note also the 'ring composition' technique: having established that Athene goes to the Phaiakians, Homer digresses, then returns to the theme in 171.6.

p. 171 line

13 ἀνέμου: cf. anemometer.

πνοιή: πνευ- as in pneumatic etc.

δέμνια: met in Section 14 (130.37), but it will need recall here.

14 'stood above her head' – cf. on p. 159.38.

πρός ... ἔειπεν: tmesis, taking a double accusative (μιν, μῦθον).

15 ναυσικλειτοῖο: the Phaiakians were famed for their nautical skills, see *Text* p. 180.27–9.

18 Almost 'How come your mother has such a lazy daughter?'

19 The εἵματα which should be σιγαλόεντα are in fact ἀκηδέα.

20 ἵνα+indicative 'where', cf. *ut* in Latin.

αὐτήν: σέ is implied = '*you* yourself'.

21 ἕννυσθαι: ἀμφιεννύς (*Text* p. 151.10) may be recalled, otherwise elicit this from the context.

ἄγωνται: the bride's father clearly had the responsibility for organizing the procession to the new home.

κε (= ἄν)+subjunctive – indefinite.

22 τοι is so common in Homer that it sometimes seems to have lost its meaning as an ethic dative – here perhaps 'from such things, you know,...' with almost as little meaning as the English colloquial, parenthetical 'you know'.

23 πότνια: a stock epithet, usually translated 'lady', with μήτηρ.

24 ἴομεν: note the form of this subjunctive.

πλυνέουσαι: ask which tense; those who remember λ-μ-ν-ρ verbs may spot that -ε- indicates a future tense and may deduce the sense of purpose.

ἠώς: often ῥοδοδάκτυλος – though this beautiful epithet does not occur in our extract. Note also the -θι/-φι termination for some datives (ἠῶθι πρό, l. 29, e.g.).

26 ἐντύνεαι: second person singular aorist subjunctive – mention this if asked (Reference Grammar p. 269 (ii)). N.B. Do not use this line to test scansion – with synizesis (twice), correption (twice) and irrational lengthening, it is an unfair example!

28 πάντων Φαιήκων: partitive genitive, probably with ἀριστῆες rather than δῆμον.

ὅθι: the antecedent is either ἀριστῆες (i.e. your peers) or Φαιήκων (i.e. your compatriots).

29 ἐπότρυνον: aorist imperative – λ-μ-ν-ρ verbs have no -σ- in the weak aorist.

30 ἡμιόνους:: has not appeared since *Text* p. 92.27; ἄμαξα (as ἄμαξα) since *Text* p. 55.12; for ἐφοπλίσαι cf. ὤπλιζε, *Text* p. 150.37. κεν (= ἄν) + subjunctive in Homer often = future.

p. 172 line

3 ἔρχεσθαι: note how Homer uses moods of ἔρχομαι rather than εἶμι (*ibo*): infinitive here, a participle in l. 25, an imperative in l. 40.

πλυνοί: hollows of some kind, either natural rock-pools or man-made basins lined with stone.

6–7 Closely imitated by Lucretius in *De rerum natura* III.18–24 [cf. Claudian, *De Nupt. Hon. et Mar.* 52–5] and by Tennyson:

> Where falls not hail, or rain, or any snow,
> Nor ever wind blows loudly (*Idylls of the King* 1.428–9).

8 ἀνέφελος: cf. Nephelokokkugia.

λευκή: cf. leukaemia (excess of leukocytes, i.e. white blood corpuscles).

10 'Ring composition' again, the first three words picking up directly from line 4.

Section Nineteen B

Commentary

p. 172 line

19 μιν: object with Nausikaa in the next line in apposition to it.

21 βῆ δ' ἴμεναι: note the otiose infinitive, a very common idiom.

22 φίλῳ: to be taken with both, almost a stock epithet, cf. ll. 27, 38. Shakespeare plays with stock epithets: *Hamlet* II.2.33–4

> KING   Thanks, Rosencrantz and gentle Guildenstern.
> QUEEN   Thanks, Guildenstern and gentle Rosencrantz.

23 ἀμφιπόλοισι γυναιξίν: another very common stylistic feature; two nouns in apposition, forming the second half of the hexameter.

24 Give first three words; emphasize the contrast ἡ μέν (l. 23) with τῷ δέ here.

25 βασιλῆας: 'chieftains', 'nobles', as often in Homer.

28 πάππα φίλ': 'Daddy dear'. Note, in this speech and throughout the rest of the book, the extraordinary clarity of character in Nausikaa – she is in some respects a more vivid character than even Odysseus himself. 'No-one else is drawn with like livingness and enthusiasm, and no other episode is written with the same, or nearly the same, buoyancy of spirits and resilience of pulse and movement, or brings the scene before us with anything approaching the same freshness, as that in which Nausikaa takes the family linen to the washing cisterns. The whole of Book vi can only have been written by one who was throwing herself into it heart and soul' (Samuel Butler, *The Authoress of the Odyssey*). Butler's book still makes fresh and amusing reading in spite of Butler's pet theories (feminine authorship, all adventures taking place around the coast of Sicily etc.); Butler knew the Odyssey inside out. Robert Graves in *Homer's Daughter* retells the *Odyssey* with Nausikaa as the first-person narrator.

28 ἀπήνη: synonymous with ἄμαξα.

30 μοι: ideal for an explanation of the ethic dative: '(and this is a matter of some concern) to me'.

31 Note the non-agreement of the participle ἐόντα with σοί: grammarians will refer to a *constructio ad sensum*.

33 γεγάασιν: = γεγόνασιν.

34 'three are blooming bachelors'.

37 αἴδετο: note GVE, 'felt reticent about' rather than 'was ashamed'. Much is made of Nausikaa's impending nuptials, though the matter of her intended has not yet been decided…

θαλερόν: possibly a stock epithet of marriage 'first, it was ordained for the procreation of children' (The Book of Common Prayer: Form of the Solemnization of Matrimony), possibly wishful.

ἐξονομῆναι: note how this verb moved from its original meaning of 'call/mention by name' and is used (e.g. VI.254, *Text* p. 180.10) when the name is not mentioned.

p. 173 line

1 ὑπερτερίῃ: some sort of awning.

ἐκέκλετο: formed from κέλομαι by augment + reduplication (reduplicated aorist, cf. p. 172.10) + syncopation (of κ⸢λ⸣-).

Section Nineteen C

---

p. 174 line

6 ἔμελλε: almost 'it was time to', as they do not start packing up until line 252 (*Text*, p. 180.8), just after our extract ends.

8 ἀλλ': emphasize in reading, noting the accent.

10   the relative+optative for purpose; cf. Latin. Note that there is only one dactyl in this line.
12   Nausikaa is the subject of both verbs. Perhaps cf. *Text* p. 163.14–15, in a totally different tone.
17   **φιλόξεινοι**: cf. 67.26!
19   **νυμφάων**: in apposition to κουράων, defining it more closely. Note the Homeric usage of ἔχω = 'I inhabit', viz. 'I have (as my home)'.
22   **πειρήσομαι**: for πειρήσωμαι, aorist subjunctive (not future indicative as it may appear).

Section Nineteen D

Background

Supplication   2.36–7

Commentary

p. 174 line
31   **ὑπεδύσετο**: cf. *Text* p. 86.24. The basic meaning of δύω is to put clothes on (cf. Latin *induo*), so ὑποδύω is to put underclothes on. Here, with 'genitive of separation', it means the opposite (as ἐκδύομαι), viz. get oneself out from under.
32   **πυκινῆς**: cf. πυκναῖς (*Text* p. 151.10).
      ὕλης: the basic meaning is 'wood', but it is also used for material generally, cf. Latin *materia*.
      κλάσε: cf. iconoclasm.
      παχείη: cf. pachyderm. Definitions help in these two lines (ll. 31–2) to avoid giving every other word!
33   **φύλλων**: not to be confused with φυλ- compounds – cf. numerous φυλλ- words, and chlorophyl(l).
      χροΐ: cf. *Text* p. 129.39.
      φωτός: beware of confusion arising over the two words φώς 'man', and φῶς 'light'.
34   **ὀρεσίτροφος**: both roots should be known. Note the savagery as the metaphor develops.
35   **ὑόμενος**: 'Tramp up Snowdon, With your woad on, Never mind if you get rained or snowed on' provides an example of a personal passive use of an impersonal verb.

ὄσσε: the exhaustive note on duals given on p. 131.15 should ensure that this is recognized.

37 κέλεται: not easily recognized from ἐκέκλετο (p. 173.2) unless the latter has been explained.

γαστήρ: various gastro- compounds in English should elicit the meaning.

39 The savagery of the simile should have been emphasized (this image is used in *Iliad* XII of Sarpedon advancing to battle) – then the sudden contrast with κούρῃσιν ἐϋπλοκάμοισιν will have its effect. How closely is the simile tied to the narrative?

40 μίξεσθαι: used (also) of sexual intercourse.

γυμνός: explain why gymnasium derives from γυμνός.

p. 175 line
29 σμερδαλέος: sounds more evocative to us than it probably did to Greeks, but the triple k in κεκακωμένος is deliberately harsh.

φάνη: that was how he *looked* to the girls: it was not intentional.

32 Note the Greek idiom: 'took the fear from her limbs', because when a person is afraid the limbs start trembling.

33 σχομένη: difficult to translate literally; perhaps simply 'halting', or 'checking herself'.

34 γούνων: for the case, cf. regular usage of λαμβάνομαι + genitive.

35 αὔτως: *GVE* 'simply', or 'as he was' viz. at a distance.

μειλιχίοισι: *GVE* 'winning, soothing' but point out the possible derivation from μέλι; 'honey-tongued' is a Greek metaphorical expression also used in English, so here 'with honeyed words' conveys the sense exactly.

36 εἰ: cf. on εἴ κως (p. 162.5); '(to see) if she would...'

37 κέρδιον: note the profit-minded motive, nicely picked up in κερδαλέον (40), an ambiguous word meaning 'shrewd' or 'crafty', depending upon the motive behind the κέρδος.

39 φρένα: accusative of respect.

Section Nineteen E

Commentary

p. 176 line
8ff. Take this speech carefully – it is full of wonderful touches, truly κερδαλέον, starting with γουνοῦμαι – 'I seize your knees'! – though he does *not*!

8 θεός νύ κτλ.: a good bit of flattery to start with – Odysseus' knowledge of psychology is faultless: 'flattery will get you everywhere'. It is also practical – one does not rape (cf. μίξεσθαι above, p. 174.40) a goddess (surely Nausikaa's main fear):

οὐ βιοθάλμιος ἀνὴρ
γίγνεται ὅς τε θεαῖς εὐνάζεται ἀθανάτῃσι
(Hom. *Hymn Aphrodite* 189–90)

9 τοί: a plural relative pronoun after a singular antecedent; *constructio ad sensum* again.

ἔχουσιν: cf. on p. 174.19.

10 Ἀρτέμιδι: a shrewd choice of deity, the goddess of chastity and maidenly modesty, not like the three who stripped off for Paris (Lucian, *Dial. Deorum* 20). Also note the 'awe' mentioned in the English note, ll. 4–6 (picked up again ll. 20, 27).

11 μέγεθος: *GVE* 'size' is hardly flattering! 'Stature' fits better, but that is given for φυή. Rieu translates 'beauty, grace and stature'.

14–16 Homer appears to 'break the rules' (a) with the genitive plural participle λευσσόντων as if σφων had been used instead of the possessive dative σφισι; (b) the feminine participle εἰσοιχνεῦσαν seems to agree with the neuter noun θάλος. Both are sense-constructions, neither presenting any problem of understanding – particularly when one bears in mind that Homer is oral poetry.

17 A final touch of opening flattery – 'how lucky your future husband' – but also highly soothing for Nausikaa. One is not normally raped by people who confess admiration for chastity, parents, family and marriage.

18 ἐέδνοισι: *GVE* 'bridal gifts' – the regular gifts to the father (to win acceptance, as he gave the bride away).

ἀγάγηται: cf. on p. 160.5.

19 τοιοῦτον: perhaps not too flattering – 'no such thing'!

20 σέβας: *GVE* 'respect', but also with the sense of 'awe, reverence' noted above, and cf. on p. 26.13. This is the feeling Odysseus has in front of Nausikaa – not, e.g. lust.

21 Δήλῳ: presumably on the way to Troy, as we know (Odyssey III.169ff.) that the return route was through the western islands. On Delos, Leto gave birth to Apollo and Artemis; in honour of this, their father Zeus created the palm and the bay tree. Euripides, *Hekabe* 458 refers to the πρωτόγονος φοῖνιξ on Delos (see Illustrations, Text p. 177).

22 This may not seem to be a very flattering comparison – 'You remind me of a date palm I once saw'; the point of the metaphor is the sanctity of the particular ἔρνος, its slender beauty and its young freshness.

23 πολύς … λαός: the 'hint at his own importance', as he must be a person of considerable power if he has a large company following him – not just another grubby, naked wretch that the sea has washed up.

25 Another point to the metaphor: so taken was he by the beauty of the plant that he stood for a long while awestruck; it was unique (l. 26). This is how he is behaving now, of course.

27 Note the mixture of emotions Odysseus claims are troubling him.

29 χθιζός: an adjective with adverbial sense.

ἐεικοστῷ: a silent tribute to his heroic endurance – twenty days without sustenance.

31 κάββαλε: Greek expressions relating to the shore seem to visualize the shore as lowest point

so to go inland or out to sea has an *ἀνά* compound, to go down to the sea or reach land a *κατά* compound.

32 καὶ τῇδε: 'here too', hoping to evoke a protective response.

ὅίω: active form of a known middle verb.

33 πάροιθεν: i.e. before the *κακόν* comes to an end, there is plenty more in store.

34 σέ: the emphatic word, widely separated from the preposition governing it and the adjective qualifying it.

37 ῥάκος: almost 'any old rag', more specifically in next line 'the old sheet in which the clothing was wrapped' to bring it for washing.

ἀμφιβαλέσθαι: an infinitive expressing purpose (not uncommon in Homer), i.e. 'a rag *to put round* me'.

39 After his own appeal for help come his pious wishes for everything good for Nausikaa.

p. 178 line

1 Note what his priorities are for her: a husband, a home – and harmony.

ὀπάσειαν: ensure that this is taken as an optative – there is a tendency to assume that it is a first-declension adjective agreeing with *ὁμοφροσύνην*.

3 ἢ ὅθ': defines what he means by harmony.

ὁμοφρονέοντε: the exhaustive note on duals (p. 131.15) should ensure that this too is recognized as a dual; add a note on the verbal dual endings at discretion.

4 Note again the pre-Christian attitude that it is right to benefit one's friends and harm one's enemies: cf. *Text* p. 103.21ff. and note at the end of Section 13.

5 ἔκλυον: GVE neatly ducks the problem of the exact meaning by giving 'be respected'; it seems to be more literally 'they hear (nice things about them from their friends, words of grudging envy from their enemies)', understanding quite a lot from the previous sentence!

Section Nineteen F

Background

Suppliants' rights 2.25, 36

Commentary

p. 178 line

14 λευκώλενος: most people had tanned skin, and therefore white was a sign of beauty (as on p. 129.18).

15 ἐπεί: the apodosis follows at νῦν δέ (l. 19).

κακῷ: nicely ambiguous, referring either to his hints at importance and nobility above, or to the possibility of his having malicious intent.

16 νέμει ὄλβον: cf. Iliad xxiv.527ff., describing how Zeus dispenses happiness and misery to mortals: to some, a mixture, to others unmixed misery, to none unmixed happiness.

17 ἑκάστῳ: in loose apposition (as often) to ἐσθλοῖς ἠδὲ κακοῖσιν. Note how the sentence ungrammatically tails off – is Nausikaa trying to sound 'grown-up' here – and failing?

21 A compressed phrase (not much helped by GVE ἐπέοικε+ dative when there is no dative in sight!). It is better to take ἐπέοικε as+ accusative+ infinitive, so ὧν (governed by μὴ δεύεσθαι understood) ἐπέοικε ἱκέτην ταλαπείριον ἀντιάσαντα (sc. 'anyone who could help him') μὴ δεύεσθαι.

25 ἐκ governs τοῦ: 'on him the power and might of the Phaiakians depend'.

26 ἦ ῥα: first occurrence of this extremely common formulaic phrase – make sure that it is understood from the start by reference to ἦ (met in ἦ δ' ὅς in Section 6D etc.) and by pointing out that ῥα = ἄρα.

27 στῆτέ μοι: not 'stand by me', but 'stop' and then the dative of advantage.

28 φάσθ': as very often, more 'consider' or 'think' than 'say'.

29 This may cause a laugh. Merry translates 'That man exists not as a creature of flesh and blood, nor ever will be born, who shall come as a foeman to the Phaeacians' land.'

32 ἀπάνευθε: Phaeacia, as other places in the *Odyssey*, is regarded as towards the extremities of the known world – yet strangely homely for all that! Cf. on p. 172.28.

35 Quoted in the *Text* p. 29.9. πρός+ genitive = 'under the protection of': cf. the very common use of πρός+ genitive in apostrophes.

36 ξεῖνοι: 'Be not forgetful to entertain strangers: for thereby some have entertained angels unawares' (*Hebrews* 13.2).

ὀλίγη τε φίλη τε: a good example of Homeric parataxis where English would probably subordinate: 'a gift, though small, is welcome'.

38 λούσατε: note the active – Nausikaa tells her servants to wash Odysseus, not just take him to a convenient place and let him wash himself.

ἐπί: adverbial, 'also', 'in addition'. Alternatively, as *GVE*, tmesis ἐπί... ἐστί.

Section Nineteen G

Commentary

p. 179 line

8 κάδ... εἶσαν: note κάδ = κατά; the root of ἕζω = ἕδος. They escorted Odysseus to the sheltered spot and sat him down there.

10 πάρ = παρά (to be learnt in this section): note the common Homeric shortening of dissyllabic prepositions to monosyllables – κάδ has just occurred, and recurs in l. 26.

εἵματα (cf. ἱμάτιον): in apposition, 'as clothing'.

14 Odysseus clearly differs from Nausikaa in his views on the propriety of being washed by her maidservants! Cf. on p. 178.38.

15–16 ἀπολούσομαι... χρίσομαι: both are actually aorist subjunctives (-ομαι for -ωμαι), though they never present any problems of translation, even if they are taken as future indicatives.

15 ὤμοιϊν: note the dual here, but even in Homer's time ordinary plurals may replace the dual – see p. 179.21.

16 ἐστίν: note that English uses a perfect here, where Greek uses a present.

ἀλοιφή: cf. ἀλείφου, *Text* p. 88.3. Also ἄλειψεν below (l. 23).

17 αἰδέομαι: Odysseus' strange coyness has already been noted. Or does it have a purpose?

21 ἄλμην: note (a) the double accusative (χρόα, ἄλμην) after νίζετο; (b) that as above (l. 15), *Text* p. 175.29 and χνόον below (l. 22), ἄλμην probably refers to the scum of caked salt.

24 ἀδμής: the root δμα- always has sense of 'tame' or 'conquer'; here 'unmarried'.

25 ἐκγεγαυῖα: in the Hesiodic version (*Theogony* 886ff.) she was born from Zeus' skull after he had swallowed Metis.

26 μείζονα... εἰσιδέειν: 'greater to look upon' – an epexegetic infinitive.

27 Presumably thick-clustering curls suggest the hyacinth flower.

28 Presumably golden hair encircling a paler face suggests this simile.

29 Παλλάς: the ancient epithet of Athene. Tzetzes (*On Lycophron* 355) makes him her father, whom she killed and flayed to make her aegis. The latter part of this version (but with the Hesiodic version of her paternity) is now also known from a papyrus fragment of Epicharmus (Köln 5604).

Hephaistos and Athene are here linked, as in the Protagoras extract (Section 17C).

31 τῷ: indirect object 'on him', with 'on his head and shoulders' in loose apposition.

36 Cf. 'non sine numine divum' (*Aeneid* II.777); note also the emphasis once again placed upon Odysseus and Nausikaa together – hence Butler's and Graves' conclusions (see on p. 172.28).

40 'I wish some such man would be (called) my husband' – 'called' is rather otiose in English.

p. 180 line

1 Invert the order of clauses for translation: 'and that he might be pleased to remain here and live among us'.

2 πόσιν: GVE avoids the problem of having two words spelt and accented identically by not including πόσις = husband.

6 ἁρπαλέως: elicit from the context, or by reference to the Harpies – the general sense of the last clause should then follow.

On concluding this section, apart from asking students to read the rest of the book in translation, try to provoke some discussion about the whole episode in its own context, drawing attention to the very valid point made by Butler about the extraordinary charm of the episode, its vivid life-like quality – and (he claims) its virtual irrelevance in the context of what follows. One should point out against this view that Odysseus is subject to varying kinds of ξενία, carrying different challenges, during his travels home (Calypso, Nausikaa, Phaiakians, Cyclops, Kirke etc.), and that the climax of the *Odyssey* is the ultimate challenge – the re-establishment of his rightful lordship in his *own* home, from which he has been rejected by villains who know nothing of these human institutions. In the charming, rather tongue-tied modesty of Nausikaa we may also like to see a parallel with Telemakhos; in Odysseus' dealings with her, a pre-figuring of the subtle relationship he will develop with Penelope, and an elegant counterpoint to his relationship with Calypso in Book 5 (e.g. their differing attitudes to baths, food and bed).

After his entertainment in Phaiakia, Odysseus is invited to tell his story at the evening banquet: he does so in Books IX–XII, so we then hear his full adventures from the sack of Troy onwards. After that, Books XIII–XXIV deal with his homecoming to Ithaca: apart from the petrification of the ship taking him back to Ithaca, the Phaiakians are no longer mentioned. What became of this charming princess whom we had assumed would be for ever romantically linked with Odysseus?

NOTES ON THE ILLUSTRATIONS IN *READING GREEK (TEXT AND GRAMMAR)*, *GREEK VOCABULARY* AND *THE TEACHERS' NOTES TO READING GREEK*

The illustrations have been chosen to assist students to understand the text, to enliven the reading and to give a selection of pictures of Greek life as shown in their figured arts.

No material later than the fourth century B.C. has been included, and little earlier than the middle of the sixth. For the most part the illustrations are of Athenian origin.

Attic black-figure and red-figure vases provide the bulk of the material, for the obvious reason that they supply the best narrative scenes. The majority of the vases chosen date from the late sixth and early fifth centuries B.C., as once again this period gives the clearest pictures for the purpose.

The illustrations chosen do not always match the text, e.g. *Text* p. 6, left is a mythological scene of Herakles destroying the house of Syleus, and has nothing to do with a boat; and *Text* p. 28, right has Telephos with the infant Orestes.

The following notes attempt to answer the sorts of questions that might be raised about the pictures. Also included are basic bibliographical information and reference to some more accessible books.

We are grateful to the museums, photographic firms, draughtsmen and individuals for supplying prints and drawings and giving permission for their use.

The following abbreviations are used:

ABSA	*The Annual of the British School at Athens*
ABV	J. D. Beazley, *Attic Black-figure Vase-painters* (Oxford, 1956)
Agora xii	B. A. Sparkes and L. Talcott, *Black and Plain Pottery of the 6th, 5th and 4th Centuries B.C.* (ASCS, 1970)
Agora xiv	H. A. Thompson and R. E. Wycherley, *The Agora of Athens* (ASCS, 1972)

The Athenian Agora Guide³   H. A. Thompson, *The Athenian Agora: A Guide to the Excavation and Museum*, 3rd edn (ASCS, 1976)

Agora Picture Books 1   B. A. Sparkes and L. Talcott, *Pots and Pans of Classical Athens* (1958)

4   M. Lang, *The Athenian Citizen* (1960)

9   J. Perlzweig, *Lamps from the Athenian Agora* (1964)

12   D. B. Thompson, *An Ancient Shopping Center: The Athenian Agora* (1971)

13   S. A. Immerwahr, *Early Burials from the Agora Cemeteries* (1973)

16   H. A. Thompson, *The Athenian Agora: A Short Guide* (1976)

Anderson, *Ancient Greek Horsemanship*   J. K. Anderson, *Ancient Greek Horsemanship* (California, 1961)

ARV²   J. D. Beazley, *Attic Red-figure Vase-painters*, 2nd edn (Oxford, 1963)

Boardman, *ABFV*   J. Boardman, *Athenian Black Figure Vases* (London, 1974)

Boardman, *ARFV*   J. Boardman, *Athenian Red Figure Vases: The Archaic Period* (London, 1975)

JHS   *The Journal of Hellenic Studies*

Kerameikos ix   *Ergebnisse der Ausgrabungen*, ix, *Der Südhügel*, U. von Knigge (Berlin, 1976)

Morrison and Williams, *Greek Oared Ships*   J. S. Morrison and R. T. Williams, *Greek Oared Ships, 900–322 B.C.* (Cambridge, 1968)

OMC³   T. B. L. Webster, *Monuments Illustrating Old and Middle Comedy*, 3rd edn, revised by J. R. Green, BICS Supplement no. 39 (London, 1978)

Para   J. D. Beazley, *Paralipomena, Additions to 'ABV' and 'ARV²'* (Oxford, 1971)

Reading Greek, Text

Cover   Detail of an Attic red-figure skyphos showing a reveller and a courtesan (*hetaira*).
Another detail from the same skyphos is figured on p. 85 and another work by the same painter on p. 110.
Paris, Louvre G 156.
The Brygos Painter, *ARV²* 380, no. 172 and 1649; *Para* 366.
Early fifth century B.C.

P. xvi   Side A of an Attic black-figure cup showing a merchant vessel on the left and a two-level warship on the right. The merchant vessel is round and capacious and powered by sails; the warship is sleek and low and propelled by oars or sail. Detail on p. 2.

London BM B 436.

Morrison and Williams, *Greek Oared Ships* 109, Arch. 85.

Late sixth century B.C.

P. 2, *t*   The route from Byzantium to Athens.

P. 2, *m*   Detail of the merchant vessel from p. xvi.

P. 2, *b*   View of the Acropolis of Athens from the south-west. On the left are the Propylaia and small Nike temple; over the brow in the centre is the Erekhtheion with the Parthenon standing out at the southern edge.

P. 6, *l*   Detail of an Attic red-figure Nolan amphora showing Herakles destroying the house of Syleus; he puts his axe to a fallen capital. Syleus of Lydia usually forced passing strangers to dig his vineyard; Herakles uprooted his vines and/or tore down his house.

Paris, Louvre G 210.

The Oionokles Painter, *ARV²* 647, no. 18; Boardman, *ARFV* fig. 363.

Second quarter of the fifth century B.C.

P. 6, *r*   Detail of an Attic black-figure oinokhoe showing a ship with one man standing on the prow and others in the forepart of the ship – the subject is uncertain. That the ship is not coming to land is shown by the raised mast and sail and by the fact that ships were beached stern first.

London, BM B 508.

The Keyside Class, *ABV* 426, no. 10; Morrison and Williams, *Greek Oared Ships* 111, Arch. 88.

Late sixth century B.C.

P. 8, *l*   Side B of an Attic red-figure amphora of Panathenaic shape showing Poseidon with some of the attributes of his realm: a trident and a fish. Poseidon is depicted as a mature man with beard and long hair.

Another work by the same painter is to the right.

Berlin F 2164.

The Kleophrades Painter, *ARV²* 183, no. 10; *Para* 340.

Early fifth century B.C.

P. 8, *r*   Side A of an Attic red-figure neck-amphora showing a rhapsode on a platform. He stands with his staff held prominently in front of him, and the painter has added words in front of his mouth –

P. 8, *r*   'Once upon a time in Tyrins [*sic*]...' – most likely the beginning of an epic in hexameters.

Another work by the same painter is to the left.

London, BM E 270.

The Kleophrades Painter, *ARV*² 183, no. 15, and 1632; *Para* 340; Boardman, *ARFV* fig. 138.

Early fifth century B.C.

P. 11. *l*   Side A of an Attic red-figure skyphos showing a Persian seated on a rock, his right hand stretched out to his large wicker shield. He wears an outfit that is furnished with trousers and long sleeves, and has a soft hat (*tiara*) on his head. This is one of a number of representations of Persians that seem to have been influenced by the contacts of the early fifth century.

Berlin inv. 3156.

Follower of Douris, *ARV*² 804, no. 65; *Para* 419.

Mid fifth century B.C.

P. 11, *r*   Interior design of an Attic red-figure cup showing a fight between a Greek and a Persian. A contrast is made between the outfit of the Greek warrior (bronze helmet, greaves and breast-plate) and the Persian trouser-suit (see previous entry). Both warriors wield curved swords, but the Greek has a shield and the Persian a bow and quiver.

Another work by the same painter is figured on the cover of the *Grammar*.

Edinburgh, Royal Scottish Museum 1887.213.

The Triptolemos Painter, *ARV*² 364, no. 46; *Para* 364; Boardman, *ARFV* fig. 303.1.

First quarter of the fifth century B.C.

P. 12   Carved frieze from the 'Treasury' of the Palace at Persepolis. On a platform in the centre sits Dareios enthroned with Xerxes behind him. He is giving audience to a Median official who is making a gesture of respect; in front of him are two incense burners. The poles of the now missing baldacchino separate the armed guards from the central characters. Behind Xerxes stand two high court officials.

Much of the architecture and sculpture of the palace at Persepolis betrays the influence and the hand of Greek craftsmen.

Teheran, Archaeological Museum.

Early fifth century B.C.

P. 14   Design on an Attic black-figure plate showing a trumpeter, hand on hip, trumpet held high, blowing a summons. The trumpeter is dressed in armour.

      London, BM B 590.

      Psiax, *ABV* 294, no. 19; Boardman, *ABFV* fig. 169.

      Last quarter of sixth century B.C.

P. 15   Attica and Salamis, with Dikaiopolis' route marked.

P. 17   Interior design of an Attic red-figure cup showing a warrior wearing a loin-cloth and greaves and carrying a shield, helmet and spear. The warrior runs to the right but looks left; is he fleeing from the fight? The painter, Skythes ('Skythian'), tends to have a humorous view on life.

      Paris, Louvre CA 1527.

      Skythes, *ARV*² 83, no. 12; *Para* 329; Boardman, *ARFV* fig. 91.

      Last quarter of sixth century B.C.

P. 19   Map of Athens and the harbours of the Peiraieus.

P. 21   Detail of an Attic red-figure oinokhoe showing a young man in front of an altar pouring a libation from a shallow bowl.

      Basel, Antikenmuseum Kä 423.

      The Berlin Painter, *ARV*² 1635, addendum to 210, no. 185 *bis*; *Para* 343.

      First quarter of fifth century B.C.

P. 22   Bronze figurine of Zeus making ready to hurl his thunderbolt. The workmanship is most likely Corinthian.

      Berlin misc. 10561.

      Second quarter of fifth century B.C.

P. 25   Detail of Attic black-figure one-handled kantharos showing a man lying on his bier. The women (painted white) had the duty of preparing the body for burial, and the men now come to pay their respects and to join in the lamentation.

      London, BM 99.7–21.1.

      Last quarter of sixth century B.C.

P. 27   Drawing of the sanctuary of the Twelve Gods in the centre of Athens. Situated near the north edge of the *agora*, this sanctuary, consisting of an altar within a fenced area, was a place of refuge and the point from which distances to other parts of Greece were measured. The sanctuary was founded by the younger Peisistratos in the year of his archonship, 522/1 B.C.

      See *Agora* xiv 129–36; *The Athenian Agora Guide*³ 96–8; *The Athenian Agora: A Short Guide* fig. 16.

P. 28, *l*   Side B of an Attic red-figure skyphos showing Theseus in cloak and travelling hat. He carries two spears. Sinis, the pine-bender, is shown on the other side of the skyphos, seated under a tree and holding a club. This is one of Theseus' adventures on his way from Troisden to Athens.
　　　Berlin F 2580.
　　　The Euaion Painter, *ARV²* 797, no. 143.
　　　Mid fifth century B.C.

P. 28, *r*   Detail of an Attic red-figure pelike showing Telephos, king of the Mysians, who has seized the infant Orestes as hostage and has taken refuge on an altar as a suppliant. His bandaged left thigh indicates the place of the wound inflicted by Achilles' spear. Agamemnon (not shown) faces him on the left.
　　　London, BM E 382.
　　　A bad imitation of the Chicago Painter, *ARV²* 632, top.
　　　Second quarter of the fifth century B.C.

P. 32   A selection of Athenian silver coins of various denominations.
　　　Cambridge, Fitzwilliam Museum.

P. 33   Bronze figurine of a horse, part of a chariot team of four. The harness is particularly clear, showing the bit with curved cheek-piece and the collar to which the traces were fastened.
　　　Olympia, Museum.
　　　Anderson, *Ancient Greek Horsemanship* pl. 19.
　　　Second quarter of the fifth century B.C.

P. 34   A clay lamp with lighted wick. This small container for oil could supply light for 2–3 hours and burn brighter than a candle.
　　　Athens, Agora Museum L 4137.
　　　Lamps from the Athenian Agora fig. 18.
　　　Last quarter of the fifth century B.C.

P. 36   These two oven bells were pre-heated and placed over already prepared dough; they were also used as fire extinguishers.
　　　Athens, Agora Museum P 8862 and P 10133.
　　　See *Agora* xii 233; *Pots and Pans of Classical Athens* fig. 36.
　　　C. 500 B.C. (left) and c. 400 B.C. (right).

P. 39, *l*   A pair of model clay travelling boots found in an Early Geometric cremation grave of a woman.
　　　Athens, Agora Museum P 19249.
　　　Early Burials from the Agora Cemeteries figs. 1 and 37; *The Athenian Agora Guide³* 230; *The Athenian Agora: A Short Guide* fig. 38.
　　　C. 900 B.C.

P. 39, r　Detail of an Attic red-figure amphora showing a pair of boots on
a small footstool under a table; above the table a man reclines on
on a couch.
Munich 2303.
The Painter of the Munich Amphora, *ARV*² 245, no. 1; *Para*
350; Boardman, *ARFV* fig. 191.
Early fifth century B.C.

P. 44　Detail of an Attic red-figure volute-krater showing a procession
to Apollo at Delphi. Apollo is seated at the right on a throne raised
on a platform. The setting is a temple represented by four columns
of the Doric order. Apollo's attributes consist of a laurel branch
and crown, and a quiver and bow on the wall; the Delphic
location is given by the naval stone and tripod in front of the
columns. An official waits for the procession to arrive; it is headed
by a young girl in festal robe carrying a sacrificial basket (*kanoun*)
on her head.
Another work by the same painter is figured on p. 68.
Ferrara, Museo Nazionale di Spina, T 57C VP.
The Kleophon Painter, *ARV*² 1143, no. 1, and 1684; *Para* 455.
Third quarter of the fifth century B.C.

P. 46　View of Delphi facing south-east. The fourth-century version of
Apollo's temple lies beyond the theatre in the foreground.

P. 48, l　The pedestal of an Attic marble votive relief showing a cobbler's
shop with men and a child at work. The inscription which starts
below this scene indicates that the dedication is by a cobbler
Dionysios and his children to the hero Kallistephanos. The main
relief above the pedestal is not preserved.
Athens, Agora Museum I 7396.
*The Athenian Agora Guide*³ 208–9.
Mid fourth-century B.C.

P. 48, r　East Greek (Samian?) rock crystal with an intaglio design of a
helmet-maker seated on a stool tapping the crown of the helmet
with a small hammer. It is a popular motif in gem carving.
Munich 36246.
Late sixth century B.C.

P. 51　Interior design on an Attic red-figure cup showing a seated man
with tablets and stylus, no doubt correcting the exercise of the
boy who stands in front of him. A flute case hangs on the wall.
Basel, Antikenmuseum BS 465.
According to Schefold, related to Apollodoros; cf. *ARV*² 117–21.
Early fifth century B.C.

P. 53   The decorated head of a gold comb from the Solokha barrow near
the Lower Dnieper. Above a row of recumbent lions is a scene of
combat between two soldiers on foot and one on horseback. The
arms and armour are a mixture of Greek and Scythian equipment,
and like many objects from the Scythian tombs, the comb was
most likely made by a Greek craftsman living in Panticapaeum.
Leningrad, State Hermitage DE 1913.1/1.
Early fourth century B.C.

P. 54   Detail of an Attic red-figure calyx-krater showing an Amazon on
horseback; she is in combat with Theseus (not shown). She wears
trousers, a top with long sleeves, and a soft hat. Her weapons are
a lunate shield, bow and quiver, and spear. Amazons were a
popular subject in Greek art and are usually dressed in a vaguely
Eastern costume.
Leningrad, State Hermitage 769.
Near the Peleus and Hector Painters, *ARV*² 1037, no. 3, below;
Para 517.
Third quarter of the fifth century B.C.

P. 56   A terracotta group of two actors taking part in an Athenian
comedy of the mid fourth century B.C. They wear short tunics
and the stylized masks of a slave and young (but bearded) man;
they are out on a spree.
Berlin 8405.
*OMC*³ 91, AT 84.
Second quarter of the fourth century B.C.

P. 60   Detail of an Attic red-figure khous showing a bearded man in
festal robe pointing to a sacrificial basket (*kanoun*) held by a second
figure. The setting is a smithy, with the furnace at the right and an
anvil between the two figures. There is more than a touch of
caricature about the scene.
Athens, Agora Museum P 15210.
C. 400 B.C.

P. 61   A sketch-plan of Athens about 425 B.C. (see caption for details).

P. 67   Detail of the interior design of an Attic red-figure cup showing
a youth standing before another who is seated with a lyre. Above
their heads is the inscription 'The boy is handsome' (καλός),
a popular comment whether in this general form or with a
particular name substituted.
Hamburg, Museum für Kunst und Gewerbe 1900.164.
The Penthesilea Painter, *ARV*² 880, no. 4, and 1673; *Para* 428.
Second quarter of the fifth century B.C.

P. 68   Detail of an Attic red-figure pelike showing a maenad beating a
tambourine as she leads the return of Hephaistos. Another work by
the same painter is figured on p. 44.
> Munich 2361.
> The Kleophon Painter, *ARV*² 1145, no. 36; *Para* 456.
> Third quarter of the fifth century B.C.

P. 70, *l*   Interior design of an Attic red-figure cup showing a she-ass with
a wooden-framed pack saddle. The ass, which was the usual pack
animal, has no bit or mouthpiece.
> Boston, MFA 10.199.
> The Antiphon Painter, *ARV*² 337, no. 26, and 1646; *Para* 361.
> First quarter of the fifth century B.C.

P. 70, *r*   Side A of an Attic red-figure pelike showing Odysseus escaping
under a ram. He is in armour and wields a sword; he clings on but
the lines across the animal make allusion to the tying of his
comrades. No Cyclops is shown; the story was so well known
and distinctive that it could be presented in extract.
> Boston, MFA 1961.384.
> Near the Goettingen Painter, *ARV*² 1638, addendum to 233-4;
> *Para* 348.
> First to second quarter of the fifth century B.C.

P. 73, *l*   Interior design of an Attic red-figure cup showing a balding man
picking his way along with a basket and stick in his left hand and
a bucket (*kados*), most likely of bronze, in his right. The garland
round his temples proclaims him a reveller.
Another work by the same painter is figured on p. 87, *l* and on
p. 132.
> Boston, MFA 95.29.
> Onesimos, *ARV*² 324, no. 65 and 1645; *Pots and Pans of Classical
> Athens* fig. 27.
> First quarter of the fifth century B.C.

P. 73, *r*   A clay bucket (*kados*) used for drawing water from the well, as
opposed to the water-jar (hydria) which was used at the fountain.
On the shoulder of this bucket the words 'I am a kados' have been
scratched; it is usual for objects to be given the power of speech
in such inscriptions. The word *kalos* has also been scratched, as
though the bucket were calling itself 'handsome': cf. p. 67.
> Athens, Kerameikos Museum 7357 (inv. 3776).
> *Kerameikos* ix pl. 95, 1 (= ES 35) and p. 192, fig. 50; for the shape,
> see *Agora* xii 201-3, and for the name, *JHS* 95 (1975) 127-8.
> Late sixth century B.C.

P. 74, *l*   Modern replicas of an Athenian water-clock (*klepsydra*) used for timing speeches in the lawcourts. A plug in the bronze tube at the base of the bowl was released at the start of a speech. The two *khis* indicate that the bowl held two *khoes* (6.4 litres), and the bowl was emptied in six minutes. The name *Antiokhidos*, meaning 'belonging to the Antiokhis tribe', may indicate that this bowl was used when the tribe was presiding in the Council chamber (*Bouleuterion*).

    Athens, Agora Museum P 2084 (the bowl on which the two replicas are based).

    See *The Athenian Citizen* figs. 25–6; *Agora* xiv 55; *The Athenian Agora Guide*³ 248–9.

    Late fifth century B.C.

P. 74, *r*   Interior design of an Attic red-figure cup showing a reveller, with a scarf round his head, a cloak over his shoulders and a stick under his arm pit, relieving himself into a jug. A flute case hangs on the right.

    Berlin inv. 3198.

    The Foundry Painter, *ARV*² 402, no. 13; *Para* 370.

    First quarter of the fifth century B.C.

P. 75   The trial of Labes from a modern Greek production of Aristophanes' *Wasps*.

P. 76   A selection of ordinary Athenian kitchen equipment: a brazier, a kettle, a barrel cooker, a grill, and a casserole on a deep firebox.

    Athens, Agora Museum P 2362, P 16512 on 16520, P 8305, P 2306 on 16521.

    See *Pots and Pans of Classical Athens* figs. 37, 39, 40, 44, 45; *Agora* xii 224–35.

    Fifth and fourth centuries B.C.

P. 77   A Boiotian terracotta figurine of a woman grating stuff into a mixing bowl.

    Boston, MFA 01.7783.

    JHS 82 (1962) 136, no. 56.

    Early fifth century B.C.

P. 85   Detail of an Attic red-figure skyphos showing a reveller and a courtesan (*hetaira*).

    Another detail from the same skyphos is figured on the cover and another work by the same painter on p. 110.

    Paris, Louvre G 156.

    The Brygos Painter, *ARV*² 380, no. 172, and 1649; *Para* 366.

    Early fifth century B.C.

P. 87, *l*   Interior design of an Attic red-figure cup showing a balding man
at a party inviting a courtesan (*hetaira*) to disrobe. The man wears
shoes and holds his walking stick; a basket and a lyre are in the
background.
Another work by the same painter is figured on p. 73, *l* and on
p. 132.
London, BM E 44.
Onesimos, *ARV*² 318–19, no. 2; *Para* 358; Boardman, *ARFV*
fig. 222.
First quarter of the fifth century B.C.

P. 87, *r*   Detail of an Attic red-figure cup with a reveller and a courtesan
(*hetaira*) together on a couch.
New York, MM 20.246.
Makron, *ARV*² 467, no. 118, and 1654; *Para* 378.
First quarter of the fifth century B.C.

P. 89   View across the agora from the north-west (*c.* 425 B.C.).

P. 91   Design on an Attic red-figure plate showing an archer drawing
a bow from his quiver as he turns his head to the right to face his
unseen pursuer. He wears an 'Oriental' suit with long sleeves and
trousers and a high-crowned Scythian cap.
London, BM E 135.
Epiktetos, *ARV*² 78, no. 93, and 1623; *Para* 329; Boardman,
ARFV fig. 77.
Last quarter of the sixth century B.C.

P. 93   Interior design of an Attic red-figure cup showing a youth holding
a cup in his left hand and a ladle in his right. Behind him stands
a mixing-bowl with a wine-cooler set inside. The garland in his
hair is a further indication that this is an extract from a party.
Compiègne, Musée Vivenel 1102.
Manner of the Antiphon Painter, *ARV*² 341, no. 1, and 1646.
First quarter of the fifth century B.C.

P. 95   Side B of an Attic red-figure cup showing a bridegroom leading
his bride towards their home. The bride, who is as usual veiled,
is followed by a woman with a torch, whilst on the left the house
is represented by a door and a column within which stands the
groom's mother also holding torches. A young man serenades the
couple on the lyre. This may be a version of the wedding of
Peleus and Thetis.
Berlin, F 2530.
The Amphitrite Painter, *ARV*² 831, no. 20, and 1702.
Second quarter of the fifth century B.C.

P. 101   The agora area of Athens, with the 'Hephaisteion' on the far left
and the Acropolis on the far right. The long building in the centre
is the recently rebuilt Stoa of Attalos, originally erected in the
middle of the second century B.C.; it then formed the east side
of the agora. The west side was below the hill on which the
'Hephaisteion' stood. The lawcourts lay in and around this area.
In the middle distance rises the peak of Lykabettos and on the
right the range of Hymettos.

P. 104   Reconstructed drawing of the monument of the Eponymous
Heroes. This consisted of a row of statues of the 'patrons' of the
ten tribes into which Athens and Attica were divided by Kleisthenes at the close of the sixth century B.C. The base of the
monument was used for the display of drafts of proposed new
laws, notices of lawsuits and lists for military service.
See *Agora* xiv 38–41; *The Athenian Agora Guide*³ 70–2; *The
Athenian Agora, A Short Guide* fig. 11.

P. 107   Detail of an Attic red-figure plaque showing extracts from the
Eleusinian cult. Precise interpretation of the scenes is not sure, but
Demeter may be represented twice at the right side with Perse-
phone by her side in the upper level and Iakkhos facing her with
torches on the lower level. The figures on the left may be initiates
approaching. An inscription on the plaque says that it was dedicated to the goddesses by Niinnion, perhaps the courtesan Nannion
of that period. Found at Eleusis.
Athens, NM 11036.
See G. Mylonas, *Eleusis and the Eleusinian Mysteries* (1961)
213–21.
Mid fourth century B.C.

P. 108   Official voting discs found in the Athenian agora. Each juror
was given two discs, one with solid hub (for acquittal), one with
hollow hub (for condemnation); by placing thumb and forefinger
over the hubs the juror could make his vote without revealing his
preference. Some discs carry the inscription 'Official ballot', some
a letter in relief, perhaps to indicate the jury-section. A less
sophisticated system of pebbles (*psephoi*) was in operation before
the fourth century B.C.
Athens, Agora Museum B 1056, 146, 728, 1058, 1055.
See *The Athenian Citizen* fig. 22; *Agora* xiv 56; *The Athenian
Agora Guide*³ 249.

P. 110   Side A of an Attic red-figure cup showing a symposium in
          progress. The men recline on couches; one girl plays the pipes
          while another prepares to give a cup of wine to one of the men.
          A youth holds a lyre by a column, an indication of an indoor
          scene. Baskets hang on the wall.
          Another work by the same painter is figured on the cover and on
          p. 85.
            London, BM E 68.
            The Brygos Painter, *ARV²* 371, nos. 24 and 1649; *Para* 365;
              Boardman, *ARFV* fig. 253; M. Vickers, *Greek Symposia*
              (n.d.) fig. 12.
            First quarter of the fifth century B.C.

P. 114   Detail of rolled-out drawing of an Attic black-figure lekythos
          showing women at work folding clothes, spinning, preparing
          wool and weaving. The lekythos may have been a wedding present
          to a bride.
            New York, MM 31.11.10.
            The Amasis Painter, *ABV* 154, no. 57, and 688; *Para* 64;
              Boardman, *ABFV* fig. 78; Agora Picture Book 12 fig. 17.
            Mid sixth century B.C.

P. 123   The side reliefs of a marble altar frame (?), the so-called Ludovisi
          Throne. A contrast is made between the veiled woman at the
          incense-burner and the naked flute-girl. The purpose, meaning and
          place of manufacture are all in doubt.
            Rome, Museo Nazionale Romano 8670.
            Second quarter of the fifth century B.C.

P. 128   Detail of an Attic red-figure onos (used in wool-working) showing
          preparations for the wedding of Alkestis (on the right). She is
          pictured at the entrance to her bridal chamber, and her friends fill
          a loutrophoros with myrtle (centre) and lebetes gamikoi with
          sprigs (left), both types of vase connected with the wedding
          ceremony. Two other friends play with a pet bird. The object may
          have been a wedding present to a bride.
            Athens, NM 1629.
            The Eretria Painter, *ARV²* 1250–1, no. 34, and 1688; *Para*
              469.
            Third quarter of the fifth century B.C.

P. 130   Detail of an Apulian red-figure loutrophoros showing Alkestis
          surrounded by her children and with her husband Admetos on the

P. 130   left. The white-haired woman on the right may be Admetus' mother or a nurse; the old man is the children's tutor (*paidagogos*). This is one of the finest of the South Italian treatments of tragic themes.
Basel, Antikenmuseum Loan s 21.
A. D. Trendall and A. Cambitoglou, *The Red-figured Vases of Apulia ii* (1982), ch. 18, no. 16.
Mid fourth century B.C.

P. 132   Drawing of one side of an Attic red-figure cup showing a brawl amongst revellers.
Another work by the same painter is figured on p. 73, *l* and on p. 87, *l*.
Leningrad, State Hermitage 651.
Onesimos, *ARV*² 325, no. 77; *Para* 511; Vickers, *Greek Symposia* fig. 21.
First quarter of the fifth century B.C.

P. 142, *l*   A bronze hydria with siren attachment at the lower end of the vertical handle, a popular motif.
Cambridge, Mass., Fogg Museum 1949.89.
E. Diehl, *Die Hydria* (1964) 219, B 147.
Third quarter of the fifth century B.C.

P. 142, *r*   Detail of an Attic red-figure pelike showing a young man carrying a couch and a small table in preparation for a party.
Oxford, Ashmolean Museum 282.
The Pan Painter, *ARV*² 555, no. 87; *Para* 388; Vickers, *Greek Symposia* fig. 5.
First quarter of the fifth century B.C.

P. 142, *b*   Drawn reconstruction of a country house near Vari in Attica.
See *ABSA* 68 (1973) 355–452 and pls. 63–86.

P. 146   Side B of an Attic red-figure skyphos showing a rare 'still-life' scene of household equipment: lampstand and buckets, casserole and grill, and chest, basket, wine jar and jug.
Malibu, The J. Paul Getty Museum, Bareiss Collection
Agora Picture Book 12 fig. 12.
Third quarter of the fifth century B.C.

P. 150   Detail of an Attic red-figure calyx-krater showing Prometheus and satyrs. He is giving them the gift of fire which they take with their torches from Prometheus' fennel stalk (*narthex*). Prometheus' name is written by him, and the satyrs are named Komos, Sikinnis and

Simos. The inspiration for the scene (and others like it) may have come from Aeschylus' satyr-play *Prometheus Pyrkaios*.
Oxford, Ashmolean Museum 1937.983.
The Dinos Painter, *ARV²* 1153, no. 13; *Para* 457.
Last quarter of the fifth century B.C.

P. 153   Side B of an Attic black-figure ovoid neck-amphora showing Zeus enthroned on the left sending Hermes on a mission. Hermes is dressed in his winged boots and his travelling hat and holds his caduceus.
Oxford, Ashmolean Museum 509.
The Affecter, *ABV* 239, no. 5; *Para* 110; Boardman, *ABFV* fig. 155.
Third quarter of the sixth century B.C.

P. 154   Side A of an Attic red-figure amphora showing Croesus seated on his funeral pyre. His royal status is shown by his throne and sceptre. He pours a libation from a dish (*phiale*) whilst Euthymos (his name is written by him) sets fire to the timber.
Paris, Louvre G 197.
Myson, *ARV²* 238, no. 1, and 1638; *Para* 349; Boardman, *ARFV* fig. 171.
C. 500 B.C.

P. 157   Map of Greece and Asia Minor showing Mysian Olympos, the site of the boar hunt in which Croesus' son is killed.

P. 163   Attic red-figure dinos showing a boar hunt. This may be a version of the Calydonian boar hunt, for although Atalante is not present and none of the participants is named, one hunter wields a battle-axe which comes to be associated with Ankaios.
Athens, NM 1489.
The Agrigento Painter, *ARV²* 577, no. 52.
Second quarter of the fifth century B.C.

P. 166   Side A of an Attic red-figure neck-amphora showing Odysseus appearing from behind a tree on which Nausikaa and her companions have spread the washing. He holds a branch in each hand and looks suitably dishevelled. Athene stands between him and Nausikaa who looks back as she runs away with her companions.
Munich 2322.
The Nausikaa Painter, *ARV²* 1107, no. 2, and 1683; *Para* 452.
Third quarter of the fifth century B.C.

P. 169   Side A of an Attic red-figure stamnos showing Odysseus and the sirens. Odysseus is tied to the mast, and his companions' ears are presumably stopped with wax, as the singing sirens are having no effect. In mortification one of the sirens is falling to her death from her perching place on the rocks.
London, BM E 440.
The Siren Painter, *ARV*² 289, no. 1, and 1642; *Para* 355; Boardman, *ARFV* fig. 184; Morrison and Williams, *Greek Oared Ships* 114, Arch. 94.
First quarter of the fifth century B.C.

P. 171   Detail of an Attic black-figure oinokhoe showing two youths and a man in a cart drawn by mules.
London, BM B 485.
The Burgon Group, *ABV* 90, no. 4.
Second quarter of the sixth century B.C.

P. 175   Lid of an Attic red-figure pyxis showing Odysseus appearing before Nausikaa and her companions with Athene to assist.
Boston, MFA 04.18.
Aison, *ARV*² 1177, no. 48; *Para* 460.
Last quarter of the fifth century B.C.

P. 177, *l*   Attic red-figure lekythos showing Artemis with bow and libation dish (phiale); a fawn makes allusion to her domain.
Basel, Market (Münzen und Medaillen).
Auktion 40 (13.12.1969) no. 99.
Second quarter of the fifth century B.C.

P. 177, *r*   Attic red-figure lekythos showing Apollo dressed in a concert performer's robes and holding a kithara in his left hand and a plectrum in his right. The palm tree makes allusion to Delos, his birthplace.
New York, MM 53.224.
The Nikon Painter, *ARV*² 651, no. 26.
Second quarter of the fifth century B.C.

Reading Greek, Grammar

Cover   Detail of side A of an Attic red-figure amphora of Panathenaic shape showing Athene with stylus and tablet acting as scorer in the Panathenaic Games. Side B shows an acontist.

Another work by the same painter is figured on *Text* p. 11 r.
Munich 2314.
The Triptolemos Painter, *ARV*² 362, no. 14, and 1648; *Para*
364; Boardman, *ARFV* fig. 307.
Second quarter of the fifth century B.C.

Greek Vocabulary

Cover Detail of side A of an Attic red-figure cup showing a school. The
teacher holds up a scroll for the boy to practise his recitation; the
lines are most likely from some lost epic poem, 'O Muse, I start
to sing of wide-flowing Scamander...' The setting of the lines
from edge to edge of the scroll should not be thought to be usual;
it is for the convenience of the vase-painter. Lines were normally
set parallel to the edges of the roll, and when one set of lines had
been read, the roll could be advanced to the next set.
Berlin F 2285.
Douris, *ARV*² 431, no. 48, and 1653; *Para* 374; Boardman,
ARFV fig. 289.
First quarter of the fifth century B.C.

Teachers' Notes to Reading Greek

Cover Side B of an Attic red-figure cup showing a bearded man with
hand to head seated facing a young boy.
Paris, Louvre G 448.
The Penthesilea Painter, *ARV*² 880, no. 5.
Second quarter of the fifth century B.C.

B. A. Sparkes

NOTES ON ATTIC VASES AND
VASE-PAINTERS

Painters

The individual identities of vase-painters have been differentiated by their styles of drawing. This being so, their real names are for the most part unimportant, provided that they are distinctive.

The actual names of some vase-painters are known, as they appear in the background of one or more of the scenes they painted (e.g. 'Douris painted'). In the case of the illustrations which accompany *Text*, painters such as Aison (p. 175), Apollodoros (p. 51), Douris (cover of *GV*), Makron (p. 87, *r*), Myson (p. 154) and Psiax (p. 14) are in this category. Not all the preserved names are proper names; contrast the name Apollodoros with those which seem to be nicknames, e.g. Epiktetos = 'newly acquired' (p. 91) and Onesimos = 'profitable' (pp. 73, *l*, 87, *l* and 132) or with Skythes = 'the Skythian' (p. 17), all perhaps indicating foreign origin and slave status.

Some painters were also potters; for instance, only one signed vase by Myson survives, but it shows him to have been both potter and painter (see Boardman, *ARFV* fig. 168). In some cases, in order to name a painter whose name has not survived, modern scholars have borrowed the known name of a potter (e.g. 'Amasis made me') and used it as the basis of a painter's name with whom he worked, e.g. the Amasis Painter (p. 114), the Brygos Painter (cover of *Text*, and pp. 85 and 110) and the Kleophrades Painter (p. 8, *l* and *r*). In these instances Amasis, Brygos and Kleophrades were the potters who fashioned some of the vases painted by the artists now linked to them by name. Again the names Amasis and Brygos suggest foreign connections, with Egypt and with Thrace. Some scholars believe that the potters' names were more likely those of the owners of pottery shops and not the actual makers of the vases.

The vast majority of vases carry no signature of either potter or painter, and so modern names of convenience have been invented. Many of them take their origin from the subject on one or more of the vases they painted. The name-vases of the Nausicaa Painter and of the Siren Painter are illustrated on pp. 166 and 169. Other names that belong to this category and are mentioned in the notes are the Amphitrite Painter (p. 95), the Foundry Painter (p. 74, *r*), the Hector Painter (p. 54), the Pan Painter (p. 142, *r*), the Peleus Painter (p. 54), the Penthesilea Painter (p. 67) and the Triptolemos Painter (p. 11, *r* and cover of *GVE*). Sometimes the *kalos*-name painted in the background of some scenes (see notes to p. 67) provides the distinctive name, e.g. the Antiphon Painter (pp. 70, *l* and 93), the Euaion Painter (p. 28, *l*), the Kleophon Painter (pp. 44 and 68), the Nikon Painter (p. 177, *r*) and the Oionokles Painter (p. 6, *l*). Other methods of naming used are by the finding-place of one or more of the vases: for instance, the onos illustrated on p. 128 was found at Eretria on the island of Euboia, and the painter is called the Eretria Painter for that reason; or by the city or town in which one or more of the vases is now to be found, e.g. the Agrigento Painter (p. 163), the Berlin Painter (p. 21), the Chicago Painter (p. 28, *r*) and the Goettingen Painter (p. 70, *r*). Occasionally one of the shapes a painter decorated gives him his name, e.g. the Dinos Painter (p. 150), and there is one instance among the painters represented in *Text* for whom the city and a shape are both used: the Painter of the Munich Amphora (p. 39, *r*, the name-vase). In rare instances the style of the painter provides the soubriquet, e.g. the Affecter (p. 153).

It will be noted that some references are not to the painters themselves, but to various types of association with them, e.g. 'near' (p. 70, *r*), 'manner of' (p. 93), 'follower of' (p. 11, *l*), 'bad imitation of' (p. 28, *r*). Also the word 'group' as in 'the Burgon Group' (p. 171) indicates vases that are closely connected in style but cannot be said to be by one hand.

Naturally there are many vases which have not yet been attached to already differentiated artistic personalities or joined with others to form the nucleus of a painter's work; examples in *Text* are on pp. 6, *r*, 25, 107, 146 and 177, *l*.

The same stylistic grouping of painters has been adopted for vases painted in South Italy and Sicily, as indeed for other areas of Greece itself. The Alkestis scene on p. 130 is an example of a vase painted in Apulia, but no other vases have been recognized as from the same hand.

Techniques

The names for the two techniques of 'black-figure' and 'red-figure' are for the most part self-explanatory, but it must be remembered that they are not precisely parallel terms: 'black-figure' indicates that the figures are silhouetted in black paint on the orange-red background of the clay, with the addition of incision and usually some added colour, whereas 'red-figure' means that the figures are reserved, i.e. left unpainted, on the orange-red ground of the clay, with the background of the painting filled with black.

Shapes

Many of the illustrations in *Text* show details only, not the shape they decorate. However, in every case the composition is arranged over, and often dictated by, the curved surface of the vase. The following list gives some basic information about shapes mentioned in the notes. The ancient names which are used by convention do not always fit the ancient usage. The drawings below are all of Attic shapes. The order of the list follows that to be found in *ABV* pp. xi–xii and *ARV*² pp. xlix–li.

amphora

Mainly used as a wine-decanter. A complete shape is shown on *Text* p. 154. There are also other varieties of shape to which modern terminology has given distinctive names, such as the Panathenaic shape from its similarity to those vases given as prizes in the Panathenaic Games, the neck-amphora with an angle of junction of neck and body, and the small Nolan amphora that takes its defining adjective from the fact that many were found at the site of Nola in South Italy.

loutrophoros

An elongated amphora shape used at weddings and at the funerals of girls who died unmarried. The Apulian shape (*Text* p. 130) is even more elaborate than the Attic.

pelike

Mainly a container for oil, with sagging pear-shaped body.

stamnos

Used as a mixing bowl for wine. A complete shape, apart from the missing lid, is shown on *Text* p. 169.

dinos

Used as a mixing bowl for wine and usually provided with a stand. A complete shape is shown on *Text* p. 163. It was also used as an ash urn for the dead. Its more likely name in ancient Greek was lebes.

volute-krater

One of the large mixing bowls with wide mouth used for mixing wine. It is named from the two rolled handles that curve above the rim.

calyx-krater

Another shape of mixing bowl, named from the resemblance of its body to the calyx of a flower.

hydria

A water jar with two side-handles for lifting and a vertical handle at the back for dipping and carrying when empty. A complete shape in bronze is shown on *Text* p. 142, *l.*

oinokhoe

There are a great many shapes of 'wine jug' under this general heading. One distinctive name, khous, is attached to a jug with squat body and trefoil mouth because of its connection with festivities at the Anthesteria.

lekythos

An oil and perfume flask produced in a variety of shapes. Two examples of a complete shape are shown on *Text* p. 177.

onos

A thigh-cover used during the preparation of wool. A more likely name in ancient Greek is epinetron. It was often given as a wedding present.

pyxis

A round, lidded trinket- or powder-box. The illustration on *Text* p. 175 shows a view down on the top of the lid.

kantharos

A deep-bodied cup with two high vertical handles, often put in the hands of Dionysos. Occasionally a one-handled version was produced (*Text* p. 25).

skyphos

A deep cup with two horizontal handles near the rim. It was one of the commonest shapes of drinking cup. A complete shape is shown on *Text* p. 146.

cup

The stemmed cup, often given the name of kylix, was one of the most elegant shapes of drinking cup, with narrow stem, broad, shallow bowl and two horizontal handles. A complete shape, tilted on its side, is shown on *Text* p. xvi.

plate

Not a common shape with black- or red-figure decoration, as it was usual to produce plates in wood.

plaque
(see *Text* p. 107)

A flat, square or rectangular shape, sometimes with moulded edges and pedimental top. Some were dedicated in sanctuaries (see *Text* p. 107).

As with painters, so with potters it is possible to attribute work to one hand or another; modern terminology makes a distinction between words used for painters and those used for potters: 'class' is used when close similarities can be discerned in a number of examples of a shape and corresponds to 'group' used in painting – compare, for instance, 'the Keyside Class' (*Text* p. 6, r) and 'the Burgon Group' (*Text* p. 171).

B. A. Sparkes

EXAMINATION PAPERS

Here are three comprehensive examinations set for candidates who have used *RG* and its associated volumes. Papers A and B were set for university students after using *RG* for one year, three to four hours a week for *c.* twenty-two weeks. Paper C is a public examination of the Oxford and Cambridge Schools' Examination Board G.C.E. Alternative 'O'-level (set in June 1981), for sixth-formers who had studied Greek for two years, using *RG* in year 1 and studying the set texts (the 'target' passages from *WoH* Herodotus and Sophocles selections) in year 2.

Note: The numbers in brackets (where given) refer to the marks allotted to each part of the paper.

Discussion

All the papers, in their different ways, attempt to cater for a wide range of abilities, and demand a grasp of the language with an understanding of the culture which produced it.

All the papers offer liberal help with vocabulary for the unseens (sight passages); and the Alternative 'O'-level paper offers it with the set texts as well (an important concession when the set texts are as sophisticated as these are; when the students' time must be limited, since Greek will only be a minority subject for them in the sixth form; and when we want to *dis*courage memorization of the translation, and encourage mature appraisal of the text).

Both papers A and C have experimented very successfully with an unseen in which the passages to be translated are intercut with passages translated already. This gives a much larger context, and duplicates more faithfully the conditions of class-work (where one's classmates translate sections as well: one does not do it all oneself).

Paper A attempts to offer something for the linguistically weak and strong:
A1 (set text) gives the lifeline to the weak (120/200 for knowing what *Neaira*
is all about, and fairly mild grammatical questions + short unseen): A2 gives
the linguistically strong the chance to show what they can do (80/200).
For full details of Paper C, the Oxford and Cambridge Schools' Examination Board JACT Greek 'AO' paper, write to: The Secretary, Oxford and
Cambridge Schools' Examination Board, Elsfield Way, Oxford OX2 8EP.

PAPER A1 (worth 120/200)

Time allowed – 3 *hours*

SET TEXT – NEAIRA (*Reading Greek* 11–13) with
UNSEEN TRANSLATION

A. Translate into English:

> ἡ γὰρ Νέαιρα πρῶτον μὲν δούλη ἐν Κορίνθῳ ἦν Νικαρέτης, ὑφ᾽
> ἧς ἐτρέφετο παῖς μικρὰ οὖσα. καὶ τόδε φανερὸν καὶ βέβαιον
> τεκμήριόν ἐστι τούτου· ἦν γὰρ δὴ ἑτέρα δούλη Νικαρέτης,
> Μετάνειρα ὀνόματι, ἧς ἐραστὴς ὢν Λυσίας ὁ σοφιστὴς πολλὰς
> 5 δραχμὰς ἔθηκεν ὑπὲρ αὐτῆς. ἀλλ᾽ ἐπειδὴ ὑπὸ Νικαρέτης ἐλήφθησαν
> πᾶσαι αἱ δραχμαὶ ἃς ἔθηκεν, ἔδοξεν αὐτῷ μυῆσαι αὐτὴν καὶ πολλὰ
> χρήματα καταθεῖναι εἴς τε τὴν ἑορτὴν καὶ τὰ μυστήρια, βουλομένῳ
> ὑπὲρ Μετανείρας καὶ οὐχ ὑπὲρ Νικαρέτης τιθέναι τὰ χρήματα. καὶ
> ἐπείσθη Νικαρέτη ἐλθεῖν εἰς τὰ μυστήρια, ἄγουσα τὴν Μετάνειραν.
> 10 ἀφικομένας δὲ αὐτὰς ὁ Λυσίας εἰς μὲν τὴν αὐτοῦ οἰκίαν οὐκ εἰσάγει
> (ᾐσχύνετο γὰρ τὴν γυναῖκα ἣν εἶχε καὶ τὴν μητέρα τὴν αὐτοῦ, ἣ
> γραῦς οὖσα ἐν τῇ οἰκίᾳ συνῴκει). καθίστησι δ᾽ αὐτὰς ὁ Λυσίας ὡς
> Φιλόστρατον, ἤθεον ἔτι ὄντα καὶ φίλον αὐτῷ.

(*Neaira* 11) (10/120)

B. *Do not translate*, but answer the appended questions:

> τί δὲ καὶ φήσειεν ἂν ὑμῶν ἕκαστος, εἰσιὼν πρὸς τὴν αὑτοῦ γυναῖκα
> ἢ παῖδα κόρην ἢ μητέρα, ἀποψηφισάμενος Νεαίρας; ἐπειδὰν γάρ τις
> ἔρηται ὑμᾶς 'ποῦ ἦτε;' καὶ εἴπητε ὅτι 'ἐδικάζομεν', ἐρήσεταί τις
> εὐθὺς 'τίνι ἐδικάζετε;' ὑμεῖς δὲ φήσετε 'Νεαίρᾳ' (οὐ γάρ;) 'ὅτι ξένη
> 5 οὖσα ἀστῷ συνοικεῖ παρὰ τὸν νόμον καὶ ὅτι τὴν θυγατέρα ἐξέδωκε
> Θεογένει τῷ βασιλεύσαντι καὶ αὕτη ἔθυε τὰ ἱερὰ τὰ ἄρρητα ὑπὲρ
> τῆς πόλεως καὶ τῷ Διονύσῳ γυνὴ ἐδόθη.' (καὶ τὰ ἄλλα περὶ τῆς
> κατηγορίας διηγήσεσθε, ὡς εὖ καὶ ἐπιμελῶς καὶ μνημονικῶς περὶ
> ἑκάστου κατηγορήθη.) αἱ δέ, ἀκούσασαι, ἐρήσονται 'τί οὖν
> 10 ἐποιήσατε;' ὑμεῖς δὲ φήσετε 'ἀπεψηφισάμεθα'. οὔκουν ἤδη αἱ
> σωφρονέσταται τῶν γυναικῶν, ἐπειδὰν πύθωνται, ὀργισθήσονται
> ὑμῖν διότι ὁμοίως αὐταῖς κατηξίουτε Νέαιραν μετέχειν τῶν τῆς

πόλεως καὶ τῶν ἱερῶν; καὶ δὴ καὶ ταῖς ἀνοήτοις γυναιξὶ δόξετε
ἄδειαν διδόναι ποιεῖν ὅ τι ἂν βούλωνται. δόξετε γὰρ ὀλίγωροι εἶναι
15 καὶ αὐτοὶ ὁμογνώμονες τοῖς Νεαίρας τρόποις.

(*Neaira* 13)

1. From what verbs, with what meanings, do the following words come:
   ἀποψηφισάμενος (l. 2); φήσετε (l. 4); ἐδόθη (l. 7); πύθωνται (l. 11); δόξετε
   (l. 14)? (10)
2. Give examples from this passage of 2 aorist subjunctives; 2 future indicatives; and 2 aorist passive indicatives. (6)
3. Why is βουλῶνται (l. 14) subjunctive? Quote two other examples of this
   construction from the text. (4)
4. Explain the constructions which account for the following forms:
   μετέχειν (l. 12); διδόναι (l. 14); φήσειεν (l. 1); ἔρηται (l. 3)   (8)
5. (a) What charges does Apollodoros think the dikasts will relay back to
       their relations at home? (3)
   (b) Why does Apollodoros think wives will be angry if Neaira is
       acquitted? (3)
   (c) What does Apollodoros think will be the effect on foolish women? (3)
   (d) How effective is this passage as oratory? (3)   (40/120)

C. *Do not translate* (except where asked), but answer the appended questions:

καὶ δὴ καὶ ἄλλο τεκμήριον βούλομαι ὑμῖν ἐπιδεῖξαι ὅτι ξένη ἐστὶ
Νέαιρα αὑτηί. ὁ γὰρ Φράστωρ, ἐν τῇ ἀσθενείᾳ ὤν, εἰσήγαγε τὸν
Φανοῦς παῖδα εἰς τοὺς φράτερας καὶ τοὺς Βρυτίδας, ὧν Φράστωρ
ἐστὶ γεννήτης. ἀλλὰ οἱ γεννῆται, εἰδότες τὴν γυναῖκα θυγατέρα
5 Νεαίρας οὖσαν, καὶ ἀκούσαντες Φράστορα αὐτὴν ἀποπέμψαντα,
ἔπειτα διὰ τὸ ἀσθενεῖν ἀναλαβεῖν τὸ παιδίον, ἀποψηφίζονται τοῦ
παιδὸς καὶ οὐκ ἐνέγραφον αὐτὸν εἰς τὸ γένος. ἀλλ' εἰ ἀστῆς
θυγάτηρ ἦν Φανώ, οὐκ ἂν ἀπεψηφίσαντο τοῦ παιδὸς οἱ γεννῆται,
ἀλλ' ἐνέγραψαν ἂν εἰς τὸ γένος. λαχόντος οὖν τοῦ Φράστορος
10 αὐτοῖς δίκην, προκαλοῦνται αὐτὸν οἱ γεννῆται ὀμόσαι καθ' ἱερῶν
τελείων ἦ μὴν νομίζειν τὸν παῖδα εἶναι αὐτοῦ υἱὸν ἐξ ἀστῆς
γυναικὸς καὶ ἐγγυητῆς κατὰ τὸν νόμον. προκαλουμένων δ' αὐτὸν
τῶν γεννητῶν, ἔλιπεν ὁ Φράστωρ τὸν ὅρκον καὶ ἀπῆλθε πρὶν
ὀμόσαι τὸν παῖδα γνήσιον εἶναι. ἀλλ' εἰ ὁ παῖς γνήσιος ἦν καὶ ἐξ
15 ἀστῆς γυναικός, ὤμοσεν ἄν.

(*Neaira* 12)

1. From what verbs, with what meanings, do the following words come:
   ἐπιδεῖξαι (l. 1); εἰδότες (l. 4); λαχόντος (l. 9); ὀμόσαι (l. 10); ἀπῆλθε
   (l. 13)? (10)

2. Explain the construction ἀλλ᾽ εἰ...ἄν (ll. 14–15). Find another example in this passage. (4)
3. Translate: διὰ τὸ ἀσθενεῖν (l. 6); πρὶν ὁμόσαι (ll. 13–14); λαχόντος οὖν τοῦ Φράστορος αὐτοῖς δίκην (ll. 9–10); ἦ μὴν νομίζειν (l.11). (6)
4. What is the argument of this passage, and what is its background? (10)
(30/120)

D. Answer one of the following questions in *not more than 2 sides*:

1. Do you think Stephanos and Neaira stood any chance of acquittal?
2. What light does *Neaira* cast upon fourth-century Greek women?
3. Discuss the relevance of the Theogenes incident to Apollodoros' case
(20/120)

E. UNSEEN TRANSLATION

Translate the passages between the double lines into English:

The orator Hyperides is defending Euxenippos on an impeachment. Hyperides begins by remembering how serious such charges used to be and comparing them with the current absurd charges which are brought under that heading. He goes on to wonder what crimes should truly merit an impeachment.

'Αλλ᾽ ἔγωγε, ὦ ἄνδρες δικασταί, ὅπερ καὶ πρὸς τοὺς παρακαθημένους ἀρτίως ἔλεγον, θαυμάζω εἰ μὴ προσίστανται ἤδη ὑμῖν αἱ τοιαῦται εἰσαγγελίαι. τὸ μὲν γὰρ πρότερον εἰσηγγέλλοντο παρ᾽ ὑμῖν Τιμόμαχος καὶ Λεωσθένης καὶ Καλλίστρατος καὶ Φίλων ὁ ἐξ 'Αναίων καὶ Θεότιμος ὁ Σηστὸν ἀπολέσας καὶ ἕτεροι τοιοῦτοι· καὶ οἱ μὲν αὐτῶν ναῦς αἰτίαν ἔχοντες προδοῦναι, οἱ δὲ πόλεις 'Αθηναίων, ὁ δὲ ῥήτωρ ὢν λέγειν μὴ τὰ ἄριστα τῷ δήμῳ. καὶ οὔτε τούτων τῶν πέντε ὄντων οὐδεὶς ὑπέμεινε τὸν ἀγῶνα, ἀλλ᾽ αὐτοὶ ᾤχοντο φεύγοντες ἐκ τῆς πόλεως, οὔτ᾽ ἄλλοι πολλοὶ τῶν εἰσαγγελλομένων, ἀλλ᾽ ἦν σπάνιον ἰδεῖν ἀπ᾽ εἰσαγγελίας τινὰ κρινόμενον ὑπακούσαντα εἰς τὸ δικαστήριον· οὕτως ὑπὲρ μεγάλων ἀδικημάτων καὶ περιφανῶν αἱ εἰσαγγελίαι τότε ἦσαν.

Personally, gentlemen of the jury, as I was just saying to those seated beside me, I am surprised that you are not tired by now of this kind of impeachment. At one time the men impeached before you were Timomachus, Leosthenes, Callistratus, Philon of Anaea, Theotimus who lost Sestos, and others of the same type. Some were accused of betraying ships, others of giving up Athenian cities, and another, an orator, of speaking against the people's interests. Though there were five of them, not one waited to be tried; they left the city of their own accord and went into exile. The same is true of many others who were impeached. In fact it was a rare thing to see anyone subjected to impeachment appearing in court. So serious and so notorious were the crimes which at that time led to an impeachment.

νυνὶ δὲ τὸ γιγνόμενον ἐν τῇ πόλει πάνυ
καταγέλαστόν ἐστιν. Διογνίδης μὲν καὶ
'Αντίδωρος ὁ μέτοικος εἰσαγγέλλονται
ὡς πλέονος μισθοῦντες τὰς αὐλητρίδας
ἢ ὁ νόμος κελεύει, 'Αγασικλῆς δ' ὁ ἐκ
Πειραιέως ὅτι εἰς 'Αλιμουσίους ἐνε-
γρά[φη] Εὐξένιππος δ' [ὑπ]ὲρ τῶν
ἐνυπνί[ων] ὧν φησιν ἑω[ρακέ]ναι· ὧν
οὐδεμ[ία] δήπου τῶν αἰτιῶν τούτων
οὐδὲν κοινωνεῖ τῷ εἰσαγγελτικῷ νόμῳ.

καταγέλαστος laughable
πλέονος μισθόω hire at a greater price
αὐλητρίς flute-girl
'Αλιμούσιος the deme Halimos
ἐνύπνιον dream
οὐδὲν κοινωνέω have no relevance to

οὔτε πλείους οἶμαι δεῖν λόγους ποιεῖσθαι περὶ ἄλλου τινὸς ἢ ὅπως ἐν
δημοκρατίᾳ κύριοι οἱ νόμοι ἔσονται,
καὶ αἱ εἰσαγγελίαι καὶ αἱ ἄλλαι κρίσεις
κατὰ τοὺς νόμους εἰσίασιν εἰς τὸ
δικαστήριον. διὰ τοῦτο γὰρ ὑμεῖς ὑπὲρ
ἁπάντων τῶν ἀδικημάτων, ὅσα ἔστιν
ἐν τῇ πόλει, νόμους ἔθεσθε χωρὶς περὶ
ἑκάστου αὐτῶν. ἀσεβεῖ τις περὶ τὰ
ἱερά· γραφαὶ ἀσεβείας πρὸς τὸν
βασιλέα. —φαῦλός ἐστι πρὸς τοὺς
ἑαυτοῦ γονεῖς· ὁ ἄρχων ἐπὶ τούτου
κάθηται. —παράνομά τις ἐν τῇ πόλει
γράφει· θεσμοθετῶν συνέδριον ἐστι.—
ἀπαγωγῆς ἄξια ποιεῖ· ἀρχὴ τῶν
ἕνδεκα καθέστηκε. —τὸν αὐτὸν δὲ
τρόπον καὶ ἐπὶ τῶν ἄλλων ἀδικημάτων
ἁπάντων καὶ νόμους καὶ ἀρχὰς καὶ
δικαστήρια τὰ προσήκοντα ἑκάστοις
αὐτῶν ἀπέδοτε.

and a point, I think, which should be dwelt
on as much as any, is how to ensure that
the laws in a democracy are binding and
that impeachments and other actions
brought into court are legally valid. It was
with this in view that you made separate
laws covering individually all offences
committed in the city. Suppose someone
commits a religious offence. There is the
method of public prosecution before the
King-Archon. Or he maltreats his parents.
The Archon presides over his case. Someone makes illegal proposals in the city.
There is the board of Thesmothetae ready.
Perhaps he does something involving
summary arrest. You have the authority
of the Eleven. Similarly, to deal with every
other offence you have established laws,
offices, and courts appropriate to each.

ὑπὲρ τίνων οὖν οἴεσθε δεῖν τὰς εἰσαγγελίας γίγνεσθαι; τοῦτ' ἤδη καθ'
ἕκαστον ἐν τῷ νόμῳ ἐγράψατε, ἵνα μὴ
ἀγνοῇ μηδείς· 'ἐάν τις,' φησί, 'τὸν
δῆμον τὸν 'Αθηναίων καταλύῃ'—
εἰκότως, ὦ ἄνδρες δικασταί· ἡ γὰρ
τοιαύτη αἰτία οὐ παραδέχεται σκῆψι[ν
ο]ὐδεμίαν οὐδενὸς οὐδ' ὑπωμοσίαν,
ἀλλὰ τὴν ταχίστην αὐτὴν δεῖ εἶναι ἐν
τῷ δικαστηρίῳ· —ἢ "συνίῃ ποι ἐπὶ
καταλύσει τοῦ δήμου ἢ ἑταιρικὸν
συναγάγῃ, ἢ ἐάν τις πόλιν τινὰ προδῷ
ἢ ναῦς ἢ πεζὴν ἢ ναυτικὴν στρατιάν, ἢ
ῥήτωρ ὢν μὴ λέγῃ τὰ ἄριστα τῷ δήμῳ
τῷ 'Αθηναίων χρήματα λαμβάνων"·

καθ' ἕκαστον specifically
καταλύω attempt to overthrow, cf.
καταλύσις 1. 18
σκῆψις excuse
ὑπωμοσία postponement
συνίῃ '(if) he is present at a meeting'
ἑταιρικόν political club

PAPER A2 (worth 80/200)

Time allowed – 3 hours

Translate into English. (Candidates are advised to work through the translated passages first, since the underlined words recur in passages to be translated, and you will get some idea of what is going on.)

A. Apollodoros describes the difficult situation Athens and its allies were in, and how he took pains to select the very best crew and equipment for his ship.

ὧν ἀκούοντες ὑμεῖς τότε ἐν τῷ δήμῳ αὐτῶν τε λεγόντων καὶ τῶν συναγορευόντων αὐτοῖς, ἔτι δὲ τῶν ἐμπόρων καὶ τῶν ναυκλήρων περὶ ἔκπλουν ὄντων ἐκ τοῦ Πόντου, καὶ Βυζαντίων καὶ Καλχηδονίων καὶ Κυζικηνῶν καταγόντων τὰ πλοῖα ἕνεκα τῆς <u>ἰδίας</u> χρείας <u>τοῦ σίτου</u>, καὶ ὁρῶντες ἐν τῷ Πειραιεῖ τὸν σῖτον ἐπιτιμώμενον καὶ οὐκ ὄντα ἄφθονον ὠνεῖσθαι, ἐψηφίσασθε τάς τε ναῦς <u>καθέλκειν</u> τοὺς <u>τριηράρχους</u> καὶ παρακομίζειν ἐπὶ τὸ χῶμα, καὶ τοὺς βουλευτὰς καὶ τοὺς δημάρχους καταλόγους ποιεῖσθαι τῶν δημοτῶν καὶ ἀποφέρειν ναύτας, καὶ διὰ <u>τάχους</u> τὸν ἀπόστολον ποιεῖσθαι καὶ βοηθεῖν ἑκασταχοῖ. καὶ ἐνίκησε τὸ Ἀριστοφῶντος ψήφισμα τουτί·

ΨΗΦΙΣΜΑ

When you heard all these tidings at that time in the assembly from both the speakers themselves and those who supported them; when furthermore the merchants and shipowners were about to sail out of the Pontus, and the Byzantines and Chalcedonians and Cyzicenes were forcing their ships to put in to their ports because of the scarcity of grain in their own countries; seeing also that the price of grain was advancing in the Peiraeus, and that there was not very much to be bought, you voted that the trierarchs should launch their ships and bring them up to the pier, and that the members of the senate and the demarchs should make out lists of the demesmen and reports of available seamen, and that the armament should be despatched at once, and aid sent to the various regions. And this decree, proposed by Aristophon, was passed, as follows:

THE DECREE

Τοῦ μὲν ψηφίσματος τοίνυν ἀκηκόατε, ὦ ἄνδρες δικασταί. ἐγὼ δ' ἐπειδή μοι οὐκ ἦλθον οἱ ναῦται οἱ καταλεγέντες ὑπὸ τῶν δημοτῶν, ἀλλ' ἢ ὀλίγοι καὶ οὗτοι ἀδύνατοι, τούτους μὲν ἀφῆκα, ὑποθεὶς δὲ τὴν οὐσίαν τὴν ἐμαυτοῦ καὶ δανεισάμενος ἀργύριον, πρῶτος ἐπληρωσάμην τὴν ναῦν, μισθωσάμενος ναύτας ὡς οἷόν τ' ἦν ἀρίστους, δωρειὰς καὶ προδόσεις δοὺς ἑκάστῳ αὐτῶν μεγάλας. ἔτι δὲ σκεύεσιν ἰδίοις τὴν

καταλεγείς selected
δημοτής demesman
ἀλλ' ἤ except
ἀφίημι (ἀφηκ-) dismiss
ὑποτίθημι (ὑποθε-) mortgage
δανείζομαι borrow
πληρόομαι man, fill
μισθόομαι hire
δωρειά bonus
πρόδοσις advance
κατασκευάζω equip

ναῦν ἅπασι κατεσκεύασα, καὶ τῶν
δημοσίων ἔλαβον οὐδέν, καὶ κόσμῳ ὡς
οἷόν τ᾽ ἦν κάλλιστα καὶ διαπρεπέστατα
τῶν τριηράρχων. ὑπηρεσίαν τοίνυν ἦν
ἐδυνάμην κρατίστην ἐμισθωσάμην.

Καὶ ταῦτα ὅτι ἀληθῆ λέγω πρὸς ὑμᾶς,
τούτων ὑμῖν ἀναγνώσεται τὰς μαρτυ-
ρίας τῶν τε τὰ στρατιωτικὰ τότε
εἰσπραττόντων καὶ τῶν ἀποστολέων,
καὶ τοὺς μισθοὺς οὓς ταῖς ὑπηρεσίαις
καὶ τοῖς ἐπιβάταις κατὰ μῆνα ἐδίδουν,
παρὰ τῶν στρατηγῶν σιτηρέσιον μόνον
λαμβάνων, πλὴν δυοῖν μηνοῖν μόνον
μισθὸν ἐν πέντε μησὶ καὶ ἐνιαυτῷ καὶ
τοὺς ναύτας τοὺς μισθωθέντας, καὶ
ὅσον ἕκαστος ἔλαβεν ἀργύριον, ἵν᾽ ἐκ
τούτων εἰδῆτε τὴν ἐμὴν προθυμίαν, καὶ
οὗτος διότι παραλαβεῖν παρ᾽ ἐμοῦ τὴν
ναῦν οὐκ ἤθελεν, ἐπειδή μοι ὁ χρόνος
ἐξῆλθε τῆς τριηραρχίας.

ΜΑΡΤΥΡΙΑΙ

τὰ δημόσια public stores
διαπρεπής magnificent

To prove that I am stating the truth to you
in this, the clerk shall read you the
depositions covering these matters, those
of the persons who at that time collected
the military supplies and of the despatching
board; also the record of the pay which I
gave out every month to the rowers and
the marines, receiving from the generals
subsistence-money alone, except pay for
two months only in a period of a year and
five months; also a list of the sailors who
were hired, and how much money each of
them received; to the end that from this
evidence you may know how generous I
was and why the defendant was unwilling
to take over the ship from me when the
term of my trierarchy had expired.

THE DEPOSITIONS

B. He goes on to discuss how difficult things become if a ship returns home
in mid-service and claims that, because of the excellence of this ship,
he frequently put in at Peiraieus on different missions.

Ὅτι μὲν τοίνυν οὐ ψεύδομαι πρὸς
ὑμᾶς περὶ ὧν εἶπον, ὦ ἄνδρες δικασταί,
τῶν μαρτυριῶν ἀναγιγνωσκομένων
ἀκηκόατε. ἔτι δὲ περὶ ὧν μέλλω λέγειν,
ἅπαντές μοι ὁμολογήσετε ὅτι ἀληθῆ
ἐστιν. τριήρους γὰρ ὁμολογεῖται κατάλυσις εἶναι, πρῶτον μέν, ἐὰν μὴ
μισθόν τις διδῷ, δεύτερον δέ, ἐὰν εἰς
τὸν Πειραιᾶ μεταξὺ καταπλεύσῃ·
ἀπόλειψίς τε γὰρ πλείστη γίγνεται, οἵ
τε παραμένοντες τῶν ναυτῶν οὐκ
ἐθέλουσι πάλιν ἐμβαίνειν, ἐὰν μή τις
αὐτοῖς ἕτερον ἀργύριον διδῷ, ὥστε τὰ
οἰκεῖα διοικήσασθαι. ἃ ἐμοὶ ἀμφότερα
συνέβη, ὦ ἄνδρες δικασταί, ὥστε
πολυτελεστέραν μοι γενέσθαι τὴν τρι-
ηραρχίαν. καὶ γὰρ μισθὸν οὐδένα
ἔλαβον παρὰ τοῦ στρατηγοῦ ὀκτὼ
μηνῶν, καὶ κατέπλευσα, τοὺς πρέσβεις

ὁμολογέω agree
κατάλυσις break-up, dispersal
μεταξύ in the middle of a voyage
καταλέω sail home
ἀπόλειψις desertion
συμβαίνω (συνέβ) happen
πολυτελής expensive
πρέσβεις ambassadors
προσταχθέν μοι 'since I have been
      ordered'
ἀντί in place of
ἀποχειροτονέω dismiss from office
ἀνάγομαι put to sea

ἄγων διὰ τὸ ἄριστά μοι πλεῖν τὴν
ναῦν, καὶ ἐνθένδε πάλιν, προσταχθέν
μοι ὑπὸ τοῦ δήμου Μένωνα τὸν στρα-
τηγὸν ἄγειν εἰς Ἑλλήσποντον ἀντὶ
Αὐτοκλέους ἀποχειροτονηθέντος, ᾠχόμην ἀναγόμενος διὰ τάχους.

(27/80)

C. After his ship has helped a convoy to Maroneia and Thasos, his admiral
Timomakhos met resistance to an attempted attack on the Maronites –
both from the Maronites and Apollodoros' exhausted crew.

Καὶ ταῦθ᾽ ὑμῖν διὰ ταῦτα ἅπαντα
διηγησάμην ἐξ ἀρχῆς, ἵν᾽ εἰδῆτε ὅσα
ἀνηλωκὼς αὐτὸς καὶ ἡλίκης μοι
γεγενημένης τῆς λῃτουργίας, ὕστερον
ὅσα ἀναλώματα ὑπὲρ τούτου ἐπὶ τὴν
ναῦν, καὶ κινδύνους ὅσους ἐκινδύνευσα
αὐτὸς πρός τε χειμῶνας καὶ πρὸς
πολεμίους.

I have told all these facts to you from the
beginning, that you may know how much
I have myself expended and how burden-
some my service as trierarch has been to
me, and all the expenses which I subsequently bore in the interest of the defendant by serving beyond my term, since he
did not come to take over the ship, and all
the dangers I myself incurred from storms
and from the enemy.

μετὰ γὰρ τὴν παραπομπὴν τῶν πλοίων
τὴν εἰς Μαρώνειαν καὶ τὴν ἄφιξιν τὴν
εἰς Θάσον, ἀφικόμενος πάλιν ὁ Τιμόμαχος μετὰ τῶν Θασίων
εἰς Στρύμην σῖτον καὶ πελταστάς, ὡς
παραληψόμενος αὐτὸς τὸ χωρίον. παρα-
ταξαμένων δὲ Μαρωνιτῶν ἡμῖν ταῖς
ναυσὶν ὑπὲρ τοῦ χωρίου τούτου καὶ
μελλόντων ναυμαχήσειν, καὶ τῶν στρατιωτῶν ἀπειρηκότων, πλοῦν πολὺν
πεπλευκότων καὶ πλοῖα ἑλκόντων ἐκ
Θάσου εἰς Στρύμην, ἔτι δὲ χειμῶνος
ὄντος καὶ τοῦ χωρίου ἀλιμένου, καὶ
ἐκβῆναι οὐκ ὂν οὐδὲ δειπνοποιήσασ-
θαι, πολεμίας τῆς χώρας οὔσης καὶ
περικαθημένων κύκλῳ τὸ τεῖχος καὶ
ξένων μισθοφόρων καὶ βαρβάρων προσ-
οίκων, ἀναγκαῖον ἦν ἐπ᾽ ἀγκύρας
ἀποσαλεύειν τὴν νύκτα μετεώρους,
ἀσίτους καὶ ἀγρύπνους, φυλαττομένους
μὴ τῆς νυκτὸς ἡμῖν ἐπιθῶνται αἱ
Μαρωνιτῶν τριήρεις.

παραπομπή conveying: cf. παραπέμπω
  convey
πελτασταί peltasts
παραλαμβάνω (fut. παραληψ-) capture
παρατάττω (+ dat.) draw up against
στρατιωτῶν i.e. our own sailors
ἀπειρηκώς refusing
ἀλίμενος harbourless
ὄν 'it being possible'
περικάθημαι be encamped around
μισθοφόρος hired
πρόσοικος neighbouring
ἐπ᾽ ἀγκύρας at anchor
ἀποσαλεύω ride
μετέωρος at sea
ἄγρυπνος unsleeping
ἐπιτίθεμαι (ἐπιθε-) + dat. attack

(25/80)

PAPER B (worth 100/100)

Time allowed – 3 *hours*

1. Translate into English: [unseen]

Dionysodorus, who is under sentence of death, sends for his wife and puts his affairs in order.

καὶ δὴ καὶ Διονυσόδωρος μεταπέμπεται τὴν ἀδελφὴν τὴν ἐμὴν εἰς τὸ δεσμωτήριον, γυναῖκα ἑαυτοῦ οὖσαν. πυθομένη δ᾽ ἐκείνη ἀφικνεῖται, μέλαν τι ἱμάτιον ἠμφιεσμένη, ὡς εἰκὸς ἦν ἐπὶ τῷ ἀνδρὶ αὐτῆς τοιαύτῃ συμφορᾷ κεχορημένῳ. ἐναντίον δὲ τῆς ἀδελφῆς τῆς ἐμῆς Διονυσόδωρος τά τε οἰκεῖα τὰ αὐτοῦ διέθετο ὅπως αὐτῷ ἐδόκει, καὶ περὶ Ἀγοράτου τουτουὶ ἔλεγεν ὅτι οἱ αἴτιος ἦν τοῦ θανάτου, καὶ ἐπέσκηπτεν ἐμοὶ καὶ Διονυσίῳ τουτῳί, τῷ ἀδελφῷ τῷ αὐτοῦ, καὶ τοῖς φίλοις πᾶσι τιμωρεῖν ὑπὲρ αὐτοῦ Ἀγόρατον· καὶ τῇ γυναικὶ τῇ αὐτοῦ ἐπέσκηπτε, νομίζων αὐτὴν κυεῖν ἐξ αὐτοῦ, ἐὰν γένηται αὐτῇ παιδίον, φράζειν τῷ γενομένῳ ὅτι τὸν πατέρα αὐτοῦ Ἀγόρατος ἀπέκτεινε, καὶ κελεύειν τιμωρεῖν ὑπὲρ αὐτοῦ ὡς φονέα ὄντα.

(LYSIAS, *Against Agoratus* 40–2)

μεταπέμπομαι: send for, summon
ἡ ἀδελφή: sister (1a)
τὸ δεσμωτήριον: prison (2b)
ἀμφιέννυμι: put on, put round (perfect passive ἠμφίεσμαι)
ἐπισκήπτω: charge X(dat.) to do Y(inf.)
τιμωρέω: take vengeance on X(acc.)
κυέω: be pregnant
ὁ φονεύς: murderer (3g)

(25/100)

2. Translate into English: [RG Section 17]

ὅτ᾽ οὖν ἀθροισθεῖεν, ἠδίκουν ἀλλήλους ἅτε οὐκ ἔχοντες τὴν πολιτικὴν τέχνην, ὥστε πάλιν σκεδαννύμενοι διεφθείροντο. Ζεὺς οὖν δείσας περὶ τῷ γένει ἡμῶν μὴ ἀπόλοιτο πᾶν, Ἑρμῆν πέμπει ἄγοντα εἰς ἀνθρώπους αἰδῶ τε καὶ δίκην, ἵν᾽ εἶεν πόλεων κόσμοι τε καὶ δεσμοὶ φιλίας συναγωγοί. ἐρωτᾷ οὖν Ἑρμῆς Δία τίνα οὖν τρόπον δοίη δίκην καὶ αἰδῶ ἀνθρώποις· ᾽Πότερον ὡς αἱ τέχναι νενέμηνται, οὕτω καὶ ταύτας νείμω; νενέμηνται δὲ ὧδε· εἷς ἔχων ἰατρικὴν πολλοῖς ἱκανὸς ἰδιώταις, καὶ οἱ ἄλλοι δημιουργοί· καὶ δίκην δὴ καὶ αἰδῶ οὕτω θῶ ἐν τοῖς ἀνθρώποις, ἢ ἐπὶ πάντας νείμω;᾽ ᾽Ἐπὶ πάντας,᾽ ἔφη ὁ Ζεύς, ᾽καὶ πάντες μετεχόντων· οὐ γὰρ ἂν γένοιντο πόλεις, εἰ ὀλίγοι αὐτῶν μετέχοιεν ὥσπερ ἄλλων τεχνῶν· καὶ νόμον γε θὲς παρ᾽ ἐμοῦ τὸν μὴ δυνάμενον αἰδοῦς καὶ δίκης μετέχειν κτείνειν ὡς νόσον πόλεως.᾽

(PLATO, *Protagoras* 322 b–d)   (13)

i. Parse (identify): εἶεν; νενέμηνται; θῶ; μετεχόντων. (4)
ii. Explain the syntax of:

(a) ὅτ᾽ οὖν ἀθροισθεῖεν
(b) τίνα οὖν τρόπον δοίη
(c) οὐ...ἂν γένοιντο..., εἰ...μετέχοιεν. (3)

iii. How does this μῦθος support the view of Protagoras that it is possible to teach people to be good citizens? (5) (25/100)

3. Translate into English: (*RG* Section 18)

> ᾽νῦν ὦν, ὀφείλεις γάρ, ἐμεῦ προποιήσαντος χρηστὰ ἐς σέ, χρηστοῖσί
> με ἀμείβεσθαι, φύλακα παιδός σε τοῦ ἐμοῦ χρηίζω γενέσθαι
> ἐς ἄγρην ὁρμωμένου, μή τινες κατ᾽ ὁδὸν κλῶπες κακοῦργοι ἐπὶ
> δηλήσι φανέωσι ὑμῖν. πρὸς δὲ τούτῳ καὶ σέ τοι χρεόν ἐστι ἰέναι
> ἔνθα ἀπολαμπρυνέαι τοῖσι ἔργοισι· πατρώιόν τε γάρ τοί ἐστι καὶ
> προσέτι ῥώμη ὑπάρχει.᾽ ἀμείβεται ὁ ῎Αδρηστος· ῾ὦ βασιλεῦ,
> ἄλλως μὲν ἔγωγε ἂν οὐκ ἦια ἐς ἄεθλον τοιόνδε· οὔτε γὰρ συμφορῇ
> τοιῇδε κεχρημένον οἰκός ἐστι ἐς ὁμήλικας εὖ πρήσσοντας ἰέναι,
> οὔτε τὸ βούλεσθαι πάρα, πολλαχῇ τε ἂν ἴσχον ἐμεωυτόν. νῦν δέ,
> ἐπείτε σὺ σπεύδεις καὶ δεῖ τοι χαρίζεσθαι (ὀφείλω γάρ σε ἀμείβεσθαι
> χρηστοῖσι), ποιέειν εἰμὶ ἕτοιμος ταῦτα, παῖδά τε σόν, τὸν διακελεύεαι
> φυλάσσειν, ἀπήμονα, τοῦ φυλάσσοντος εἵνεκεν, προσδόκα τοι
> ἀπονοστήσειν.᾽

(13)

i. Parse (identify): ἤια; ἐμεωυτόν; διακελεύεαι; προσδόκα. (4)
ii. Explain the syntax of:

(a) ἐμεῦ προποιήσαντος
(b) μή...φανέωσι.
(c) οὔτε τὸ βούλεσθαι πάρα. (3)

iii. Comment on the role of Adrastos in the Croesus episode. (5)
(25/100)

4. Translate into English: (*RG* Section 19)

> ἦ ῥα, καὶ ἀμφιπόλοισιν ἐϋπλοκάμοισι κέλευσε·
> ῾στῆτέ μοι, ἀμφίπολοι· πόσε φεύγετε φῶτα ἰδοῦσαι;
> ἦ μή πού τινα δυσμενέων φάσθ᾽ ἔμμεναι ἀνδρῶν;
> οὐκ ἔσθ᾽ οὗτος ἀνὴρ διερὸς βροτὸς οὐδὲ γένηται,
> ὅς κεν Φαιήκων ἀνδρῶν ἐς γαῖαν ἵκηται
> δηϊοτῆτα φέρων· μάλα γὰρ φίλοι ἀθανάτοισιν.
> οἰκέομεν δ᾽ ἀπάνευθε πολυκλύστῳ ἐνὶ πόντῳ,
> 204 ἔσχατοι, οὐδέ τις ἄμμι βροτῶν ἐπιμίσγεται ἄλλος.

205 ἀλλ' ὅδε τις δύστηνος ἀλώμενος ἐνθάδ' ἱκάνει,
τὸν νῦν χρὴ κομέειν· πρὸς γὰρ Διός εἰσιν ἅπαντες
ξεῖνοί τε πτωχοί τε, δόσις δ' ὀλίγη τε φίλη τε.
ἀλλὰ δότ', ἀμφίπολοι, ξείνῳ βρῶσίν τε πόσιν τε,
λούσατέ τ' ἐν ποταμῷ, ὅθ' ἐπὶ σκέπας ἔστ' ἀνέμοιο.'

(HOMER, *Odyssey* VI.198–210)   (13)

i. Parse (identify): ἔμμεναι; ἵκηται; ἄμμι; ἀνέμοιο. (4)
ii. Scan lines 204–5. (3)
iii. What does this passage contribute to our understanding of the character of Nausikaa? (5)   (25/100)

PAPER C1

(No full mark scheme given with this examination)

Unprepared translation

Important: Read the Greek and the English of the translated sections A and C, and use them to help you with your translation of the remainder (sections B and D). The words underlined in the Greek of A and C will be particularly useful. Words underlined in sections B and D are given in the glossary at the end of the passage.

Translate into English sections B and D of the following passage:

Euxitheos, a Mytilenean, is on trial for the alleged murder of Herodes, an Athenian. This is the defendant's account of what happened on the night that Herodes disappeared after a convivial party on board a ship in harbour.

A

ἔγωγε δὲ τὸν μὲν πλοῦν ἐποιησάμην ἐκ τῆς Μυτιλήνης, ὦ ἄνδρες, ἐν τῷ πλοίῳ πλέων ᾧ Ἡρῴδης οὗτος ὃν φασιν ὑπ' ἐμοῦ ἀποθανεῖν. ἐπλέομεν δὲ εἰς τὴν Αἶνον, ἐγὼ μὲν ὡς τὸν πατέρα (ἐτύγχανε γὰρ ἐκεῖ ὢν τότε), ὁ δὲ Ἡρῴδης ἀνδράποδα Θρᾳξὶν ἀνθρώποις ἀπολύσων. συνέπλει δὲ τὰ ἀνδράποδα ἃ ἔδει αὐτὸν ἀπολῦσαι, καὶ οἱ Θρᾷκες οἱ λυσόμενοι. ἡ μὲν πρόφασις ἑκατέρῳ τοῦ πλοῦ αὕτη· ἐτύχομεν δὲ χειμῶνί τινι χρησάμενοι, ὑφ' οὗ ἠναγκάσθημεν κατασχεῖν εἰς τὴν Μηθύμνην, οὗ τὸ πλοῖον ὥρμει τοῦτο εἰς ὃ μετεκβάντα φασὶν ἀποθανεῖν τὸν Ἡρῴδην.

I made the voyage from Mytilene, gentlemen, sailing as a passenger in the same ship as Herodes, the man the prosecution say I murdered. We were bound for Ainos, – I to visit my father, who was living there just at that time, and Herodes to arrange the ransom of some slaves to certain Thracians. Both the slaves and the Thracians who were to purchase their freedom were on board with us. Such were our several motives for making the voyage. In the course of it we encountered a storm, as a result of which we were forced to put in at Methymne, where there was lying at anchor the boat to which – according to the prosecution –, Herodes transshipped, and met his death.

B

καὶ πρῶτον μὲν αὐτὰ ταῦτα σκοπεῖτε ὅτι οὐ τῇ ἐμῇ προνοίᾳ
ἐγίγνετο μᾶλλον ἢ τύχῃ. οὔτε γὰρ ἔπεισα τὸν ἄνδρα συμπλεῖν
μοι, ἀλλ' αὐτὸς καθ' αὑτὸν τὸν πλοῦν ἐποιήσατο ἕνεκα
πραγμάτων ἰδίων. οὔτε αὖ ἐγὼ ἄνευ προφάσεως ἱκανῆς φαίνομαι
5 τὸν πλοῦν ποιησάμενος εἰς τὴν Αἶνον, οὔτε κατέσχομεν εἰς
Μήθυμνην ἀπὸ παρασκευῆς οὐδεμιᾶς, ἀλλ' ἀνάγκῃ καὶ χειμῶνι
χρησάμενοι. οὔτ' αὖ, ἐπειδὴ ὡρμισάμεθα, ἡ μετέκβασις ἐγένετο
εἰς τὸ ἕτερον πλοῖον οὐδενὶ μηχανήματι οὐδ' ἀπάτῃ, ἀλλ'
ἀνάγκῃ καὶ τοῦτο ἐγένετο. τὸ μὲν γὰρ πλοῖον ἐν ᾧ ἐπλέομεν
10 ἀστέγαστον ἦν, εἰς ὃ δὲ μετέβημεν, ἐστεγασμένον. τοῦ δὲ ὑετοῦ
ἕνεκα ταῦτ' ἦν.
ἐπειδὴ δὲ μετεξέβημεν εἰς τὸ ἕτερον πλοῖον, ἐπίνομεν. καὶ ὁ
μὲν Ἡρώδης φαίνεται ἐκβὰς ἐκ τοῦ πλοίου, καὶ οὐκ εἰσβὰς
πάλιν. ἐγὼ δὲ τὸ παράπαν οὐκ ἐξέβην ἐκ τοῦ πλοίου τῆς νυκτὸς
15 ἐκείνης. τῇ δὲ ὑστεραίᾳ, ἐπειδὴ ἀφανὴς ἦν ὁ ἀνήρ, ἐζητεῖτο
οὐδὲν μᾶλλον ὑπὸ τῶν ἄλλων ἢ καὶ ὑπ' ἐμοῦ, καὶ εἴ τινι τῶν
ἄλλων ἐδόκει δεινὸν εἶναι, ἐδόκει καὶ ἐμοὶ ὁμοίως. καὶ εἰς
τὴν Μυτιλήνην ἐγὼ αἴτιος ἦν πεμφθῆναι ἄγγελον, καὶ ἄλλου
οὐδενὸς ἐθέλοντος βαδίζειν, ἐγὼ τὸν ἀκόλουθον τὸν ἐμαυτοῦ
20 πέμπειν ἕτοιμος ἦν.

C

ἐπειδὴ δὲ ὁ ἀνὴρ οὔτε ἐν Μυτιλήνῃ
ἐφαίνετο ζητούμενος οὔτ' ἄλλοθι οὐδα-
μοῦ, καὶ πλοῦς ἡμῖν ἐγίγνετο, καὶ
τἆλλα ἀνήγετο πλοῖα ἅπαντα, ᾠχόμην
καὶ ἐγὼ πλέων.

There was no trace of the man, in spite of
search being made for him in Mytilene and
elsewhere. Our voyage could now be
resumed;–all other boats were now putting
to sea, so I likewise sailed and went my
way.

D

Euxitheos bases his defence on arguments from probability (τὰ εἰκότα): if the
prosecution had a real case, they would have been likely to have preferred it at once
in Methymne.

τὰ μὲν γενόμενα ταῦτ' ἐστίν. ἐκ δὲ τούτων σκοπεῖτε τὰ
εἰκότα· πρῶτον μὲν γὰρ πρὶν ἀνάγεσθαί με εἰς τὴν Αἶνον,
ὅτε ἦν ἀφανὴς ὁ ἀνήρ, οὐδεὶς τούτων ᾐτιάσατό με, ἤδη
πεπυσμένων τὴν ἀγγελίαν. εἰ γὰρ ᾐτιάσαντο, οὐκ ἄν ποτ'
25 ἐγὼ ᾠχόμην πλέων. ἐπειδὴ δὲ ἐγώ τε ᾠχόμην πλέων καὶ
οὗτοι ἐξ ἐπιβουλῆς ἐμηχανήσαντο ταῦτα κατ' ἐμοῦ, τότε
ᾐτιάσαντο.

ANTIPHON, *Murder of Herodes* 20–5

Vocabulary

σκοπέω	I consider	ἀστέγαστος-ον	with no cover (on deck)
πρόνοια, ἡ	deliberate plan	ὑετός, ὁ	rain
αὐτὸς καθ' αὐτόν	on his own initiative	ἀφανής-ές	disappeared without trace
ἴδιος-α-ον	private	αἴτιος-α-ον	+ inf. = responsible for
παρασκευή ἡ,	contrivance	ἀκόλουθος, ὁ	servant
μηχάνημα, τό	scheming	ἐξ ἐπιβουλῆς	in a conspiracy

PAPER C2

Set Texts

Answer **all** *the questions on both Set Texts.*

Words underlined are given in the glossary below each passage.

HERODOTUS

The Battle of Thermopylai

1. Translate into English:

Λακεδαιμονίων δὲ καὶ Θεσπιέων τοιούτων γενομένων ὅμως
λέγεται ἀνὴρ ἄριστος γενέσθαι Σπαρτιήτης Διηνέκης· τὸν τόδε φασὶ
εἰπεῖν τὸ ἔπος πρὶν ἢ συμμεῖξαί σφεας τοῖσι Μήδοισι, πυθόμενον πρός
τευ τῶν Τρηχινίων ὡς ἐπεὰν οἱ βάρβαροι ἀπίωσι τὰ τοξεύματα, τὸν
ἥλιον ὑπὸ τοῦ πλήθεος τῶν ὀϊστῶν ἀποκρύπτουσι· τοσοῦτο πλῆθος
αὐτῶν εἶναι· τὸν δὲ οὐκ ἐκπλαγέντα τούτοισι εἰπεῖν, ἐν ἀλογίῃ
ποιεύμενον τὸ τῶν Μήδων πλῆθος, ὡς πάντα σφι ἀγαθὰ ὁ Τρηχίνιος
ξεῖνος ἀγγέλλοι, εἰ ἀποκρυπτόντων τῶν Μήδων τὸν ἥλιον ὑπὸ σκιῇ
ἔσοιτο πρὸς αὐτοὺς ἡ μάχη καὶ οὐκ ἐν ἡλίῳ. ταῦτα μὲν καὶ ἄλλα
τοιουτότροπα ἔπεά φασι Διηνέκεα τὸν Λακεδαιμόνιον λιπέσθαι
μνημόσυνα. μετὰ δὲ τοῦτον ἀριστεῦσαι λέγονται Λακεδαιμόνιοι δύο
ἀδελφεοί, Ἀλφεός τε καὶ Μάρων Ὀρσιφάντου παῖδες.

Θεσπιέες, οἱ	Thespians	ἀλογίη, ἡ	contempt
Διηνέκης ὁ	Dienekes	σκιή, ἡ	shade
πρὶν ἤ	before	τοιουτότροπος -ον	of such a kind
τευ = τινός		μνημόσυνον, τό	memorial
Τρηχίνιος ὁ	Trachinian	ἀριστεύω	I am distinguished
ἐπεάν = ἐπεὶ ἄν			by valour
ἀπίωσι = ἀφίωσι	(subj. of ἀφίημι)	Ἀλφεός, ὁ	Alpheos
οϊστός, ὁ	arrow	Μάρων, ὁ	Maron
ἐκπλήσσω (ἐκπλαγ-)	I astonish	Ὀρσίφαντος, ὁ	Orsiphantos

2. Answer the questions set on **both** of the following passages:

(a)   ὁ μὲν ταῦτα εἰρώτα, ὁ δὲ ὑπολαβὼν ἔφη · 'βασιλεῦ, κότερα
ἀληθείῃ χρήσωμαι πρὸς σὲ ἢ ἡδονῇ;' ὁ δέ μιν ἀληθείῃ χρήσασθαι
ἐκέλευε, φὰς οὐδέν οἱ ἀηδέστερον ἔσεσθαι ἢ πρότερον ἦν. ὡς δὲ ταῦτα
ἤκουσε Δημάρητος, ἔλεγε τάδε · 'βασιλεῦ, ἐπειδὴ ἀληθείῃ διαχρήσασθαι
5   πάντως κελεύεις – ταῦτα λέγοντα τὰ μὴ ψευδόμενός τις ὕστερον ὑπὸ σεῦ
ἁλώσεται - τῇ Ἑλλάδι <u>πενίη</u> μὲν ἀιεί κοτε σύντροφός ἐστι, ἀρετὴ δὲ
<u>ἔπακτός</u> ἐστι, ἀπό τε σοφίης κατεργασμένη καὶ νόμου ἰσχυροῦ · τῇ
<u>διαχρεωμένη</u> ἡ Ἑλλὰς τήν τε πενίην <u>ἀπαμύνεται</u> καὶ τὴν δεσποσύνην.
<u>αἰνέω</u> μέν νυν πάντας τοὺς Ἕλληνας τοὺς περὶ ἐκείνους τοὺς Δωρικοὺς
10   χώρους <u>οἰκημένους</u>, ἔρχομαι δὲ λέξων οὐ περὶ πάντων τούσδε τοὺς
λόγους, ἀλλὰ περὶ Λακεδαιμονίων μούνων, πρῶτα μὲν ὅτι οὐκ ἔστι
ὅκως κοτὲ σοὺς δέξονται λόγους <u>δουλοσύνην</u> φέροντας τῇ Ἑλλάδι, <u>αὗτις</u>
<u>δὲ ὡς ἀντιώσονταί τοι ἐς</u> μάχην καὶ <u>ἢν</u> οἱ ἄλλοι Ἕλληνες πάντες τὰ σὰ
φρονέωσι. ἀριθμοῦ δὲ πέρι μὴ πύθῃ ὅσοι τινὲς ἐόντες ταῦτα ποιέειν οἷοί
15   τέ εἰσι · ἢν τε γὰρ τύχωσι <u>ἐξεστρατευμένοι</u> χίλιοι, οὗτοι μαχήσονταί τοι,
ἤν τε ἐλάσσονες τούτων, ἤν τε καὶ <u>πλεῦνες.</u>'

(i) When did this conversation take place? Who was Demaratos? What question had he been asked?

(ii) What picture of Greek life and culture is presented in lines 6–8 (τῇ Ἑλλάδι . . . δεσποσύνην)?

(iii) What does this conversation contribute to our understanding of the differences between Greeks and Persians?

ἀηδής -ες	displeasing	δουλοσύνη, ἡ	slavery
πενίη, ἡ	poverty	αὗτις δέ	and secondly
ἔπακτος -ον	acquired	ἀντιόομαι + dat. ἐς...	I suppose someone in...
ἀπαμύνομαι	I ward off	ἤν = ἐάν	
δεσποσύνη, ἡ	despotism	ἐκστρατεύομαι	I take the field
Δωρικός -η -ον	Dorian	πλεῦνες = πλέονες	
οἴκημαι	I dwell		

(b)   ἐπείτε δὲ οἱ Μῆδοι <u>τρηχέως περιείποντο</u>, ἐνθαῦτα οὗτοι μὲν
ὑπεξήισαν, οἱ δὲ Πέρσαι ἐκδεξάμενοι ἐπήισαν, τοὺς ἀθανάτους ἐκάλεε
βασιλεύς, τῶν ἦρχε Ὑδάρνης, ὡς δὴ οὗτοί γε εὐπετέως κατεργασόμενοι.
ὡς δὲ καὶ οὗτοι συνέμισγον τοῖσι Ἕλλησι, οὐδὲν πλέον ἐφέροντο
5   τῆς στρατιῆς τῆς Μηδικῆς ἀλλὰ τὰ αὐτά, ἅτε ἐν <u>στεινοπόρῳ</u> τε
μαχόμενοι καὶ δόρασι βραχυτέροισι χρεώμενοι ἤ <u>περ οἱ</u> Ἕλληνες καὶ
οὐκ ἔχοντες πλήθεϊ χρήσασθαι. Λακεδαιμόνιοι δὲ ἐμάχοντο ἀξίως
λόγου, ἄλλα τε ἀποδεικνύμενοι ἐν οὐκ ἐπισταμένοισι μάχεσθαι
ἐξεπιστάμενοι, καὶ ὅκως ἐντρέψειαν τὰ νῶτα, ἁλέες <u>φεύγεσκον</u> δῆθεν, οἱ
10   δὲ βάρβαροι ὁρῶντες φεύγοντας βοῇ τε καὶ <u>πατάγῳ</u> ἐπήισαν, οἱ δ' ἂν

καταλαμβανόμενοι ὑπέστρεφον ἀντίοι εἶναι τοῖσι βαρβάροισι,
μεταστρεφόμενοι δὲ κατέβαλλον πλήθεϊ ἀναριθμήτους τῶν Περσέων·
ἔπιπτον δὲ καὶ αὐτῶν Σπαρτιητέων ἐνθαῦτα ὀλίγοι. ἐπεὶ δὲ οὐδὲν
ἐδυνέατο παραλαβεῖν οἱ Πέρσαι τῆς ἐσόδου πειρώμενοι καὶ κατὰ τέλεα
15 καὶ παντοίως προσβάλλοντες, ἀπήλαυνον ὀπίσω. ἐν ταύτῃσι τῇσι
προσόδοισι τῆς μάχης λέγεται βασιλέα θηεύμενον τρὶς ἀναδραμεῖν ἐκ
τοῦ θρόνου, δείσαντα περὶ τῇ στρατιῇ.

(i) Distinguish between the two contingents of Xerxes' army mentioned in
the first sentence. Why did Xerxes call the second of them into action?

(ii) To what does Herodotus attribute the Greek success in this engagement?

(iii) In what ways is this passage typical of Herodotus' narrative style and
technique?

τρηχέως	roughly	ὑποστρέφω	I turn about
περιέπω	I handle	ἀντίοι εἶναι + dat.	to face...
Ὑδάρνης, ὁ	Hydarnes	μεταστρέφομαι	I turn about
εὐπετέως	easily	καταβάλλω	I kill
φέρομαι	I succeed, achieve	ἐδυνέατο = ἐδύναντο	
στεινόπορον	pass, narrow defile	παραλαμβάνω (λαβ-)	I gain an advantage
ἐντρέπω	I turn round	κατὰ τέλεα	squadron by squadron
ἀλέες	in close order	ἀνατρέχω (-δρακ-)	I leap up
φευγέσκω: -σκ-	*indicates repeated action*	θρόνος, -ου, ὁ	throne
πάταγος, ὁ	rattle of arms		

3. **Either,** (*a*) Discuss the strategic advantages of holding Thermopylai.

Or,   (*b*) In what way, according to Herodotus, was Athens the Saviour
of Greece?

SOPHOCLES

The Fall of Oedipus

1. Translate into English:

XO. τί ποτε βέβηκεν, Οἰδίπους, ὑπ' ἀγρίας
ᾄξασα λύπης ἡ γυνή; δέδοιχ' ὅπως
μὴ 'κ τῆς σιωπῆς τῆσδ' ἀναρρήξει κακά.

OI. ὁποῖα χρῄζει ῥηγνύτω· τοὐμὸν δ' ἐγώ,
κεἰ σμικρόν ἐστι, σπέρμ' ἰδεῖν βουλήσομαι.
αὕτη δ' ἴσως, φρονεῖ γὰρ ὡς γυνὴ μέγα,
τὴν δυσγένειαν τὴν ἐμὴν αἰσχύνεται.
ἐγὼ δ' ἐμαυτὸν παῖδα τῆς Τύχης νέμων
τῆς εὖ διδούσης οὐκ ἀτιμασθήσομαι.
τῆς γὰρ πέφυκα μητρός· οἱ δὲ συγγενεῖς

μῆνές με μικρὸν καὶ μέγαν διώρισαν.
τοιόσδε δ' ἐκφὺς οὐκ ἂν ἐξέλθοιμ' ἔτι
ποτ' ἄλλος, ὥστε μὴ 'κμαθεῖν τοὐμὸν γένος.

ἀΐσσω (ἀξ-)	I rush out	σπέρμα, τό	origin
λυπή, ἡ	grief	δυσγένεια, ἡ	lowly birth
ἀναρρήγνυμι (-ρρηξ-)	I break out	μείς (μην-), ὁ	month

2. Answer the questions set on **both** of the following passages:

(a) *ΟΙ.* τί φής, ξέν'; αὐτός μοι σὺ σημήνας γενοῦ.
 ΑΓΓΕΛΟΣ
   εἰ τοῦτο πρῶτον δεῖ μ' ἀπαγγεῖλαι σαφῶς,
   εὖ ἴσθ' ἐκεῖνον θανάσιμον βεβηκότα.
 ΟΙ. πότερα δόλοισιν, ἢ νόσου ξυναλλαγῇ;
5 *ΑΓ.* σμικρὰ παλαιὰ σώματ' εὐνάζει ῥοπή.
 ΟΙ. νόσοις ὁ τλήμων, ὡς ἔοικεν, ἔφθιτο.
 ΑΓ. καὶ τῷ μακρῷ γε συμμετρούμενος χρόνῳ.
 ΟΙ. φεῦ φεῦ, τί δῆτ' ἄν, ὦ γύναι, σκοποῖτό τις
   τὴν Πυθόμαντιν ἑστίαν, ἢ τοὺς ἄνω
10 κλάζοντας ὄρνεις, ὧν ὑφηγητῶν ἐγὼ
   κτενεῖν ἔμελλον πατέρα τὸν ἐμόν; ὁ δὲ θανὼν
   κεύθει κάτω δὴ γῆς· ἐγὼ δ' ὅδ' ἐνθάδε
   ἄψαυστος ἔγχους, εἴ τι μὴ τὠμῷ πόθῳ
   κατέφθιθ'· οὕτω δ' ἂν θανὼν εἴη 'ξ ἐμοῦ.
15 τὰ δ' οὖν προδόντα συλλαβὼν θεσπίσματα
   κεῖται παρ' Ἅιδῃ Πόλυβος ἄξι' οὐδενός.
 ΙΟ. οὔκουν ἐγώ σοι ταῦτα προὔλεγον πάλαι;
 ΟΙ. ηὔδας· ἐγὼ δὲ τῷ φόβῳ παρηγόμην.
 ΙΟ. μή νυν ἔτ' αὐτῶν μηδὲν ἐς θυμὸν βάλῃς.
20 *ΟΙ.* καὶ πῶς τὸ μητρὸς οὐκ ὀκνεῖν λέχος με δεῖ;
 ΙΟ. τί δ' ἂν φοβοῖτ' ἄνθρωπος ᾧ τὰ τῆς τύχης
   κρατεῖ, πρόνοια δ' ἐστὶν οὐδενὸς σαφής;
   εἰκῇ κράτιστον ζῆν, ὅπως δύναιτό τις.
   σὺ δ' ἐς τὰ μητρὸς μὴ φοβοῦ νυμφεύματα·
25 πολλοὶ γὰρ ἤδη κἀν ὀνείρασιν βροτῶν
   μητρὶ ξυνηυνάσθησαν. ἀλλὰ ταῦθ' ὅτῳ
   παρ' οὐδέν ἐστι, ῥᾷστα τὸν βίον φέρει.
 ΟΙ. καλῶς ἅπαντα ταῦτ' ἂν ἐξείρητό σοι,
   εἰ μὴ 'κύρει ζῶσ' ἡ τεκοῦσα· νῦν δ' ἐπεὶ
30 ζῇ, πᾶσ' ἀνάγκη, κεἰ καλῶς λέγεις, ὀκνεῖν.
 ΙΟ. καὶ μὴν μέγας γ' ὀφθαλμὸς οἱ πατρὸς τάφοι.
 ΟΙ. μέγας, ξυνίημ'· ἀλλὰ τῆς ζώσης φόβος.
 ΑΓ. ποίας δὲ καὶ γυναικὸς ἐκφοβεῖσθ' ὕπερ;

(i) What is the significance of the messenger's interruption in the last line of the passage?

(ii) How do Oedipus and Iokaste react to the messenger's news? In what way are their reactions typical of their characters?

(iii) How does this scene fit into the story of Oedipus' search for the truth? Assess its dramatic effectiveness.

σημήνας γενοῦ	tell me	ὑφηγητής, ὁ	guide
θανάσιμος -ον	dead	κεύθω	I lie hidden
δόλος, ὁ	treachery	ἄψαυστος -ον	without touching
ξυναλλαγή, ἡ	visitation	πόθος, ὁ	longing
εὐνάζω	I put to sleep	καταφθίνομαι (φθι)	I waste away
ῥοπή, ἡ	turn of the scale	συλλαμβάνω	I carry off
συμμετρούμενος	in due measure with	θέσπισμα, τό	prophesy
Πυθόμαντις ἑστία	the seat of the Pythian oracle	παράγω	I mislead
κλάζω	I scream	εἰκῆ	at random
ὄρνις, ὁ	bird	ὀφθαλμός, ὁ	comfort

(b)   *ΟΙ.*   οὗτος σύ, πρέσβυ, δεῦρό μοι φώνει βλέπων
         ὅσ᾽ ἄν σ᾽ ἐρωτῶ. Λαΐου ποτ᾽ ἦσθα σύ;
      ΘΕΡΑΠΩΝ
         ἦ, δοῦλος οὐκ ὠνητός, ἀλλ᾽ οἴκοι τραφείς.
      ΟΙ.   ἔργον μεριμνῶν ποῖον ἢ βίον τίνα;
   5 *ΘΕ.*   ποίμναις τὰ πλεῖστα τοῦ βίου συνειπόμην.
      ΟΙ.   χώροις μάλιστα πρὸς τίσι ξύναυλος ὤν;
      ΘΕ.   ἦν μὲν Κιθαιρών, ἦν δὲ πρόσχωρος τόπος.
      ΟΙ.   τὸν ἄνδρα τόνδ᾽ οὖν οἶσθα τῇδέ που μαθών;
      ΘΕ.   τί χρῆμα δρῶντα; ποῖον ἄνδρα καὶ λέγεις;
  10 *ΟΙ.*   τόνδ᾽ ὃς πάρεστιν· ἢ ξυναλλάξας τί που;
      ΘΕ.   οὐχ ὥστε γ᾽ εἰπεῖν ἐν τάχει μνήμης ἄπο.
      ΑΓ.   κοὐδέν γε θαῦμα, δέσποτ᾽. ἀλλ᾽ ἐγὼ σαφῶς
         ἀγνῶτ᾽ ἀναμνήσω νιν. εὖ γὰρ οἶδ᾽ ὅτι
         κάτοιδεν ἦμος τὸν Κιθαιρῶνος τόπον
  15   ὃ μὲν διπλοῖσι ποιμνίοις, ἐγὼ δ᾽ ἑνὶ
         ἐπλησίαζον τῷδε τἀνδρὶ τρεῖς ὅλους
         ἐξ ἦρος εἰς ἀρκτοῦρον ἐκμήνους χρόνους·
         χειμῶνι δ᾽ ἤδη τἀμά τ᾽ εἰς ἔπαυλ᾽ ἐγὼ
         ἤλαυνον οὗτός τ᾽ ἐς τὰ Λαΐου σταθμά.
  20 *ΘΕ.*   λέγω τι τούτων, ἢ οὐ λέγω πεπραγμένον;
      ΘΕ.   λέγεις ἀληθῆ, καίπερ ἐκ μακροῦ χρόνου.
      ΑΓ.   φέρ᾽ εἰπὲ νῦν, τότ᾽ οἶσθα παῖδά μοί τινα
         δούς, ὡς ἐμαυτῷ θρέμμα θρεψαίμην ἐγώ;
      ΘΕ.   τί δ᾽ ἔστι; πρὸς τί τοῦτο τοὔπος ἱστορεῖς;
  25 *ΑΓ.*   ὅδ᾽ ἐστίν, ὦ τᾶν, κεῖνος ὃς τότ᾽ ἦν νέος.

ΘΕ. οὐκ εἰς ὄλεθρον; οὐ σιωπήσας ἔσῃ;
ΟΙ. ἆ, μὴ κόλαζε, πρέσβυ, τόνδ', ἐπεὶ τὰ σὰ
  δεῖται κολαστοῦ μᾶλλον ἢ τὰ τοῦδ' ἔπη.
ΘΕ. τί δ', ὦ φέριστε δεσποτῶν, ἁμαρτάνω;
30 ΟΙ. οὐκ ἐννέπων τὸν παῖδ' ὃν οὗτος ἱστορεῖ.
ΘΕ. λέγει γὰρ εἰδὼς οὐδέν, ἀλλ' ἄλλως πονεῖ.

(i) What vital information is elicited from the old shepherd in this passage?
(ii) Show, with examples, how the old shepherd consistently tries to evade the issue. Why does he behave like this?
(iii) How does Sophocles contrive to make both the messenger and the shepherd important agents in this dialogue?

ὠνητός -ον	bought	διπλοῦς -οῦν	double
τραφείς	bred	πλησιάζω + dat.	I associate with
μεριμνῶ	I am occupied with	ἦρ, τό	spring
συνέπομαι + dat.	I tend	ἀρκτοῦρος, ὁ	the rising of Arcturus in September
ξύναυλος -ον	living in	ἑκμηνος -ον	of six months
πρόσχωρος -ον	neighbouring	ἔπαυλα, τά	sheep-fold
ξυναλλάσσω	I have dealings with	θρέμμα, τό	baby
ἀγνώς (ἀγνωτ-)	ignorant	κολαστής, ὁ	punisher
ἀναμιμνήσκω (μνησ-)	I remind	φέριστος -η -ον	best
ἦμος	when		

3. **Either,** (*a*) Is it true to say that nothing 'happens' in *Oedipus Tyrannus*?

Or,   (*b*) Sophocles increased the number of actors from two to three. How does this innovation enhance the dramatic effect of the scenes you have read?

YEAR-PLANS

Here are three year-plans. *A* represents a good average for a university beginners course over the year; *B* (second term only) represents a good university beginners' class going flat out; *C* shows what might be done in three to four 40-minute periods a week in the first year of the sixth form, with committed and intelligent pupils.

A (average) *Three hours per week*

    1st term week 1 Alphabet, pronounciation etc; 1A
                  2 1B–G
                  3 1H–J, 2A–B
                  4 2C–D, 3A–E (teacher translating D-E)
                  5 4A–B inc. written test
                  6 4C–D, 5A–B
                  7 5C–F
                  8 5G–H, 6A
                  9 6B–F
                10 6G–H

Vacation: revision of grammar and vocabulary; looking at Language Surveys; learning pp. 74-5 of *GVE*.

    2nd term week 1 7A–C
                  2 8A–F
                  3 8G–J
                  4 9A–E
                  5 10A-C
                  6 11A (one hour only)
                  7 11B–G (omitting conversations)
                  8 11 H–I, 12A–I (omitting some parts)
                  9 13A-F
                10 14A–C

Vacation: revision of grammar and vocabulary; preparing 15A; writing out p. 155.

3rd term week 1 15A–H
2 16A–D (omitting E)
3 17A–E
4 18A–F
5 revision

Alternatively, revise 11–13 while reading on through 15 and 16 (to prepare for Examination A).

B (intensive) *Three hours per week, c. 60 lines to be prepared for each session*

Wed. 17 Jan.	8A–B	
Thur. 18	8C–E	
Tues. 23	8F–G	
Wed. 24	8H–J	Test Exercise 8 (p. 129)
Thur. 25	9A–B	
Tues. 30	9C–D	
Wed. 31	9E–10A	9 (p. 142)
Thur. 1 Feb.	10B–C	
Tues. 6	11A–C	
Wed. 7	11D–F	10 (p. 150)
Thur. 8	11G–I	
Tues. 13		
Wed. 14	READING WEEK	
Thur. 15		
Tues. 20	12A–D	
Wed. 21	12E–I	11 (p. 173) and 12 (p. 191)
Thur. 22	13A–F	
Tues. 27	14A	
Wed. 28	14B–C	13 (p. 200)
Thur. 1 Mar.	15A–B	
Tues. 6	15C–E	
Wed. 7	15F–H	15 (p. 219)
Thur. 8	16A–B	
Tues. 13	16C–E	
Wed. 14	17A–C33	16 (p. 234)
Thur. 15	17C34–E	
Tues. 20	HOMER	
Wed. 21		
Thur. 22		

C (first year, sixth form) *three to four 40-minute periods a week*

Week	
1	Alphabet practice and 1A
2	1B–G
3	1H–2A
4	2B–D
5	3A–E (ending rushed)
6	revised 3C–E; 4A–B
7	4C–5A
8	5B–E
9	5F–H
10	6A–C
11	6D–G
12	6H–7A
13	7B–C (ending rushed)
14	Consolidation
15	8A–D (teacher translated 8C)
16	8E–G
17	8H–J
18	9A–B
19	9C–E
20	10 (ending rushed)
21	11A–B
22	11C–G (teacher translated 11C, E)
23	11H–12D
24	12E–13B
25	13C–F
26	14
27	15A–C
28	15D–F
29	15G–16A
30	16B–E (teacher translated c. 20 lines)
31	17
32	18A–B
33	18C–E
34	18F

APPENDIX

Here are lists of regular verbs, nouns and adjectives taken from the learning vocabularies of Sections 1–6, listed by section. These can be used in any exercise you care to add to those already in GVE. Use these lists to check quickly on regular words which students *should* know, and which should be utilized in testing.

A list of *irregular verbs* learnt in Sections 1–5 is also added. We recommend that principal part learning should be a feature of the Course from Section 6 onwards; the list taken from 1–5 will ensure that you do not miss any important ones.

Nouns

Section learnt	Type 1a	1b	1c	1d	2a	2b
1A–G	σωτηρία	θάλαττα	ναύτης κυβερνήτης		ἄνθρωπος	πλοῖον
1H–J					ῥαψῳδός στρατηγός	ἔργον
2A–D	βοή νίκη	ἀπορία ἐλευθερία ἡσυχία θεά ναυμαχία ὁμόνοια στρατιά	τόλμα		λόγος πόλεμος	
3A–E	γῆ εὐχή σπονδή	οἰκία θύρα		κελευστής	κίνδυνος νῆσος θόρυβος τριήραρχος	ὅπλα
4A–B				δεσπότης	γεωργός θεός νεκρός νόμος νόσος φόβος	
4C–D		ἀνομία ἀσεβεία		ἱκέτης	δοῦλος ξένος βωμός	ἱερόν
5A–B	δίκη			νεανίας οἰκέτης	βίος γάμος ἵππος	
5C–D		αἰτία διάνοια		μαθητής σοφιστής		
5E–F	κεφαλή Ἀθῆναι				δῆμος οὐρανός	
5G–H	γνώμη σελήνη	δεξιά			ἥλιος	χωρίον
6A–C	ἀνάγκη διαβολή	ἀλήθεια σοφία	δόξα	ποιητής		
6D–F	ἀρετή	φιλοσοφία			νεανίσκος διδάσκαλος	

3a	3b	3c	3d	3e	3f	3g	3h
Ἕλλην							
ἀνήρ γείτων λαμπάς λιμήν νύξ παῖς πατρίς σωτήρ							
γυνή δαίμων	πρᾶγμα	πλῆθος σκεύη		πόλις οἴκησις τάξις	ἄστυ		
κῆρυξ				ὕβρις	βασιλεύς		
πατήρ	χρήματα						
φροντίς ποῦς							ὀφρῦς
γέρων			τριήρης Σωκράτης				

Adjectives

Type Section learnt	-os -η -ον	-os -α -ον	-os -os -ον*
1A–G	κακός καλός φίλος ὁ	σῶος	
1H–J	ἄριστος, δῆλος	μῶρος	ἔμπειρος
2A–D	ἀγαθός ὅσος ἐμός κάλλιστος	'Αθηναῖος βέβαιος ἐλεύθερος πολέμιος	βάρβαρος
3A–E	δεινός ἄλλος ναυτικός ἐκεῖνος	Λακεδαιμόνιος ἡμέτερος	
4A–B	ὀλίγος θνητός		
4C–D	ὀρθός -όμεν-ος (mid. part.)		
5A–B	ὅλος χρηστός	αἴτιος νέος	
5C–D	σοφός	δίκαιος	ἄδικος
5E–F	ἄγροικος	ῥᾴδιος	ἀδύνατος
5G–H	πρῶτος ὁπόσος σός χρήσιμος	δεξιός ἕτερος πότερος	
6A–C			
6D–F	-σάμεν-ος (mid. part.)	ἀνδρεῖος	

Notes

1. Adjectives in bold type are of almost universal applicability in any adj. + noun 'addition' exercise. ὁ and οὗτος are *especially* important.

irr. 2nd	3rd decl. (mf/n)	3rd decl. (m-f-n)
μέγας πολύς οὗτος		
	κακοδαίμων εὔφρων τίς τις	οὐδείς -ων -ουσα -ον (-οντ-) (act. part.)
	ἥττων κρείττων	
		εἰδ-ώς -υῖα -ός (-οτ-)
		-σας -σασα -σαν -(σαντ-) (act. part.)

2. Note the importance of *participles* in the last column. These should be thoroughly tested in Sections 4 and 6.

* Two-termination adjectives are not properly introduced till Section 10.

Verbs

Dominant consonant of fut./aor. stem

Type Section learnt	-σ-	-ξ-	-ψ-
1A–G	ἀκούω (fut. mid) σῴζω	λέγω διώκω	βλέπω ῥίπτω
2A–D			
3A–E	θύω κελεύω	εὔχομαι	
4A–B	κωλύω ἀτιμάζω		
4C–D	παύομαι		
5A–B	παύω κολάζω		ἅπτω
5C–D	πείθω	δέχομαι διδάσκω	κόπτω
5E–F	λύω θαυμάζω		
5G–H	βιάζομαι		κλέπτω
6A–C	ἐξετάζω		
6D–F		ἐκδέχομαι	προτρέπω

When constructing short exercises on aorists and imperfects indicative, progress from plain -σ- stems to contract verbs and others; then from plain augments in ἐ-, to lengthening an initial vowel, and finally augments involving prepositions. Include *middle* as well as active forms.

-ησ- (-εσ-)	-ησ- (-ασ-)	-ωσ-
ἀποχώρεω βοηθέω ποιέω		
ἀπορέω ἀναχωρέω	νικάω σιωπάω τολμάω	ἐλευθερόω
χωρέω ζητέω καλέω (-εσ-)	θεάομαι (-ασ-)	δηλόω
κρατέω	τιμάω	
μισέω		
φιλέω		
	πηδάω δράω (-ασ-)	
νοέω	πειράομαι (-ασ-)	
ὁμολογέω ἐπαινέω (-εσ-)	γελάω (-ασ-)	

The irregular learning verbs of Sections 1–6 are on p. 214. These can be used for certain exercises (e.g. present and imperfect forms), but must be thoroughly learnt before they can be used for future and aorist exercises.

Irregular verbs in Sections 1-5

1A–G   *βαίνω ἀναβαίνω καταβαίνω *ἀποθνῄσκω *ἔχω *λέγω *ὁράω πλέω *φεύγω φροντίζω
1H–J   παίζω *γιγνώσκω *εἰμί *οἶδα
2A–D   *πίπτω ἡσυχάζω σκοπέω *ἔρχομαι διέρχομαι ἐπέρχομαι προσέρχομαι φοβέομαι
     *γίγνομαι μάχομαι
3A–E   *ἀφικνέομαι *ἐρωτάω σπεύδω πορεύομαι *φαίνομαι *λαμβάνω *μανθάνω *τρέχω ἐμβαίνω
     σπένδω
4A–B   *διαφθείρω τύπτω *φέρω
4C–D   *ἀπάγω ἀποφεύγω *ἀποκτείνω ἀφέλκω *ἐπικαλέομαι *λανθάνω ὀλοφύρομαι *πάσχω
     *τρέπομαι *τυγχάνω *φθάνω
5A–B   διαλέγομαι εἰσφέρω ὀφείλω ἔνειμι πείθομαι
5C–D   διανοέομαι
5E–F   δάκνω ἐκβάλλω
5G–H   *ἀπέρχομαι ἐξευρίσκω

Notes

1. These verbs can be used in exercises involving the formation of the present or imperfect (with one or two exceptions) indicative, and present participles, but care should be taken if you ask students to start forming the future and aorist with them.

2. We recommend that principal part sheets (there is one with the morphology charts) should be kept from Section 6 onwards. When the time comes to keep them, check the above list for important verbs they may miss.

3. Asterisked verbs in the above list appear in the morphology charts, and are of prime importance. They occur in *unprefixed* form: look under ἱκνέομαι, not ἀφικνέομαι, etc.

THE GRAMMATICAL INDEX TO
READING GREEK

Bold figures indicate the numbered paragraphs in *GVE*

215

elision, pp. 55–6, 57 (1); p. 204, **178** (i)
ellipsis
    of verb, of εἰμί, p. 22, **19** (i)
    of verbs in context, p. 40, **37** (a)
enclitics, accentuation of, p. 67, **66**; pp. 265–6
epic dialect, *see* Homeric dialect
etacism, p. 245, **214**; p. 255, **225** (viii)
euphony, pp. 263–4 (viii)

fearing, verbs of
    φοβοῦμαι and constructions, p. 209, **182**
    μή+subj., p. 209, **182** (iii); p. 304
    μή+opt., p. 218, **194**; p. 305
    μή+indic., p. 305
    μὴ οὐ, p. 320, (iv) (b)
final clauses, *see* purpose clauses
Formation of words
    of nouns, p. 328 (i)
    of adjs., pp. 328–9 (ii)
    of advs., pp. 329–30 (iii)
    of vbs., pp. 330–1 (iv)
    changes in root syllables, p. 331 (v)
    useful verb stems, pp. 332–4 (vii)
future perfect tense, middle and passive
    form, p. 203, **177**; p. 278
future tense
    summary of regular endings, p. 277;
        p. 279
    summary of principal parts of vbs.,
        pp. 284–9
    fut. indic. active, p. 65, **61**; p. 277;
        middle, p. 65, **62**; p. 277
    fut. indic. passive, p. 171, **157**; p. 277
    of contracted vbs., p. 66, **62** (iii)
    irregular, p. 66, **63**; p. 66, **64**; pp. 281–3
    fut. inf. active and middle, p. 124, **121**;
        p. 277
    fut. participles, active, middle, passive,
        p. 176, **159**; p. 277
    fut. opt., p. 277
    ὅπως+fut. indic., p. 167, **154**
    ὡς+fut. participle of purpose, p. 176, **160**
    οὐ μή+fut. indic., p. 320 (iv) (c)

gender, p. 14, **9**
    of 1st declension nouns, p. 29, **24**
    of 3rd declension nouns, p. 38, **29** (ii);
        p. 46, **39**
genitive
    gen. pl. form and function, p. 30, **25**
    all forms of gen. s. and pl., pp. 100–2, **91**;
        pp. 270–2
    gen. in -εω, -έων (Ionic), p. 246, **218**

gen. sing. in -οιο (Homeric), p. 255,
    225 (iv)
    survey of main uses of, pp. 323–5
    morphology of, p. 321
    word order with, p. 30, **26**
    of possession, p. 102, **92** (i) (a)
    of description, p. 102, **92** (i) (b)
    of source, origin, p. 102, **92** (i) (c)
    partitive, p. 102, **92** (i) (d); p. 324
    of price and value, p. 324
    of crime and penalty, p. 324
    of comparison, pp. 102–3, **92** (v); p. 324
    of time, p. 114, **104**; p. 324
    with ἀκούω, p. 102, **92** (iv); p. 126, **128**
    with ὑπό and passive, p. 147, **138**
    absolute, p. 147, **139**
    adjs.+gen., p. 102, **92** (ii)
    preps.+gen., p. 102, **92** (iii); pp. 290–2;
        p. 325
    vbs.+gen., p. 102, **92** (iv); p. 324
gerunds and gerundives, *see* infinitives:
    τό+inf., as noun; verbal adjectives
Greek language, pp. 308–10

Herodotus' dialect, *see* Ionic dialect
hexameter, pp. 256–7, **226**
hiatus, p. 264 (viii)
Homeric dialect, main features of, p. 255,
    225; pp. 267–9

iambic trimeter, p. 205–6, **179**
imperative
    summary of endings of, p. 279
    pres. active, p. 12, **6**; p. 123, **118**; p. 275
    pres. of vbs. in -άω, -έω, p. 12, **6**; in -όω,
        p. 28, **22**
    pres. middle of regular and contracted
        verbs, p. 29, **23**; p. 123, **118**; p. 276
    weak and strong aorist imperative active,
        p. 118, **110**; p. 124, **119**; p. 276
    weak and strong aorist imperative middle,
        p. 118, **110**n; p. 124, **120**
    aorist passive, p. 231, **204**; p. 277
    perf. active, p. 277
    perf. middle and passive, p. 277
    of irregular verbs, p. 119, **112**; p. 124,
        120 (iii); p. 231, **205**; pp. 281–3
    3rd person imperatives, pp. 123–4, **117–20**
    1st person – subjunctive, p. 217, **192**
    negation – μή+pres. imp., p. 13, **6** (ii);
        μή+aor. subj., p. 209, **181**
    aspect of pres. and aor. imp., p. 118, **111**
    commands, pp. 306–7

imperfect tense
  indic. active, regular and contracted,
    p. 60, **58**; p. 276
  indic. middle, regular and contracted,
    p. 60, **59**; p. 276
  of εἰμί (be), p. 61, **59** (vi); p. 281
  of εἶμι (go), p. 83, **77**; p. 282
  of φημί, p. 88, **81**; p. 283
  passive, pp. 146–7, **137–8**; p. 276
  in pres. unfulfilled conditions, p. 167, **152**;
    p. 305 (ii)
impersonal verbs, p. 300
  δεῖ, p. 83, **75**
  ἔξεστι, p. 119, **114**
indefinite adjective/pronoun
  inflection of τις, τι, p. 48, **46**
  inflection of ὅστις, p. 139, **136**
indefinite adverb, p. 67, **66**
indefinite constructions, p. 315 (a)
  with subj., p. 198, **175–6**
  with opt., p. 214, **187**
  relative clauses, p. 198, **175**; p. 304
  temporal clauses, p. 198, **175–6**; p. 303
  with ἕως, pp. 217–18, **193**; p. 226, **198**n;
    p. 222, **195**
  with πρίν, p. 226, **198**
indirect commands, p. 301
indirect object, dat. of, p. 113, **104** (i); p. 325
indirect questions, p. 67, **66**; p. 301
indirect statements
  survey of, pp. 301–3
  verbs introducing, pp. 160–1, **146**
  acc. + inf., p. 161, **147**; p. 302
  tense of inf., p. 161, **148**
  nom. + inf., p. 161, **149**; p. 302
  acc. + participle, p. 170, **156**; pp. 302–3
  opt. in secondary sequence, p. 185, **167**;
    p. 214, **188**
  οὐ φημί, p. 247, **224**
  ὅτι, ὡς, p. 301
infinitives
  summary of endings, p. 279
  summary of main uses of, pp. 299–301
  pres. active and middle, p. 82, **74**;
    pp. 275–6
  pres., of contracted vbs., p. 82, **74** (i)
  weak and strong aor., active, middle,
    p. 117, **108**; p. 276
  aor. passive, p. 176, **158**; p. 277
  fut. active, middle, p. 124, **121**; p. 277
  fut. passive, p. 277
  perf. active, middle, passive, p. 188, **170**;
    p. 277

inf. of irregular vbs., p. 82, **74** (ii);
  p. 105, **101**; pp. 281–3
Homeric inf. endings, p. 255, **225** (v);
  p. 269
negative with, p. 83, **74** (iii); p. 300n
aspect of pres. and aor. inf., pp. 117–18,
  109
acc. + inf. in indirect statement, pp. 160–1,
  146–9
vbs. + inf., p. 83, **75**; p. 119, **114**; p. 299 (i);
  p. 300
ἐπίσταμαι + inf., p. 125, **125**; p. 299 (ii);
  p. 302
adj. + inf., p. 119, **115**; p. 299 (ii), (iii)
fut., with vbs. of hoping, promising etc.,
  p. 125, **122**
πρίν + inf., p. 177, **161**
τό + inf., as noun, p. 180, **163–4**; p. 300 (vi)
in result clause, p. 228–9, **200–2**; pp. 300–1
in parenthetical phrases, p. 299 (iv)
as imperative, p. 300 (v)
with vbs. of prevention, hindrance,
  p. 300 (vii)
instrument, dat. of, p. 113, **104** (iii); p. 147,
  138; p. 325
interrogative adjective/pronoun
  inflection of τίς, τί, p. 48, **46**
  τί = why?, p. 75, **73**
  τί + participle, p. 105, **100**
interrogative adverb, direct and indirect
  speech, p. 67, **66**
Ionic dialect, main features of, pp. 245–7,
  214–22
iota subscript, p. 2
irregular verbs
  principal parts of εἰμί, εἶμι, οἶδα, φημί,
    pp. 281–3
  important principal parts, pp. 284–9
  see also -μι verbs

jussive subjunctive, see subjunctive: in
  prohibitions

Latin transcriptions, p. 332 (vi)
lexicon form of words, pp. 335–6

manner, dat. of, p. 113, **104** (iv); p. 325
means, dat. of, p. 325
metre
  syllabic nature of verse, p. 205, **179**
  iambic trimeter, pp. 205–6, **179**
  hexameter, pp. 256–7, **226**
  basic rules of scansion, pp. 257–8, **228**

GREEK INDEX

Paradigms of declensions and conjugations are marked with asterisks.